RAINBOW NATION REVISITED

Other books by Donald Woods

Biko
Asking for Trouble
In Black and White
A Guide to Apartheid
South African Dispatches
Filming with Attenborough

RAINBOW NATION REVISITED

South Africa's Decade of Democracy

Donald Woods

André Deutsch

First published in 2000
This paperback edition published 2003 by

André Deutsch
an imprint of the
Carlton Publishing Group
20 Mortimer Street
London W1T 3JW

A catalogue record for this book is available from the British Library

ISBN 0 233 00052 6

The publishers would like to thank the following sources for their kind
permission to reproduce the pictures in this book:

SECTION ONE
Page 1 (top) Universal Pictorial Press and Agency; (bottom-l) PictureNET;
(bottom-r) Kenneth Muller/ PictureNET Africa. Page 2: Greg Marinovich/
PictureNET Africa; Paul Velasco/ PictureNET Africa; Adil Bradlow/ PictureNET
Africa. Page 3: Guy Tillim/ Afrapix. Page 4: Neil van Niekerk/ PictureNET Africa.
Page 5: (top)Geoff Dalglish; (bottom) Henner Frankenfeld/ PictureNET Africa.
Page 6: Frank Connor. Page 7: (top) Frank Connor; (bottom) Daniel J. Edelman.
Page 8: (top) Geoff Dalglish; (bottom) Daily Express

SECTION TWO
Page 1: (top) Television Viewpoint/ BBC; (bottom) Gary Horlor. Page 2: (top)
John Bridcut; (bottom) Fay Foto Service. Page 4: (top) Denis Farrell/ Associated
Press; (bottom) Adil Bradlow/ PictureNET Africa. Page 5: Popperfoto/ Reuters.
Page 6: Shaun Harris/ PictureNET Africa. Page 8: Charles Green.

Every effort has been made to acknowledge correctly and contact the source
and/or copyright holder of each picture, and Carlton Books Limited apologies
for any unintentional errors or omissions which will be corrected in future
editions of this book.

Typeset in Liverpool by Derek Doyle & Associates
Printed and bound in Great Britain by Mackays

This book is dedicated to

STEVE BIKO

who died for the dream

and

NELSON MANDELA

who made the dream come true

Contents

Foreword

I have no doubt that Donald Woods is a very remarkable man, possibly unique. No one else I have known has made such a complete moral journey, from one extreme to the other, and, at the end of it, found himself exactly where he had so passionately hoped to be.

Before his first encounter with Steve Biko in King Williamstown during 1975, Donald was not radically opposed to the injustices of apartheid. Brought up in the Transkei, he was originally, like thousands of other white South Africans, quite prepared to accept a status quo which, for them, underpinned a leisurely and luxurious lifestyle.

Meeting Biko changed that.

It was then, for the first time, that Donald began to question the profound inequalities and worst excesses of a system based solely on the colour of someone's skin, which, since 1948, had been enshrined in the law of his homeland. And it was Biko's brutal murder whilst in police custody – a crime ultimately admitted and proven some twenty years later during the Truth Commission's enquiries – that galvanized him into action.

In 1977, as editor of the *East London Daily Dispatch*, he wrote a courageous editorial – printed on the front page – which defied the whole apartheid regime by accusing and naming those responsible for Biko's death.

As a result, Donald was 'banned', becoming a non-person, forbidden to communicate with others and a prisoner in his home. Silenced in his own country, he decided the only way to alert the world to the outrageous repression being practised in South Africa was to leave.

It was, of course, no easy decision. To give up his home and livelihood, possibly for all time, and to risk the safety of his beloved family, possibly being parted from them for years to come, took enormous courage.

But leave he did, arriving in Britain with his wife and five children, virtually penniless. Then he wrote a biography, simply entitled *Biko*, and that was how I came to know him. Based on another of Donald's books, *Asking for Trouble*, I made a film which we called *Cry Freedom*.

Donald and his equally remarkable and enchanting wife, Wendy, acted as our full-time advisors and, because they were there with us throughout the time we filmed in Zimbabwe, I came to know them very well. We have remained firm friends ever since.

Rainbow Nation Revisited is an account of Donald's eventual return to South Africa following Nelson Mandela's release from prison, the ending of apartheid and the establishment of democracy.

Donald had and still has the belief, echoed by Nelson Mandela and so many, many of their compatriots that, in the end, good always does triumph over evil. But, at that moment of triumph as Mandela walked free, the burden of black South Africans' expectation was dangerously high.

Happily, as Donald details in this book, so much is going well and life everywhere is perceptibly improving. Houses are being built. Clean water supplies are becoming more plentiful. The possibility of a job is no longer a mirage. And the children are being educated.

If the miracle of full equality and shared prosperity can be fully implemented – and in this book Donald is unequivocal in his optimism – then he and Wendy and their quintet of offspring will have made a very significant contribution indeed to its realization.

They are people who were and are prepared to back conviction with action. Donald is one of the bravest men I have ever met; possessed of passionate conviction, outrageous powers of persuasion, burning loyalty and an irresistible sense of humour. My life is the fuller and the better for knowing him and his family.

Richard Attenborough

Introduction

Events occurred in South Africa in 1977 which brought a newspaper editor there, Donald Woods, into the international arena in a way neither he nor his persecutors in the South African government could have foreseen. What triggered the process was the tragic death in a South African political prison of a young black activist against apartheid, Steve Biko, and the campaign his friend Woods and others launched to brand senior officials of the South African government guilty of this murder.

A white South African of British and Irish descent, Donald Woods was born in the Transkei territory of South Africa's Eastern Cape Province, and like most young whites of his generation was raised to support the racist views embodied in the apartheid system of the white minority government. As a law student in Cape Town and subsequently as a journalist working for two years in Britain, Canada and the United States, Woods came to reject the apartheid philosophy, and when he was appointed editor of the *Daily Dispatch* newspaper in East London, Cape Province, in 1965, he began an editorial crusade against apartheid which resulted in several state prosecutions against him under South Africa's strict publication laws.

But it was only after he met and befriended Steve Biko in 1975 that his editorial campaign intensified towards a head-on collision with the South African government, and when Biko was killed in Security Police custody in 1977 Woods published a front-page accusation against the Minister of Police holding him and his administration accountable for the crime. Shortly after, on 19 October 1977, Woods was arrested at Johannesburg airport and served with Banning Orders – state-imposed decrees forbidding him to travel,

xi

write, speak in public or be quoted in any publication. Under virtual house arrest, he was subjected to constant surveillance and forbidden to speak to more than one person at a time, or even to be in a room in his house with more than one person at a time, except for members of his immediate family. His telephone was tapped, his house bugged and his mail monitored, and he, his wife and five children were subjected to threats and attacks by Security Police officers.

On New Year's Eve of 1977 the Woods family escaped from South Africa; he alone, disguised as a priest, and his wife Wendy and their five children travelling by a different route across the border to Lesotho, where they were reunited and whence they flew via Botswana, Zambia and Tunisia to London, where they now live. Their escape was given front-page coverage in newspapers all over the world, and widespread television and radio coverage emphasizing the gravity of the situation in South Africa led to heightened international pressure against the South African government. In the following month, January 1978, Donald Woods became the first private citizen to be invited to address the United Nations Security Council, and the theme of his address was the need for economic sanctions as the only non-violent pressure that would eventually force the South African government to abandon its racial laws.

During the next twelve years, working as a freelance journalist, lecturer and broadcaster against apartheid, he campaigned all over the world for increased pressure against the Pretoria regime, and his first book, *Biko*, a biography, was published in twelve languages. His second, *Asking for Trouble*, was an award-winning autobiography, and these two books became the basis for Sir Richard Attenborough's major motion picture *Cry Freedom*, released in 1987 by Universal Pictures. During his exile Donald Woods wrote six books about apartheid, personally briefed heads of government in thirty-seven countries and functioned as a special adviser on the South African situation to the Secretariat of the forty-nine-nation Commonwealth and to the Commission of the European Community in Brussels. His activities on the international scene during his exile led to two five-year renewals of his banning orders by the South African administration of President P. W. Botha, to prevent his being quoted in the South African media and to keep alive the threat of long-term imprisonment if Donald Woods should attempt to return to his country.

But in February 1990 the new president of South Africa, F. W. De Klerk, released Nelson Mandela and lifted the bans on all dissidents and exiles previously outlawed by state decree, and further statements several months later committed the De Klerk administration to abolishing retrospective prosecutions for past deeds by dissidents, making it possible for exiles to return.

Donald Woods was therefore able to return to South Africa in August 1990, going three times on journalistic commissions to test the reality of change there before bringing his family back to revisit their country with him. His first three trips were to report for BBC-TV, *Time* magazine and the *Observer* of London, and the fourth was the Woods family's Christmas and New Year vacation – back in their country for the first time as a family since they had escaped twelve years previously. These were to be the first of many journeys back to and inside South Africa, to all parts of the country at various stages of the great transition to democracy, and during these visits, which included an eighteen-month period ending in 1998 as Executive Director of the Institute for the Advancement of Journalism, headquartered in Johannesburg, he met and interviewed many leading political figures, including Nelson Mandela, F. W. De Klerk and Archbishop Desmond Tutu, and kept a diary. This book is the result of that diary – the diary of an exile back in his country of birth, celebrating the redemption of a nation long tortured by fear and oppression.

The Publisher

CHAPTER 1

Meeting Mr Mandela

Suddenly the long nightmare of apartheid was ending, and the horrors of four decades of racial oppression began to give way to the bright hopes that had seemed such a distant dream to so many for so long. Suddenly the whole world seemed changed, and the human race capable of so much more.

'Even the trees look different!'

That phrase had been uttered in 1948 by an exultant zealot as his party took power in South Africa to introduce a racist republic reserving all privilege for whites, and political power for Afrikaner Nationalists. It seemed to him that his people had reached the promised land, reversing the result of the Boer War, wresting power from British hands and stopping what he saw as an alarming trend towards incremental rights for blacks. And as these white Afrikaner Nationalists passed more and more racial laws, up to 317 altogether, and issued more and more restrictions on criticism and opposition during their four decades of control, how strong and unassailable they seemed to be!

Yet now, almost overnight, this power was eroding before our eyes and Nelson Mandela was walking free after twenty-seven years in political prison.

The whole world watched in awe as this tall old man strode slowly but steadily out of his prison gates to establish a nation rid of racism and based on the most advanced of all democratic constitutions.

And it wasn't only Mandela walking to freedom. At first dozens, then hundreds, then thousands of political prisoners of various

1

sorts were to follow him out of several kinds of restrictions, and many exiles in various parts of the world knew this was also the end of their own varieties of exclusion from their homes and national birthright.

In my own case it was the Banning Order imposed on 19 October 1977. I had been arrested in Johannesburg by three Security Police officers and served with page after page of restrictive edicts signed by the Minister of Police, J. T. Kruger, prohibiting me from travelling, writing, public speaking, association with others and a range of specific activities – all for using my position as a newspaper editor to write editorials accusing the apartheid government of responsibility for the murder of the young black leader, Steve Biko. I was arrested to stop me repeating these accusations, and banned to stop me being a journalist.

Such a ban amounted to a form of house arrest, under constant Security Police surveillance, and although it was imposed for a total of twelve years my family and I escaped less than three months after its imposition, crossing the border into Lesotho then travelling via Botswana, Zambia and Tunisia to London, unable to return until the lifting of the ban following the release of Mandela.

So Mandela's release was not only a great international and national occasion for me, it was also of personal significance. It meant I could go home at last, after all the years of exile, without the threat of arrest or state punishment, and I excitedly prepared to return for my first look at the new South Africa. It was 1990, and it was to be the first of many visits of varying lengths to my homeland, my place of birth, the places of my youth and schooling, and later political activities. It was also the initial phase of the all-important question: whither South Africa?

This was the question the whole world was asking, ten years after the release of Nelson Mandela. It was a summary of many subsidiary questions: Could South Africa make it? Could the rainbow nation succeed? Could the idealistic new government create enough wealth to sustain the high expectations of the masses who now supported it? Would South Africa's new leaders break new ground in Africa to entrench civil liberties, individual freedoms and total democracy? Could South Africa carry the whole impoverished region of Southern Africa into an era of future economic growth and social advancement? Could the other African giant, Nigeria, be engaged in a partnership to regenerate the entire continent?

These were the issues I was able to explore and address in the decade since Mandela's release, along with questions about how the whites were coping with change, how effective racial reconciliation was proving in various parts of the country, and what kind of leadership was emerging among young South Africans of all factions as the new millennium began.

South Africa had already confounded many prophets of doom by achieving a remarkable and virtually bloodless transfer of power. Could the country bring off a second miracle – the creation of enough wealth for its forty million citizens and all their regional neighbours to provide an even more astonishing example for the Third World to follow?

Such was the focus of my concerns as I interviewed South Africans of all shades of opinion and ideology during the most dynamic decade of our remarkable history. With Mandela's successor, Thabo Mbeki, formally installed in the presidency, all eyes turned now on the new generation of leaders as they took up the challenge.

But there could be no quick forgetting of their extraordinary predecessor, Nelson Mandela, by now universally acknowledged as the hero of heroes, the man for all seasons, ages and continents and the inspirational icon of several generations.

Though I was born within only a few miles of his own birthplace in the Transkei region of the Eastern Cape, I had never seen or met Mandela before he began his long imprisonment, nor had my wife Wendy, also born in the same region. We looked forward to our first glimpse of our fabled fellow-countryman. We shared the excitement of the large contingent of South African exiles when the newly released Mandela decided to come to London to thank the international supporters of the campaign against apartheid.

A mammoth concert for 100,000 people was planned for Wembley Stadium, with leading entertainers from the world of music, film and theatre coming to honour Mandela. Meanwhile, London's South African exiles began to bring gifts to the home of Oliver and Adelaide Tambo, where he would be staying during his visit.

Wendy and I discussed what we should give him. 'It should be something small, easy to carry,' she said, aware that Mandela would probably receive thousands of gifts. After much discussion we decided to have a tie made for him, a pure silk necktie in the colours of the African National Congress, since London was, after all, a great tie-manufacturing centre.

We set off for Jermyn Street, where most of the famous tiemakers are to be found, and asked one of the best to fill the order. He took down the details in a precise copperplate handwriting, specifying high-quality silk with diagonal stripes one centimetre wide in green, gold and black. 'It will be expensive,' he cautioned. 'As a single order it will cost about £300.'

We asked him to go ahead anyway, as a gift costing £300 seemed to us little enough for someone who had been in political prison for twenty-seven years. He waved away an offered deposit, took down our address and undertook to start on the tie immediately, adding: 'It'll take about three months, just to order the precise material . . .'

No, no, we said. We had to have the finished tie in three weeks.

Impossible, he said. Out of the question.

We looked disappointed, and he asked what the urgency was.

'You've heard of Nelson Mandela?' we said.

He nodded. 'Wonderful man,' he said, puzzled.

We said: 'It's a present for him, and he'll be here in three weeks for the big concert at Wembley. That's why we need it so soon.'

There was a long silence, then he smacked his hands together decisively: 'And you shall have it,' he cried. 'For Nelson Mandela we shall achieve the impossible!'

He did, too, and we wrapped up the tie and left it at Adelaide Tambo's house where so many other presents awaited him. We were in the nick of time, delivering it on the Friday, Mandela being due to fly into London on the Saturday to attend the concert at Wembley on the Sunday.

On the Saturday afternoon I was watching sport on television when the programme was interrupted to show the Mandela plane landing at Heathrow, and as we returned to the sports programme it struck me as remarkable that Mandela was actually now in London, centre of so many demonstrations and initiatives over so many years to pressure the apartheid government to set him free.

After what seemed barely an hour, but must surely have been more, my daughter Jane came into the room with her eyes wide. 'There's a phone call for you, Daddy,' she said. 'And the caller says he's Nelson Mandela!'

'He can't be,' I said. 'His plane landed only a short while ago. And he wouldn't be phoning me anyway. It must be a hoax.'

Jane said: 'Well, *he* says he's Nelson Mandela.'

I took the receiver from her and said a hesitant hello, and as Mandela's familiar booming voice replied my children were amused to see me jump up from my chair and stand respectfully to attention. They told me afterwards that I referred to him throughout the conversation as 'sir'.

In his slow, measured way, he spoke of having arrived from the airport to see all the presents, having by chance opened ours first and having been so touched at the 'care and expense and thought' that had gone into it that he had got my phone number from Adelaide Tambo in order to say thanks immediately.

Still dazed at the thought of this legendary figure actually telephoning me, I said rather lamely: 'I hope you like the tie . . .'

'Like it? I *love* it!' he boomed. 'I'm going to wear it to the concert tomorrow!'

He added that another reason he was glad to be speaking to me was that during some of the worst times on Robben Island he and other prisoners had been cheered by my editorials in the *Daily Dispatch*. They had been able by devious means to smuggle the paper on to the island and occasionally into their maximum security block, and they had seen the issue reporting Steve Biko's death.

'We felt you spoke for us, that though you were born with white privilege you supported our cause and were a good friend to Steve Biko – that's the other reason I'm saying thanks to you.' Then came the booming laugh before he added: 'That and the beautiful tie!'

True to his word, he wore the tie to the concert and it duly appeared in many colour pictures of the event. And I enjoyed pointing out to Wendy that few clothes designers were privileged to have their work seen simultaneously by hundreds of millions of television viewers worldwide.

But in retrospect the most remarkable aspect of the incident was the generosity of spirit of this extraordinary septuagenarian who had just completed an exhausting eleven-hour flight from 6,000 miles away, yet went to the trouble of reacting immediately to say thanks for what he saw as a thoughtful gift.

I met him for the first time that evening, at a reception at the home of the Commonwealth Secretary-General, Sir Shridath Ramphal, and was enveloped for the first of many times in the famous Mandela bear-hug. Not knowing what else to say – what, after all, do you say on first meeting a living legend? – I addressed him in the traditional Xhosa way with the salutation *'Ah! Rolihlahla!'* using the first of his four names, which is his birth-name.

Mandela gave a broad grin and replied: *'Owu! Molo mhlobo wam'!'* meaning: 'Oh! Greetings, person of my region!' then came the bear-hug and the volley of questions about my health, the well-being of my wife and children and all the unhurried courtesies of a gracious Mthembu chief, regardless of the long line of dignitaries waiting to be presented to him by Secretary-General Ramphal.

Mandela's four names were all interesting in their derivation and significance. His birthname, *Rolihlahla*, means 'Bring out the broom'. *Rola* means 'bring out', and when joined to another word loses the 'a'. The word *ihlahla* refers usually to twigs bound together to make up a broom, and *Rolihlahla* could mean metaphorically: 'Sweep out the rubbish' or 'Clean the place up' or simply 'Make things better!' There are those who think it could mean 'Stir up the dust!' The pronunciation of Rolihlahla sounded harsh to European ears, with the 'r' sounding like the 'ch' in Loch Lomond and the 'hl' identical to the Welsh double 'l', as in Llanelli.

His school name, Nelson, was bestowed on him by his teacher who admired the great British admiral Horatio Nelson, and his clan name, Madiba, derives from the fact that he and his family belong to the Diba clan, and could all be called maDiba, or more usually Madiba. In the same way members of the Jola clan are called Majola.

But Mandela's most important name, his initiation name given when he was initiated into manhood at the age of sixteen, was the most remarkable in its prescience. It is Dalibunga, meaning: 'Prepare the Parliament!'

Few people called him Nelson when speaking to him, and most of his followers referred to him affectionately as Madiba, but his closest friends called him Rolihlahla and those from his home district and his close relatives tended to use the initiation name Dalibunga.

On at least one occasion this fact was exploited for journalistic purposes. During South Africa's first democratic election campaign in 1994 I was covering the events for BBC radio on a key day when Mandela was addressing conservative white farmers at Potchefstroom and then black farmworkers in the same area.

Hundreds of journalists from all over the world were there for the occasion, but all were frustrated because Mandela's press officer had ruled out any individual interviews. My BBC producer, John Bridcut, kept insisting that I use my personal acquaintanceship with Mandela to scoop all the other journalists and I kept refusing, feeling this would be unfair.

But there is nothing more unstoppable than a quietly determined Englishman, and John finally talked me into it. As Mandela was moving along in the middle of a sea of foreign journalists, all trying to put individual questions to him and all drawing no more than a good-natured smile and a regretful headshake, I called out: *'Ah! Dalibunga!'*

The effect was electrifying. He peered about him delightedly, then seeing me called out: *'Tyini! Mhlobo wam'!'* ('Well! My country-man!') and gave me his undivided attention, and a very good radio interview, for several minutes while his press officer went into a fit of justified fury as many of the foreign journalists badgered him for 'equal time'.

Since my first meeting with Mandela I was to meet him on many occasions in many places and circumstances during the following decade and he was always unvaryingly himself – charming, friendly and unhurried. This last quality used to drive his poor staff to distraction. They would impress on you the need to limit your appointment to five minutes, then nearly tear their hair out with frustration when you rose to make your departure according to this schedule only to be pressed back into your chair by the insistent Mandela, who would say: 'No, no, there is so much to talk about.'

The long-suffering Professor Jakes Gerwel, who ran his office and oversaw his appointments, used to point out that there were visiting delegations from various parts of the world, that each was slotted into a full day's schedule of appointments planned to the minute, and that an overrun of even one minute on any of them threw the rest of the day increasingly into chaotic over-scheduling.

Yet that was repeatedly what happened because of the good nature and generosity of spirit of Mandela, to whom all visitors and all people were important. While maddening to his staff, it was precisely that quality of his, that part of the Mandela magic, that had saved South Africa from disaster and had led to the peace talks and negotiations that had ended the apartheid crisis. If this long-term political prisoner had not been sufficiently generous of spirit to signify that he was ready to negotiate with his captors, South Africa's remarkable transformation could not have occurred as it did. Other things were necessary to enable the transformation to take place, and generous concessions by other key players were part of the formula, but Mandela's was the crucial role without which the entire process could not have proceeded with relatively so little violence or difficulty.

And the key element of Mandela's character and personality which facilitated the process and ultimately enthralled his captors was humility. Not deference, not self-abasement, but that kind of humility which involves a refusal to take oneself too seriously or claim an importance which is not readily accorded by others.

One of the enduring images from the account of Mandela preparing for his first meeting with the then President P. W. Botha back in 1989 had been that of Mandela, incapable after all those years in prison uniform and sandals of dressing himself completely in a suit and shoes. He had forgotten how to tie a necktie or do up shoelaces, and high-ranking prison officers had stepped in to perform these duties for him.

There had surely been something strongly symbolic in the scene of Major Marais kneeling to tie the Mandela shoelaces while Mandela reviewed his notes of points he wished to raise with the dreaded P. W. Botha. Indeed, the senior prison and security officers had been more tense than Mandela about this meeting, because they knew P. W. Botha and had often seen him suddenly lose his temper in a fit of shouting and screaming. As usual, they hadn't known what to expect from the old crocodile, as Botha was called by aides behind his back.

P. W. Botha had a notoriously short temper, and many were the stories of his outbursts at public functions. One had only to witness a real crocodile's behaviour to understand immediately the reason for his nickname, because like the real crocodile Botha would appear to be calm to the point of almost dozing, then would suddenly leap into violent action. I had first seen this phenomenon in Zimbabwe when filming a big crocodile as it slept under some trees. A fairly large bird had alighted on a branch some eight or nine feet above the crocodile, and without any prior movement that huge croc had leapt straight up and its jaws had snapped shut on the slender branch. It had missed the bird but had got a mouthful of foliage, and I had got the fright of my life because I hadn't known that crocs could jump that high or move that fast. With the same sudden viciousness Botha had pounced on critics at public functions, shouting loudly at them and having to be led away by cabinet colleagues or aides from his office. He had once railed at army chiefs during a reception, saying that if it hadn't been for their timidity they could have captured Luanda during the Angolan war. He shouted: 'We could have taken Luanda! We could even have taken Lagos! We could even have taken Cairo!' In Afrikaans this phrase contained the frenzied screech by emphasis of the word 'Cairo' as 'Ka- *ee* – ru!'

So, to sum up in the most charitable terms, P. W. Botha had long shown himself to be a highly excitable man. As a newspaper editor before my arrest and banning I had had several meetings with him during his term as Minister of Defence, and the last of these had been nothing short of spectacular.

I had written a satirical article about him, alluding to his earlier nickname 'Piet Broek' ('Piet Pants'), earned while he was in charge of the stormtroopers of the National Party, which had been pro-Nazi during the Second World War, when he had led elements such as the *Swarthemde* (Blackshirts), *Gryshemde* (Greyshirts) and *OssewaBrandwag* (Oxwagon Sentinels) to break up meetings of the anti-Nazi parties. Soldiers on leave from the fighting in North Africa and Italy had laid a trap for Botha and his toughs, and when cornered in a back room behind the stage of a meeting hall Botha had got away through a high window leaving his trousers in the clutches of the pursuing soldiers. But he had been a young man then, and it was only in his later years that 'Piet Broek' had given way to 'Old Crocodile'. And it was about this time that I had also alluded to a decoration P. W. had received, as Minister of Defence, from the eccentric President Bongo of Gabon, up in the western coastal area of Central Africa. Bongo, it seems, had wanted a military airfield, and Botha had offered to build one for him on condition that he allowed South African planes to land there. Bongo had agreed, and on completion of the job had conferred on Botha a medal called something like 'Supreme Grand Order of Gabon'.

Botha had been inordinately proud of this award, and had worn it everywhere and on all occasions, and must have been angry indeed when I had suggested in print that he probably pinned it on his pyjama jacket at night when he went to bed. In fact, I later heard from General Constand Viljoen that he and Admiral H. H. 'Boozy' Biermann had had to walk Botha around his office to calm him down immediately prior to a meeting where he was due to brief twenty-seven of the nation's editors, including myself, on matters in Angola. He had said he was going to 'nail this Woods right now' and they had convinced him that this would be undignified and would only draw further attention to the offending article.

Hoping he hadn't yet read the piece, I had slipped through into his briefing room behind the other editors who were being greeted, and had taken the most remote seat from Botha's chair at the big briefing table. But when he had finished greeting the others he had come straight to where I was sitting, held out his hand and said: 'Welkom in Kaapstad, *Meneer* Woods.'

I had therefore concluded that he hadn't read the article, but knew it was purely a matter of time before he did, as it was syndicated in all seven of the country's biggest morning newspapers in Johannesburg, Durban, Cape Town, Port Elizabeth, East London, Pietermaritzburg and Kimberley.

I resolved to keep a low profile during question time, and as the meeting drew to a close thought all was well until a persistent line of probing from Ray Louw, editor of the Rand *Daily Mail*, caused something to snap in Botha's mind. Pointing a shaking finger at me he went into a wild frenzy, shouting that I had 'tried to help Marxist terrorists' by making fun of him personally, and accusing the other editors who took my syndicated column of conspiring in this campaign of contempt. He swore to act against them and concluded by shouting at me behind a wagging finger: 'I'm going to get you! I'm going to get you!'

The next morning I had arrived at his office to make the point that the other editors couldn't be blamed for the article and that Ray Louw, in particular, hadn't even been in the country but had been in New York when his paper had received and printed the article. But I had found a different Botha. Apologizing for his outburst, he had poured me a cup of conciliatory coffee and readily agreed that it had been unreasonable to blame the other editors. Then he had said, in a low and emotional voice and speaking now in English: 'To tell you the truth, Mr Woods, I was more hurt than angry at your article. This award from President Bongo means a lot to me.' He had pointed to the award on his suit lapel, and tears had come into his eyes and a catch into his voice as he had added: 'It may be a big joke to you, Mr Woods, but it means a *great deal* to me.' I remember finding this emotional turnabout, from the man with his finger on the national trigger, more worrying than his rantings and threats.

This, then, was the highly volatile P. W. Botha that senior prison officials and government aides were nervous about exposing to Nelson Mandela, the man Botha and his colleagues had regarded for more than two decades as their arch-enemy. Even more emotional and prone to outbursts as President than he had been as Minister of Defence, he now felt all-powerful and was even more likely to go into a tirade if Mandela provoked him in any way, intentionally or unintentionally.

But here, again, the magic of Mandela had come to the rescue. He had greeted Botha with dignified deference, having come to 'pay his respects' to the head of state and to exchange views, and this had hardly been the ogre that P. W. Botha had expected to see after all the years of official vilification.

It later became scarcely possible to give an adequate impression, to people who had never experienced it, of the extent of hatred and fear which the apartheid leaders had felt for Mandela all those years ago. And their Security Police 'experts', knowing their superiors wanted to hear ill of such 'terrorists', had fed them ever more exaggerated accounts of Mandela and the other leading political prisoners. I remember as far back as 1970 having suggested to the then Premier, B. J. Vorster, that he should at least consider meeting Mandela and the others, and Vorster becoming so angry that his voice emerged in a sort of trembling whisper as he grated out that he would never demean himself to meet such a person, and that Mandela would only emerge from prison, as Vorster put it, 'over my dead body' – a prophetic statement indeed.

In 1976 I had asked Police Minister J. T. Kruger to let me go to Robben Island to see Mandela and he had flatly refused. When I had suggested that he himself should meet Mandela he had said: 'We don't have to. We have our eye on him every day. And I can tell you he just sits there eating all the time, he's grown very fat in prison.'

Could anything more eloquently have illustrated the quality of Security Police reports to their rulers about political prisoners, or even political opponents? Today the whole world knows that Mandela remained the same weight throughout his twenty-seven years of imprisonment, and even throughout the decade since his release, and if the chubby little Minister Kruger had shown the same ascetic discipline and commitment to exercise as Mandela, he might have survived more than a few years after his insulting inaccuracies about the prison experiences of Nelson Mandela and Steve Biko. Kruger had described the latter's death in Security Police custody as the result of 'a hunger strike', and when first told about the death had commented: 'Biko's death leaves me cold.'

These were the people, the Vorsters, the Krugers and the P. W. Bothas, who for so long had had so much control over the fates of such political giants as Biko and Mandela. P. W. Botha's first meeting with Mandela must have chipped away at his own certainties, because even such bigoted people as the P. W. Bothas would have found it hard to keep believing the massive lies they had to sustain about the personalities upon whose defamation their delusions depended, if they hoped to continue their control of them.

To the relief of the generals and prison officials, the meeting between Botha and Mandela had gone off fairly smoothly, with Botha matching Mandela's courtesy as they discussed South African history and the role of the Afrikaners. Mandela had made a shrewd reference to the armed uprising of the Afrikaner Nationalist militants during the First World War, drawing the implied parallel between these heroes of Botha's and his own African National Congress resort to armed conflict after fifty years of peaceful protest. The only tense moment during the meeting had been when Mandela had asked for and Botha had refused the release of all political prisoners.

But it was generally felt on both sides that a start had been made on a process of negotiation, and that this meeting was a sort of ceremonial beginning to the process rather than part of its detailed workings which would presumably come later. Mandela was astonished that Botha himself had poured the tea for them all, and Botha was clearly somewhat surprised at the lack of hostility in Mandela's bearing. Bloodthirsty terrorists do not usually act like gentle old grandfathers.

But Botha was only the first of his leading opponents to fall prey to the charms of Mandela. Nine years later, when Mandela had emerged as President in South Africa's first-ever democratic election, he had incurred the anger of Tony Leon, leader of the Democratic Party in the South African Parliament. Leon, a white Johannesburger with a sharp tongue and a keen brain, had been somewhat too abrasive in his attacks on the ANC for Mandela's liking, and Mandela had referred to Leon as 'a Mickey Mouse politician ... the Mickey Mouse leader of a Mickey Mouse party'. Leon had been outraged, and had still been seething with anger some days later when he had fallen ill and had had to have emergency heart surgery.

After his operation in a Johannesburg hospital, nurses had approached his bed to tell him a visitor had arrived to see him, and from beyond the screens the astonished Leon had heard the familiar booming voice announcing: 'Mickey Mouse! Here is Goofy, come to visit you.'

It was yet another example of the magic of Mandela, that trait of his character which had saved South Africa, rescued it from the disaster of apartheid, set it firmly on course for freedom, and made it possible for me to revisit my home in what author Alan Paton had so memorably identified to all the world as the Beloved Country.

CHAPTER 2

Heading for Home

It was 15 August 1990, and at 37,000 feet over the Sahara Desert it felt good to be heading home for the first time in more than twelve years. I'd had my own celebration banquet in the aircraft in fulfilment of a promise made to myself when my family and I were escaping from South Africa in January 1978. We had been so cramped into a small nine-seater plane, and for two hours had been under such frightening threat of being forced down by South African Air Force jets until we were clear of their airspace, that I had promised myself that if we came through all this and I was able to return it would be with all the trimmings in first class – vodka and caviar, champagne, and a meal rounded off with cheese and vintage port.

Take-off from London had been only five minutes late. In my years of exile I had kept a private log of more than 800 take-offs all over the world, of which only three had been exactly on time. The average delay had been from ten to twenty minutes, and the worst delays had been in Dublin in 1979 (eight hours), Bombay in 1982 (seven hours), Detroit in 1985 (six hours), Lagos in 1983 (five hours), Boston in 1984 (four hours) and Mombasa in 1986 (three hours). But though few flights ever took off on time, most had managed to land on schedule, so pilots could obviously make up time in the air.

This had been quite a day. When I had woken up I had realized with an immediate rush of excitement that the great day of return had finally arrived, and it had opened up a sudden flood of memories of our departure from South Africa and the circumstances of that escape; the death of our friend Steve Biko; our part in the campaign to find out the truth about his death; our own persecution by the Security Police; my arrest and banning; the attacks on our house and members of our family; the constant surveillance and finally our escape. It had been a remarkable twelve years. Because of the unusual interest in our story – it wasn't often that a family of seven had to run away from home under governmental threat – my life had changed from newspaper editor in South Africa to London-based campaigner, hence the constant travel to broadcast, lecture and lobby internationally against apartheid.

And now, by all accounts as I relished that first return journey home, apartheid was on its last legs. I still found it hard to believe, and decided to suspend judgement until the following morning when I would be able to see for myself.

Meanwhile, I reflected that we were living in times of momentous change all over the world, and thought of Wordsworth's 'Bliss was it in that dawn to be alive!' Eastern Europe, the Soviet Union, South America, all were now stirring at last towards the long-denied vision of freedom. Suddenly it seemed a warmer, more positive world, and a more optimistic human race. The only cloud on the horizon was over the Middle East – Saddam Hussein's invasion of Kuwait two weeks previously. I had been in Kuwait in 1982, and could actually see Iraq from my hotel window. The Iraqis had been fighting Iran at the time, and I remembered thinking that if ever they got greedy for Kuwait's oil they wouldn't find it hard to saunter over the border. I had hoped selfishly that they'd wait until I got out of town. Like most people I had equated Kuwait only with oil wealth, and had been intrigued at the pride of Kuwaitis in the fact that their country had had wealth long before oil had been discovered there. 'What wealth?' I had asked, pointing out that all I could see was sand. 'We were the traders of the world,' they told me. 'We brought materials here and made things, and traded them.'

We South Africans tended to see the only real wealth as gold, diamonds and other minerals in the soil, forgetting that small countries like Belgium, Holland and Switzerland had no comparable physical wealth yet outproduced our Gross National Product to an embarrassing extent. One thing seemed certain – South Africa's gold, diamonds, platinum, vanadium, manganese, ferrochrome and other valuable minerals alone would not support our 40 million people in South Africa, and the sooner we stopped depending on being the world's richest repository of such minerals the sooner we would confront the real economic challenge, which could be met only with an educated and trained populace. That was clearly going to be our biggest problem – finding an answer to the poverty and sociological mayhem promoted by apartheid policies for forty-two years. The papers that morning were full of the violence in the South African townships, ascribing it to tribalism instead of to the real cause – the legacy of forty-two years of community fragmentation and sociological devastation. I could hardly believe I would soon be seeing it all for myself.

Flying by now over Africa's great lakes, I wondered what my ancestor would have said back in 1820 when he arrived in South Africa from Britain five generations ago, if he'd known one of his descendants would one day travel the same distance in twelve hours that had taken him three months by sailing ship. That ancestor of mine among those few thousand settlers was my twenty-one-year-old great-grandfather, Frederick Woods. Like the others, he'd been promised a farm in return for helping to populate the eastern frontier of the Cape Province, and like the others he hadn't realized that he had been deceived.

After the Napoleonic wars, culminating in Wellington's victory over Napoleon in the Battle of Waterloo, there had been widespread unemployment in Britain, and my great-grandfather had been one of 4,000 young Britons to accept their government's offer of 160 acres of farmland in return for helping to settle the frontier of Britain's latest colony. He might have emulated a number of his fellow settlers who had exaggerated, or at least stretched the truth, in describing themselves as farmers, believing this would help their application. But when they had arrived in South Africa in 1820 they had discovered that instead of settling down to become landed gentry they were really required to form a buffer strip between the warring Boers, as the Afrikaners were then called, and the blacks along the eastern frontier of the Cape Province. If not cannon fodder, they were to be rifle fodder and spear fodder. What further fooled them was that the part of South Africa they had landed in, near what is now Port Elizabeth, looked exactly like England, with green rolling hills and downs as in Hampshire and Sussex, and they had the naive notion that 160 acres there would be as productive of crops as 160 acres in England. But beneath the benevolent greensward they had found an awful lot of rock, and the irregular rainfall and regular droughts later drove most of them to urban life in Grahamstown and Bathurst, and to their former trades as coopers, wheelwrights, carpenters and thatchers. One of the settler diarists noted ironically: 'We had hoped to find precious stones here, but the stones we found were precious big.' The funny thing was that when they built their houses in all that vast space, out of English habit they built small cottages with tiny railed gardens, as if they were back in their crowded island.

Their English-speaking South African descendants were often to romanticize these 1820 settlers, investing them with lofty ideals and far-sighted principles, but the truth was that they were ordinary people who had left England not to transplant democracy and enlightenment to what they regarded as the Dark Continent, but basically to earn a living because they had been out of work. Still, they were hardy people who realized there could be no turning back; that, in the words of one of them, they had to 'take root or die', and part of what they brought to South Africa was the notion of a free press. Not that they saw this as some lofty ideal; just that they were used to outspoken newspapers. They had, in effect, brought with them to South Africa the habits of free people, and one of these habits was the reading of uppity newspapers. This was to lead them into early conflict with the colonial governor in Cape Town. Two of the settlers, Fairbairn and Pringle, established the *Grahamstown Journal*, and after prolonged campaigns and court actions finally won the right to publish independent criticism of the authorities. I believed it was that legacy that had led me into collision with the South African government through my editorials about the death of Steve Biko, and I thought that great-grandfather Frederick and his fellow settlers of 1820 would have approved. I fell asleep with that happy thought.

I was awake again only four hours later, and instantly excited, as I hadn't wanted to miss the sunrise and my first sight of Southern Africa as an unbanned political prodigal, and right on cue the dawn began to break with a pink glow from the left side of the aircraft. We were somewhere over Zambia about to cross over into Zimbabwe, where I used to go on school holidays from Kimberley. What a train journey that had been – up through Botswana then across to Bulawayo, then by car to Gwanda where my school friend's parents had had a small family gold mine. In those days Zimbabwe had been called Southern Rhodesia, Zambia had been Northern

Rhodesia, Malawi Nyasaland, and Botswana Bechuanaland. Since I had gone into exile Zimbabwe had achieved its independence, and so had Namibia, so I was certainly heading back to a changed subcontinent and couldn't wait to see how far such change had penetrated into what had become the last bastion of white minority rule – South Africa itself.

Now the sun was emerging and magical rays of colour were spreading everywhere. Down below, Africa looked green and fertile, unlike the arid parts of the north we had been flying over earlier. Only thirty minutes later we were crossing over the South African border, the river Kipling called the 'great, grey, greasy Limpopo', and I was struck by how similar parts of the scenery of the northern Transvaal were to Montana and Wyoming. It was a moment of immense emotion to be back in South African airspace again. This, for more than twelve years, had been enemy territory in my mind, and during the years in exile I had tried to explain to friends in America, in Britain, Australia and elsewhere the unique awfulness of regarding your own country as enemy territory. It was hard for people from the democracies to grasp this. In wartime one could understand how a paratrooper behind enemy lines in a foreign country saw menace in every shadow, every tree and every person – more so when one didn't know the local language. But to have been outlawed in your own country, forbidden beyond the normal processes of law to move about your own home town as you wished, banned from talking to your own friends or relatives as you wished – that had been an especially weird restriction.

Now here I was flying to the same airport, Johannesburg, where I had been arrested and served with banning restrictions back in 1977. I recalled how eerily similar the real event had been to its re-enactment by Kevin Kline in *Cry Freedom*, and the subsequent scenes showing how I had been driven overnight by the Security Police back to my house and told to stay there and write nothing for the next five years. In the event the ban had been renewed twice, because after escaping I had campaigned for international economic sanctions against Pretoria – one of the more serious statutory crimes against apartheid.

And now here, right under the wing of the aircraft, was Pretoria itself. It all looked benevolent from up in that aircraft. Down there I didn't know how benevolent the burghers of

Pretoria would be towards one they had so long regarded as a traitor to the white race. It felt safe to be officially unbanned and officially rehabilitated, but the unofficial reaction might well be something else. There were still some extreme rightwingers down there with lots of guns, and they had always thought it was their patriotic duty to eliminate those they regarded as renegades.

Soon I could see the northern suburbs of Johannesburg in the distance. Before the turn of the century, when the Transvaal had been a Boer republic, old President Paul Kruger had habitually stayed in Pretoria, avoiding Johannesburg like the plague. He had believed the earth was flat, had read nothing but the Bible, and had regarded Johannesburg as a combination of Sodom and Gomorrah. Growing like a mushroom because of the discovery of the world's richest seam of gold, and teeming with saloons and brothels catering to miners from every corner of the world, Johannesburg to him had been a city of sinners, infidels and foreigners. When the Jewish community of Johannesburg had asked him as President to open their new synagogue, his dedication speech had actually concluded with the words: 'I declare this synagogue open, in the name of our Lord Jesus Christ.'

Now, suddenly, the skyscrapers of central Johannesburg were rearing up ahead of the aircraft, and the northern suburbs were right below, gleaming with hundreds of private swimming-pools. I couldn't see the massive black township of Soweto in the distance, but I knew it wouldn't gleam with swimming-pools. That disparity in swimming-pools seemed suddenly to sum up and symbolize the greatest single challenge that would dominate the new South Africa – how to redistribute the wealth without massive social disruption. The whites couldn't expect the blacks to be content with a continuation of their grinding poverty while whites alone had barbecues in the backyard at the poolside. How could Mandela deliver on what would undoubtedly be huge black expectations? And how could he restrain those impatient for economic as well as political change? But as suddenly as they had come, all such thoughts flew out of my mind as the aircraft banked sharply to begin its landing approach to Johannesburg.

My immediate concern after landing was to get past the officials at the airport. I had had the lingering worry that some last-minute technicality might yet get me barred from entry. Stranger things had happened to me at that airport, including summary arrest. I had handed over my passport with a slight twinge, and the woman who accepted it had hesitated for only an instant as she consulted some list. Her eyes had flickered sideways to an official standing beside her, he had given a barely perceptible nod, and I was through – emerging in the concourse to a battery of cameras clicking away and volleys of questions from reporters about how it felt to be back. After twelve years during which any publication quoting anything I said, even 'good morning', would have been guilty of a statutory crime in South Africa, it felt strange to be quotable in my own country again.

There was a general press conference, and I didn't censor my replies. It was a heady experience, on South African soil, to be saying exactly what I wanted to say, and I simply answered as directly as I would have in any part of the free world. Unbeknown to me my arrival had been filmed by the television crew for a BBC programme I had agreed to do on returning to South Africa, and from that moment they were with me constantly – John Bridcut, the director, and the cameraman and sound recordist.

After the press conference I looked over towards the departure lounge, which I had last seen on 19 October 1977, when three Security Police officers had stepped forward to arrest me. But today things were different. There was a festive air as old friends rushed over in welcome, including Terry Briceland and Glyn Williams from my old paper, the *Daily Dispatch*, and Ray Louw and Allister Sparks, both former editors of the Rand *Daily Mail*. Also my old friend John Ryan, who had seen us off from Maseru in early 1978 when my family and I had begun our illegal flight out of the country.

The first impact on me of my arrival was a combination of high excitement, like a degree of intoxication, with the accompanying thought that it somehow didn't feel like the country I had left so long ago – a country full of tension, menace, constant Security Police surveillance and scowling officials with frequently raised voices. Everything seemed friendlier and more laid back now, and I was staggered at the dramatic sight of two black soldiers lounging and joking at the airport entrance, armed with automatic rifles. Black soldiers! Armed! This certainly wasn't the South Africa of 1977.

I was driven through downtown Johannesburg and Hillbrow, which looked very 'black' now. Back in 1977 no blacks were allowed to have homes in the white city, but now Hillbrow seemed to have a majority of black residents. Also, startlingly, there were ANC colours everywhere, openly displayed. That, too, used to be illegal. Now there were black, green and gold scarves, shawls, flags, caps, posters all over. Parts of Johannesburg that used to look like Denver, Colorado, now had the look of Lagos and Nairobi with thousands of open-air pavement stalls and vendors and hawkers everywhere supplanting and indeed obscuring what used to be fashionable shops.

I had lunch with Allister and Sue Sparks at their house in Rivonia, only a mile or two away from the spot where the 'Rivonia Plot' was discovered by the Security Police more than a quarter of a century ago, culminating in the life sentences for Mandela, Sisulu and the others. Allister and his friends were bubbling with optimism for the new South Africa, and we kept laughing at my expressed hope that this wasn't all a dream from which I would awake in disillusion. After lunch I was off to Pretoria with the TV crew, doing my first piece to camera in the car. As I'd promised myself, I was starting my return visit to South Africa with formal calls at the American and British embassies in Pretoria, because of the wonderful welcomes my family and I had had in both countries and because of the warm hospitality Britons and Americans, in particular, had extended to us during our exile. Now was the time to say thanks. By a happy coincidence, the US Ambassador to South Africa was now our old friend of many years, William L. Swing. More than twenty years back, Bill Swing had been a young US Consul in our Eastern Cape, and it was great that he was now back as ambassador. We laughed together about the story of how Bill, newly wed in those long ago days to a German lady named Hannelore, had taken her back to High Point, North Carolina, to meet his family. One of the locals had heard her unlocal accent and had said quite seriously to Bill's dad: 'Ah didn't know Bill had married a Yankee!'

We had a great reunion at the embassy, talked over harrowing old times and interesting new times, Bill looking quite ambassadorial with his grey hair, almost as grey as mine. We certainly looked different from the thin-necked, dark-haired young men we had been when we had first met in the 1960s.

At the British Embassy I formally said my thanks to Her Majesty's representative for giving us political asylum in Britain, telling the story of how, soon after my escape, I had been invited to the White House and had been taken in to the Oval Office to meet President Carter, who had asked why we had chosen political asylum in Britain rather than America, though both countries had made the offer. Slightly flustered, I had replied: 'Sir, I like your country – but you people don't play much rugby or cricket.' More seriously, I had of course explained that the British Embassy had happened to be nearer when I had arrived so desperately in Maseru, and that friends in London had rallied around to get the kids into schools there, so we had stayed put rather than disrupt them again by going on to the US which had also generously offered safe haven. At the British Embassy I was given a ceremonial toasting with champagne, and told that Her Majesty's government had been delighted to take us in. Her Majesty's representative also noted that champagne seemed more appropriate than tea, a joking reference to what had happened when I had asked the High Commissioner in Maseru so long ago for political asylum, and his reply had been: 'Of course, of course. Now would you like a cup of tea?' When Richard Attenborough had included the incident in the film *Cry Freedom* many had assumed, including the crew, that the joke was made up, and I had had to explain that Her Majesty's representative in Maseru, Jim Moffatt, had indeed said exactly those words. What I didn't tell the embassy staff, or anyone else, was that Jim Moffatt had rubbed his hands together and added undiplomatically but with feeling: 'Given the bastards the slip, eh? Bloody good!'

With my thank-yous to the British and Americans completed, I went with the TV crew to the Voortrekker Monument, noticing that blacks could now go in at any time, not only on Tuesday afternoons as in the old days. Few had gone then, and few seemed inclined to go now, but it was another sign of change that they could now go in as often as the whites. The custodian said that blacks visiting the monument were usually schoolkids doing historical projects. I wondered how they felt about all the graphic depictions of spear-wielding black warriors being shot by white horsemen . . .

Back in Johannesburg in the early evening we filmed some footage in Hillbrow, then went on to a welcome-home party at the Sparks house, with Ray and Jean Louw and Richard and Elizabeth Steyn, Richard having moved up from the *Natal Witness* to become editor of the *Johannesburg Star*, and later in the evening Bill Swing dropped in, looking less ambassadorial in casual clothes.

Inevitably it was an evening of reminiscence, hilarity and conviviality, with the Cape wine flowing freely. Ray, Allister and I gave a choral rendition of *'Bobbejaan klim die berg'*, which translates inadequately as 'Baboon climbs the mountain', and were stuck with the rhyming line *'om die Boere te vererg'* ('to vex the farmers'), since the word Boer had long ceased in South Africa to mean only farmers but was also the term for Afrikaners generally. Since both Ray Louw and Richard Steyn had English first names and Afrikaans surnames, we reckoned they were the embodiment of Boer–Brit harmony in the land.

In the midst of our revelry there was a surprise phone call for me from Washington DC, from South African Ambassador Piet Koornhof, welcoming me home. He had seen my arrival that morning on the American television news later in the day, and had felt like telephoning. This was appropriate, because Dr Koornhof had reportedly been the only member of the 1977 cabinet to oppose my arrest and banning. We had been working closely together in those days to get rid of apartheid in sport, and he as Sports Minister had relied on me for contacts with the black sports officials. I related to the others at the party the story of how Piet Koornhof and I had integrated cricket in the Eastern Cape with a signature on the back of a cigarette packet. While the black cricketers then had been ready to break the law if necessary to play multiracial sport, the white cricketers had first wanted it made legal, and would only risk playing if the Sports Minister guaranteed in writing that they wouldn't be arrested. Koornhof, as the minister, had said I could assure them of this privately but that he couldn't officially state it in writing. 'Good God, man, I would be thrown out of the government if I put that on my official letterhead – it's still officially against the law to play multiracial sport,' he had fumed. I had pointed out that the white officials hadn't said anything about official letterheads, only that they wanted his permission 'in writing', and I had scribbled out a suggested wording on the back of a Stuyvesant packet of thirties, suggesting he sign that. Koornhof's deputy, Dr Beyers Hoek, who was one of the most conservative men in government, was horror-struck, crying out in Afrikaans: 'You cannot sign that, Dr Koornhof! It's against the policy! It's against the law!' I had kept mumbling to Koornhof, offering him my pen, that simply signing it would 'solve the whole problem' and for a while Koornhof had responded to these conflicting statements by glancing unhappily from Hoek to me with furrowed brow. Eventually, though, he had sighed heavily, taken my proffered pen, and signed over the protesting cries of Dr Beyers Hoek, saying: 'Ach, man, Beyers, we've got to blerry well start somewhere.'

When I had returned to the Eastern Cape the white administrators had taken some convincing, but had eventually settled for the signed cigarette packet. And when, three days later, we had started the first multiracial cricket match in the official Border League, and the Security Police had arrived to photograph us and take the names of all who were 'breaking the law', I had suggested they telephone the office of the Minister of Sport first. They had gone away, puzzled, and had failed to return.

Recounting this anecdote to Bill Swing and the others was a happy reminder of how different a country South Africa had become compared with the darkest days of apartheid. As we sat around the table drinking and exchanging memories of that time, we took turns relishing and considering the new possibilities now stretching before us in the new South Africa. It still seemed scarcely credible that in the final days of apartheid things could have swung around so completely, or that so much despair could have given way so quickly to so much exultation and hope, and we were all rather like excited children at a vacation resort which had magically replaced a grim reformatory. The anecdotes and reminiscences ranged over thirty years or more, and many were the stories of stalwarts of the old parliamentary press gallery such as Anthony Delius and Stanley Uys, who had both been expelled from the precincts of parliament at sword-point in 1961 by the serjeant-at-arms, Mr Retief, who had muttered apologies to Delius out of the side of his mouth as he had led him away. The crime for which Delius had been expelled had been cited as 'writing disrespectfully about parliament', and this in respect of a 'parliament' which had made itself a laughing stock among all the real parliaments of the world.

When the National Party had sought to increase its tiny majority of five seats in parliament in order to implement apartheid, it had resorted to all sorts of unparliamentary devices to do so. First it had, in effect, handed itself an additional six seats by unconstitutionally giving the whites of Namibia (then South West Africa) representation in the Cape Town parliament. Then, unable to get a two-thirds majority of the Assembly and Senate sitting together to deprive the

24

'coloured' people of the Cape Province of their votes, the government had simply appointed dozens of bogus 'senators' to make up the numbers. Right from the start in 1948 these new rulers of South Africa with their new apartheid policy had therefore soon shown themselves to be devoid of any respect for basic democratic principles or parliamentary procedures, and as the illusion of their invincibility had grown in their minds they had become ever more deluded into believing that their arrival on the stage of South African history had become permanent and irreversible.

But they had after all proved impermanent indeed, as we were there to celebrate late into the night, and for me it was a wonderful first night back home in South Africa.

CHAPTER 3

Those Familiar Places

That memorable party had ended in the early hours of the following morning with a phone call confirming that my BBC television crew had got us a flight for East London, where they would film me in my old home and office, so only a few hours later we were up in the air bleary-eyed, and I spent the flight reading newspaper accounts of my arrival and press conference. These reports were full and generous, including in the Afrikaans press, which was change indeed because in the old days reports about me in the Afrikaans papers had invariably been pejorative if not defamatory. The flight down to the coast was little more than an hour long, and when we landed this was a far more moving homecoming for me than arriving at Johannesburg had been, because this really was home territory.

We circled over the bright blue ocean before landing on a calm and sunny morning, with the big waves rolling in to the beaches. When I had last been here the beaches had all been racially zoned with separate swimming areas for whites, blacks, 'coloureds', Indians and Chinese – even for Chinese, although out of a total of a million people there had been only a few dozen Chinese. Most of the younger ones had left, and in exile I had met some of them in countries like Canada, Australia, New Zealand and America, where they were mostly specialist physicians or surgeons, architects or scientists – a huge loss to South Africa.

Driving along Settlers Way into the city was a poignant experience. Memories kept crowding in. When the kids had been small we had brought them on Sunday drives out to the airport to watch the planes landing and taking off, then on to the beach or to Marina Glen with its miniature train. Mary, the youngest, had been only three years old then, two years before the attack on her by the Security Police, when they had mailed her a T-shirt with Steve Biko's face on it but with the inside sprayed with acid powder called Ninhydrin. I still found it hard to think of that attack without wanting to shoot the two perpetrators, Security Police officers Van Schalkwyk and Marais, but both were now dead. One had drowned in his own swimming-pool only a year later, and the other had died of a heart attack not long after. But this wasn't a day for gloomy thoughts – it was a day to relish, with the city looking so clean and bright, with a freshly painted look. I had forgotten how colourful South African gardens were, at least in the white suburbs, where the semi-tropical shrubs and flowers provided that polychromatic appearance. The suburbs had grown, and the new highway system looked impressive, but before I could revisit my old house and office the crew wanted to do some filming in the local black township, so we drove straight into Duncan Village.

Duncan Village had long been one of the most notorious townships in South Africa, in terms of poverty, despair, political rage and revolutionary zeal. It had also been the scene of some particularly horrific killings by a small but feared group of political fanatics, whose actions had included setting alight and burning to a terrible death Joseph Matoti, a former ANC man thought to have turned informer, and the murder many years before of a white medical nun, Sister Mary Aidan Quinlan, during a riot in the township. She had been a greatly loved figure in the township, where she had run a clinic for three years and had become one of the few whites welcomed and accepted there every day. Driving from the clinic one afternoon in 1952 she had run into an angry political riot where speakers were urging blacks to 'kill the whites', and the crowd had stoned her car, dragged her out, stabbed her to death and set her body alight, some having cut parts of her corpse away to eat in the belief that her goodness would pass to them. The apartheid government had made much of this gruesome killing to emphasize their claim that all blacks were savage and bestial. The authorities had not recorded the widespread horror that had swept through the township, and would certainly not have added that virtually all blacks in Duncan Village, apart from the small fanatic fringe, had grieved for the popular nun and had been revolted at what had been done to her.

Remembering all this and much else that had happened down the years in Duncan Village, I was ill at ease as we entered the township. It was hard to explain to British television people that even at this time of change white people were not entirely safe in any black township anywhere in South Africa, and for very understandable reasons. The legacy of apartheid, of all the bitterness and hatred engendered by it, could not possibly be swept away overnight by any number of reforms, and the townships were full of frustrated young blacks who were unemployed, uneducated, angry and seething with potential aggression – especially towards people with white skins. An apparently calm situation could in seconds turn into an explosion of violence, triggered off by a word, a look, a wrong move or even a wrongly interpreted move.

I had tried to articulate this to John Bridcut, the director of our television crew, but John was very British, and the British tended to feel invulnerable in almost any situation, so I tensely held my peace while he and the crew started filming scenes of appalling poverty and deprivation among the shacks and shelters of Duncan Village in the bright morning sunshine. Within moments a large crowd of young blacks had gathered about us, and an angry-looking young man, who seemed to be a leader, pushed forward asking a lot of brusque questions: 'What are you doing here? Who are you people? Where are you from?'

I suddenly thought my first morning back in my South African home town might end in tragedy. Here were we four whites, with our new-looking rental car and expensive camera equipment, literally surrounded by a large crowd of young blacks waiting for the answer to these questions. John Bridcut, quite unconcerned, said as if directing a cameraman on the Thames embankment near Westminster: 'We're doing a television programme for the BBC in England on the return of Donald Woods to South Africa.' The young man said: 'What? Which of you is Donald Woods?' John waved his hand in my direction, and the frowning young man suddenly grinned broadly and shook my hand and then embraced me, and the young blacks around us crowded in to welcome me back. They had all, apparently, seen *Cry Freedom*, and seemed soon able to relate my grey hair and glasses to what Richard Attenborough's make-up department had done to give Kevin Kline that same appearance. 'See?' said John Bridcut, busily filming this welcome, 'you had nothing to worry about.' I forbore to explain that the danger period for us had been those first few moments during which the crowd hadn't known who we were. The young leader, Koko Qebeyi, said he was the ANC director in the area, and would be glad to help us, and he was of considerable assistance to us in our subsequent filming.

On leaving Duncan Village I telephoned ahead to arrange my visit to our former family home in the suburb of Vincent, and was told I was welcome to go there right away. The house, which had been a company residence for me as editor of the *Daily Dispatch*, was now occupied by the family of the newspaper's current financial director, Alan Beaumont, and I had heard they had looked after it wonderfully well. Heading for our old home was for me a very moving pilgrimage.

There it was, number 61 Chamberlain Road, in the familiar, surprisingly unchanged avenue, and memories came crowding back as I opened the gate. I wished the whole family were there with me, in my mind's eye seeing a collage of scenes from the past – Dillon dribbling a football across the lawn, Duncan running off with the cricket bat (he always hated to be out and thought if he retained control of the bat he could somehow keep on batting), Wendy, Jane and Mary out by the swimming-pool, Gavin in a small cowboy outfit with fringed shirt and toy six-shooter.

Though it had for the last months of 1977 been a place under siege, a place where telephoned threats had become regular, and bullets had been fired by the Security Police to keep us on edge, I saw it now only as a place where we had known mostly happiness. In the bright morning sunshine it looked solid, safe and huge. It was, in fact, an enormous house.

We had bought a big house to begin with, then in an orgy of building I had added as much house again in an overall concept designed by an architect friend in the style of a Mediterranean villa with a large terrace, an arched courtyard with a fountain, and a big garden in which Wendy had lovingly planted trees and shrubs. It now seemed sumptuous beyond all exile experience, with the extra-large swimming-pool, barbecue patio and a lawn that must have seemed like a prairie to the children.

With our five kids running around and my golf-chipping practice the lawn had never stood much chance in our time, but now it looked manicured and lush. Wendy's big palm tree was flourishing, as were the four msintsi trees with their bright red flowers. I sat under the tree where Wendy and I had planned our escape, unable to talk inside the house in those days because of the listening devices of the Security Police, and it all seemed so safe now, without the air of menace that had permeated the place in our last months there and without the two Security Police observers posted to monitor us. There were still marks in the outside wall and near an upper window from the bullets fired at the house, but now with the garden stretching all around and the birds twittering in the trees the place looked as unthreatening and unthreatened as a stockbroker's mansion in Surrey, England, or Scarsdale, New York.

I looked inside the double garage where my escape had begun, where I had lain on the floor of the car covered with a coat before Wendy had opened the garage doors to drive past the Security Police observer prior to letting me out at the city limits to begin my hitch-hike disguised as a priest, with my hair dyed black. Each room, each part of the house, held its own memories, and in the big lounge where our two pianos had stood I heard again in my mind the music of that time. During my banning I had actually learned two complete movements of Chopin's B minor sonata, and now I could hear the lovely slow movement all over again as if it had all happened yesterday. There, and in the dining room, were the beautiful, butter-coloured yellow-wood ceilings given to us by Wendy's father, and in my old study I remembered looking at the familiar shelves wondering if I would ever see them again. After our escape the Security Police had confiscated all the contents of the house, including all my books, no doubt looking for subversive literature. I'd often wondered how subversive they had found all my books on cricket, rugby and chess.

Above the study, at a second-floor window which still had a bullet hole from the Security Police, was the bathroom which had once enabled us to cheat the pass laws. I had arrived home one afternoon from the office to find several white policemen swarming around our front gate, had asked the sergeant what was happening and had been told that he believed two 'unregistered Bantu' had run into our house. Apparently two black men, without documentary permission to be in our white suburb, had been looking for work as gardeners, and when the police van had stopped next to them and challenged them for their 'passes', passport-like passbooks allowing them to be in white areas, they, not having them, had run until they had entered our house. The police had been about to burst in, not needing search warrants, when I had arrived. I had replied to the sergeant: 'Right, I'll go in and see if they are there!' South African policemen had been so attuned to tones of authority from others that they had accepted this for a while, before following me in after a few moments. Inside the house Wendy told me she had hidden the two men in the guest bedroom upstairs. As the policemen started coming up the stairs we decided she should take the two men into the upstairs bathroom and stay with them in there. The policemen searched everywhere, looking under beds and even behind curtains that only hung to the window sill. In the guest room I stood in front of a cupboard I knew to be empty, saying with what I hoped was a guilty look on my face: 'There's nobody in here. Nobody.' They insisted I move away from the cupboard so that they could look inside, and it was a good moment when they opened it and found it empty. Then they came to the bathroom and seized the handle, whereupon Wendy called out: 'I'm in here!' and the police sprang back, apologizing, never being able to imagine that a white woman might be locked in a bathroom with two black men. And eventually they had concluded that the two must have jumped off a balcony and escaped over the back wall. After sitting a while in my old study, thinking of this and other strange adventures we had had in the house, I telephoned the *Daily Dispatch* to say I was on my way down to the paper. Terry Briceland, now managing director, and Glyn Williams, now editor, had wanted more time to organize a full staff welcome, but I told them I'd rather arrive without any formality.

It was great to see the old building again. The *Daily Dispatch* had been an extraordinary newspaper in many ways. For more than a hundred years it had maintained maverick editorial policies, often upholding liberal values in an extremely conservative region. All its shareholders had been staff members and its seven directors had been elected from the staff.

Two-thirds of its profits each year had gone to charities, mostly black charities, in the region, and although it had been frequently reviled by whites for its 'pro-black' policies its circulation had continued to rise so that it was now the biggest and most profitable newspaper in the Eastern Cape, bigger than either of the two papers in the much larger city of Port Elizabeth. The *Dispatch* had been unique in South Africa in having its entire board composed of newspaper people, and I remembered having said to my fellow directors at one board meeting that they should mandate me as editor to speak for the board on all editorial matters, as frequently attacks on our editorial policies came from the government late at night when I couldn't consult my colleagues on the board about a reply. They had readily granted this mandate, and not long afterwards I had had the enjoyable opportunity of using it. Late one night in a parliamentary debate a government member had said that he 'appealed to the *Daily Dispatch* board of directors to dismiss Donald Woods as editor', and I was able within one minute to send over the wires a statement issued under my name saying on behalf of the board of the *Daily Dispatch* that we the board had decided to reject the request. It wasn't often that editors had this luxury.

Arriving at the *Daily Dispatch* I walked into a warm welcome from the staff, many of whom had been there in my time. I was especially moved when old Julius Lugalo, chief doorman for many years, embraced me and said in Xhosa with tears in his eyes: 'I have prayed for you every day since you have been gone.'

I sat again in my editorial chair, reflecting that I hadn't even been able to clear out my desk back in 1977 when the banning axe had fallen. My successor as editor, Glyn Williams, brought out my personal files, hoarded faithfully for me throughout my years of exile. They tactfully left me alone for a while in the big panelled office from which I had edited the paper for twelve years, and again this triggered off more memories of past campaigns and controversies.

It was an old newspaper in South African terms – founded in 1872, it had had only a dozen or so editors in more than a century. One of the most colourful had been Vernon Barber, the first editor I had worked under, a Yorkshireman who had been editor for about thirty years. As a junior reporter I had often sat on the other side of this same desk while he commended me or chastised me for something or other. Sitting there reminiscing I remembered the day he had called me in to tell me the board of directors had decided to have me groomed as editor. A year later he had called me in again to say the board had decided that I was too 'dangerous' and that they were now going to groom someone else.

I remembered the shock of that announcement, and how I had tried to cover it up with flippancy, replying: 'The board gaveth, the board hath taken away; blessed be the name of the board.' However, his successor had died within a year and I had been appointed anyway. This highly unusual newspaper had certainly had its moments, and I felt honoured to have been at the helm for twelve years at this heavy old desk with its polished brass fittings.

Calling a halt to my reminiscences, I decided to rejoin the others in the newsroom, and there I found many old stalwarts from my time – Fred Croney, who still looked like Johnny Carson; Percy Owen, the sports editor; Dave Denison, now grey-haired like me; Robin Ross-Thompson, now assistant editor, and a lot of new young faces, black and white. When I entered the newsroom they all stood and applauded, which was a moving experience, and all work stopped while we talked about the intervening years. Glyn Williams was a gracious host, and not once did I see him glance up at the edition clock in concern at this hiatus in production.

Having completed my pilgrimage to the house and the newspaper, I set out now to see the Biko family in King William's Town, driving along the road I had so often taken to see Steve Biko. This, too, was so familiar, having also been the road I had taken during my escape. I relived the anxieties of that night. How could people understand, unless it had actually happened to them, what it felt like to be in a car that could be stopped at any time at a roadblock, where if your identity was discovered you were in serious trouble if not mortal danger? Initially I had been surprised at how reassuring my disguise had seemed. Without my glasses, and my hair dyed black and wearing a priest's collar it was astonishing how different I looked, and the fact that I was playing a role made me realize for the first time how even those actors who were shy people could escape into another identity, almost as if the whole thing was for fun, taking the edge off the nervousness. But only to a limited extent, because I soon learned that one kept forgetting one was in disguise. Whenever a policeman had looked me in the face that night, which had happened twice, I had at first assumed he was seeing the real, undisguised me. But luckily the disguise had worked, and the whole crazy scheme had worked. Merely to be thinking about it now, a dozen years later in the safe sunshine, had brought a clamminess to the palms and it was a relief to be able to laugh at it all now that it was in the past.

How quickly we forget all sorts of things we thought would haunt us constantly and for ever, like scenes of ghastly carnage at road accidents. Somehow the nerve-endings lose their rawness and we return to 'normal'. It felt quite normal to be driving to King

William's Town again, off to 'King' to see Steve, like in the old days. Only now he wouldn't be waiting at his place in Leopold Street, ready for company and conversation, prowling around the backyard behind the old church thinking up some new stratagem to outwit the Security Police, full of the latest news of resistance in Soweto or Port Elizabeth.

I remembered how the Security Police had always been parked at the kerb, openly signalling that they had listened to our telephone arrangement of a meeting (which we had assumed anyway) and openly watching him to see that he didn't break his ban by talking with more than one person at a time. In greeting me, Biko had used to exhibit a total disregard for their presence, as if they were stones in the road or leaves on the trees, and somehow they had sensed this, picking up from his attitude that he wasn't the 'nonperson' they had declared him to be; that if there were 'nonpersons' around the description fitted them, not him. He was often halfsmiling at such times. It had amused him, I think, that a white newspaper editor in his forties had regularly driven a fair distance to defer to a young black 'outlaw' in his twenties, and that their conversations had influenced the columns of a white-owned newspaper. It had interested me, in turn, to find that in this weedinfested backyard I could learn more about my own country than in all the metropolitan clubs and editors' dinners in cities such as Johannesburg, Cape Town and Durban.

On reaching King William's Town I drove directly to Leopold Street, parking outside the old church door as I had so often those days, and walked around the side of the church to the backyard. But there was nothing there. Steve's office had been dismantled, the big old willow tree was gone and even the weeds were no more. There was just an expanse of cut grass, empty and lifeless. It seemed sad that no one had preserved Steve Biko's office, the little room and verandah from which so many dynamic thoughts and ideas had poured out to all parts of the country, and later to many parts of the world. As the philosopher said, the weeds take over everything in the end, but here the irony was that the weeds would have been more evocative of what this place had meant than this empty stretch of nothing.

The church, too, which had been a hive of activity as a black community centre in the 1970s, was now a freshly painted venue for bible study – now as empty as the backyard.

I went to the hospital where Steve's wife Ntsiki still worked as a nursing sister and found her as positive about things as ever, full of questions about Wendy and the kids and bringing me up to date with news about her two sons and mutual friends. The younger boy, Samora, was more like Steve physically, she said, but his elder brother, Nkosinathi, was more like him in character. On matters such as politics he was, she said, 'serious, like Steve'.

Ntsiki had known I would want to visit Steve's grave, and had thoughtfully arranged for Nkosinathi, as the eldest son, to take me there. I had never seen Steve's grave with its headstone, because by the time it was in place I had been banned myself and therefore forbidden to travel.

Nkosinathi arrived to drive me to the cemetery, and I was struck by much in his appearance and personality that reminded me immediately of Steve. Physically he looked like a blend of Steve and Ntsiki, though he was, at eighteen, considerably shorter than his father. But there was an air to him that was similar, a quietness, a stillness. Like his father, he didn't go in much for small talk, though after a while as we drove he began to talk quite readily of his school, his ideas and some of his experiences. He had the same sense of humour as Steve, telling me how he had seen *Cry Freedom* twice, going alone the second time into the crowded cinema and rather enjoying his anonymity in the audience. He said with a smile: 'Nobody in that place knew me – I was the only one in there who knew I was Steve's son.'

The television crew and some reporters were waiting at the cemetery, and they respected my request to use their long lenses rather than intrude too closely into what was essentially a private moment. I was glad afterwards that they had done their job so well because the results were a series of pictures I would really value, and at no time were they intrusive – which showed that good journalists could indeed function properly without being callous cretins. I felt moved to be there with Steve's son as I placed some flowers I had brought, and as we stood there with our thoughts the impact of it all came back to me. I remembered the hard time Ntsiki and I had had finding Steve's body, and initially the difficulty even in locating which mortuary it was in. Thoughout much of the afternoon officials had given us the runaround, and then finally when we had found it there had been the shock of that body lying there among others. Never had I seen the contrast between life and death so starkly – the utter polarity between the vibrant personality of Steve Biko and this inert and empty shell.

Now he was buried in this neglected, overgrown little cemetery – a bleak and unkempt place for the remains of someone who had during so short a life had such an impact on the history of his country. Standing there I thought of certain moments I had experienced in various parts of the world: in Portland, Oregon, where a small radio station run by young people had structured entire programmes of music and poetry in honour of Steve Biko; in Gisborne, New Zealand, where I had heard soaring from the windows of young people's apartments the powerful Peter Gabriel song 'Biko'; in Amsterdam, Holland, where a city square was renamed Steve Biko Square; in Bradford, England, where the university pub had engraved on its glass doors 'The Steve Biko Pub'; in Norwich, where the University of East Anglia had 'The Steve Biko Library'; in Australia, Canada, Sweden, Ireland, Nigeria and India, where young people had written in huge letters on overpasses or walls: 'BIKO LIVES'.

This remarkable young man's name had echoed around the world, and his death had intensified international pressure on the South African government to the point where, in conjunction with other pressures internally and externally, the end of apartheid had been hastened. As to his posthumous fame, as a politician he would have valued its practical impact politically in helping to end apartheid, but as a person he would have been amused at the comment of one of his friends as he prepared a poster: 'Thank God his name wasn't Steve Zweliyashukuma!' During most of the time I was at his grave it was Steve Biko the good companion that I thought of more than Steve Biko the political leader. He had always been good company, and one of the readiest partygoers imaginable. What a tragedy that someone who had loved life so much should have died so young.

Leaving the cemetery we went to the house, the same house Steve and Ntsiki had lived in throughout his banning, and his mother Mamcete said: 'You were my son's good friend, so you are also now my son.'

With Mamcete and Ntsiki at the house had been Steve's younger son, Samora, who though three years younger than Nkosinathi, already seemed to have the height of his father. More extrovert than

Nkosinathi (over the telephone he had said boisterously: 'Hi, Donald! So I'll get to see you at last!'), he had nevertheless been fairly shy on being introduced, but as the conversation developed he had become animated and outgoing, telling me he wanted to be a doctor one day.

Steve's sister, Bandi, arrived, looking as always startlingly like Steve, and with her bubbling personality visibly buoyed up her mother's spirits. Mamcete seemed not to have aged a day in these last twelve years, though she had had ill health. She obviously doted on the boys. We made plans for a big reunion of the two families when Wendy and the children arrived for Christmas. 'Heyi!' called Ntsiki, clapping her hands. 'What a party that will be!'

Back in East London where I was checked into the hotel with the television crew, we had a meeting to discuss future filming. The cameraman and his sound recordist were leaving in the morning, and John Bridcut was due back in London over the weekend, which was no problem as most of our filmed interviews with Nelson Mandela and other leaders were scheduled for several weeks hence, when the crew would return. This would give me time to look around and set up material for the programme and the two articles I had to write. It would also give me time to see relatives and friends, and I drove out to Gonubie for dinner, about ten miles east of the city, to the home of my sister Joan. She and her husband, Jim Inglis, several members of their family and some old ex-Transkeians were there to welcome me.

One of them was Billy O'Hagan. When I was five years old I had seen Billy and his brother Vernon set off in their new uniforms to fight in North Africa and Italy in the Second World War. His accent was typical of the region, and I'd forgotten how strong it was. Europe became 'Yorap', 'syrup' became 'serrup' and Xhosa words were often resorted to in mid-sentence. It was Vernon who had explained how to squeeze a button through a tight buttonhole: 'Man, you've got to sort of *nyanzela* it!' (*Nyanzela* means 'push' or 'force'.)

Wendy's parents, Harold and Kay Bruce, lived only a few blocks away, so I went on to see them in their new beachfront duplex until around midnight, then called on another round of friends until 2 a.m. – returning to the hotel exhausted, having been on the go since the early departure that morning from Johannesburg. I had spent much of the day behaving like a dog returning home excitedly after a stretch in the boarding kennels – rushing everywhere, sniffing long-left places and all but barking with pleasure.

CHAPTER 4

Down Memory Lane

The following morning I slept late, rang room service and was told it was too late for breakfast, but that they would send toast and coffee. When the room service waitress arrived with the tray she looked hard at my signature and printed name and said: '*Ungumhleli? u*Donald Woods?' ('Are you that editor, Donald Woods?'). I said I was and she put down the tray and came forward to shake both my hands, saying: 'How much breakfast do you want? How many eggs, and what else?' I duly ordered a substantial breakfast, and off she went with a broad smile on her face. A short while later she returned with the breakfast and with two other members of the kitchen staff who had come to shake hands. Out in the corridor were three more, waiting to shake hands.

It being a Saturday I decided to head for the rugby stadium, and there I felt a bit like Rip Van Winkle because Swifts were playing Old Selbornians, and in the grandstand and in the members' enclosure were many familiar faces. There we all were, all twelve years older and greyer, doing the same thing we had done before, Ron Grobler, Jacko Reed, Bill Loppnow, Pip Sutton, Rolf Bryant ... These men had gone on watching Swifts play Old Selbornians regardless of anything else in the world, regardless of Irangate, the Contra deal, Noriega, *glasnost*, the fall of the Berlin Wall, Saddam Hussein or the disintegration of apartheid.

But I noticed a difference in attitude of some of the rugby officials and committee men compared to their attitudes in 1977. Back then I had been studiedly ignored by some of the more conservative ones who had resented my liberal editorials, but now on my return every one of them had come forward to shake hands and welcome me back, and one had actually said: 'We should have listened to people like you a long time ago.' This, too, was change, as was the fact that a fair number of the rugby players now on the main stadium field in the featured match were black.

The following morning my sister Joan and brother-in-law Jim called to take me to Palm Springs, a resort some miles down the coast run by our friends Roy and Joan Crawford. Roy, a colourful character, had once helped me to break more apartheid laws in one day than I had thought possible. It had been back in the early 1970s – I had planned a weekend conference of black and white leaders from all over the country at Roy's former coastal resort, the Glengarriff Hotel.

We had had to apply to no fewer than five government departments to get permission for whites, blacks, 'coloureds' and 'Indians' to be allowed on the same premises, to be served food and alcohol together and to use the same toilets – and right up to the day of the conference no permission had been granted from any of these government departments.

I had asked Roy what he thought we should do, since he could lose his hotel licence and we could both be prosecuted if we didn't have the necessary permits. There had been no precedents to follow, because no such event had been held in South Africa before. Roy had said: 'Let's go ahead. Let 'em do what they like. Fuck 'em.' In spite of unusual police interest in the proceedings the conference had gone off without untoward incident.

Now Roy and Joan had moved from the Glengarriff and were running a new resort at Palm Springs, and as we got nearer we began to see nailed to various trees and written in chalk on fences and walls, a succession of signs reading WELCOME HOME DONALD. Roy and Joan looked unchanged by the years, and more than a decade faded away as we sat down to a typical Crawford gourmet lunch featuring big mussels and oysters, followed by giant prawns in *piri-piri* sauce and my favourite soulfood, *umnqusho*, made with stamped maize, while before us as we ate a lovely river flowed through a pretty little forest into the ocean. I was reminded of facets of typical South African hospitality, such as the custom of flipping off the top of a beer bottle as it was extended to the visitor at regular intervals with no interruption in the talk and no enquiry as to whether it was required. Certain things were simply assumed.

That evening I dined with my old friend Terry Briceland and

40

some friends he had invited from the old days, and it seemed to me that most of them had grown fairly conservative during my absence. Though all supported the recent reforms and all agreed that apartheid had to go, their consensus extended to a deep apprehension about how standards would fall in South Africa under black majority rule, not because they regarded blacks as inherently inferior but because blacks for so long had been denied education and experience in administration.

They had been strongly against economic sanctions, and I had tried to make the point that if sanctions hadn't pressured De Klerk into freeing Mandela and beginning the reform process there would have been much more violence in South Africa on a widespread national scale, during which more whites as well as blacks would have lost their lives. But they weren't convinced.

Still it was a new experience for me to hear whites in South Africa talking about black rule as an inevitability, regardless of its merits, and the next morning I went to listen to what a diehard old Afrikaner Nationalist had to say about De Klerk's reforms. I called at the home of Robbie De Lange, for many years the governing party's leader in our city, and his loyalties were unambiguous. 'We've got to support De Klerk, man! These Conservatives under Treurnicht are living in the past.' I wondered if my friends abroad would have realized how strange it was to hear people like Robbie De Lange saying such things. In American terms it would have been like returning to the US after many years away to find that Jesse Helms was now supporting Jesse Jackson.

I set out to revisit parts of my city that had had special meaning for me and that I hadn't seen for so long. First I drove along Fleet Street to the site of my first lodgings in the city when I had arrived to become a junior reporter on the *Dispatch*. Called Tenby Apartments, the building looked much as it had that day back in 1957. Not far away was Gleneagles, where I had later had an apartment when I became somewhat more upwardly mobile salarywise. Then I drove to Polana Court, where Wendy and I had had our first flat after we were married in 1962, then to our first house in the suburb of Baysville, where we had lived until our fourth child, Gavin, was born. It was in search of more space for our growing family that we had moved to Chamberlain Road in Vincent.

I drove to St Mark's Road, Selborne, to the maternity hospital where all our children had been born. Opposite still stood the first boarding school I had attended on coming to East London from the Transkei territory at the age of eleven. That had been in 1945, and I recalled having seen my first newspaper headline at that big stone gate – a banner across nine columns celebrating the end of the Second World War. I remember the songs that had blared out everywhere at that time – 'Don't Fence Me In' by Bing Crosby and the Andrews Sisters, and 'Paper Doll' by the Mills Brothers. The Ink Spots had also been big that year.

I drove around for hours, just looking at such places as the children's schools, friends' former houses, my favourite golf courses and the best beaches. I even parked outside the Security Police building where I used to be taken for interrogation. I picked out the window of the room, up on the second floor, where Colonel Van den Heever used to shout: 'We're going to lock you up.' Colonel Van der Merwe, more silent in style, used to say: 'We're going to get you. My men hate you – they can't wait to get you.' I couldn't resist a rather childish two-fingered gesture up at that second-floor window, and the thought: well, I'm back, and in better circumstances than you lot.

This set me to thinking about Donald Card, one of the most extraordinary people I had ever met. Don and I had both been born in the Transkei territory, and unlike most white South African kids we had grown up speaking an African language – Xhosa. He was several years older, and by the time I was a junior reporter starting on the *Dispatch* he had become a police sergeant with the Criminal Investigation Department. At the police college he had been the only English-speaking rookie in his entire class – police recruits had invariably been Afrikaners.

This had caused him to become fluent in Afrikaans as well as English and Xhosa, and his fellow rookies had referred to him as '*die Engelsman*' ('the Englishman'). When his temper, allied to his fighting skills, had become known – he won the police heavyweight boxing title – they had called him '*die mal Engelsman*' ('the mad Englishman').

As a reporter I had done a story about him in the *Dispatch*, because as a detective he had had an unusually high success rate in solving crimes. Behind his desk in his office had been an entire wall covered with weapons he had confiscated from criminals who had attacked him with them. He had been shot at, once at point-blank range when the revolver had misfired, he had been stabbed with a

42

variety of knives, attacked with bicycle chains, pangas and clubs – and they were all up on the wall. But he had stood little chance of being promoted, because he wasn't an Afrikaner, and in those early days of the Afrikaner Nationalist government in the middle to late 1950s non-Afrikaners had stood little chance of advancement in any state departments including the army and police.

When I had returned in 1960 from two years abroad I had found he was in the dreaded Security Police because of his language skills. He hadn't seemed too pleased about this, but felt he couldn't question orders, seeing it as just another branch of police work. In the Security Police he had progressed to the rank of warrant officer, and had become quite a legendary figure among whites, and a hated figure among political blacks, because of his success rate in arresting and imprisoning members of the African National Congress and the Pan-Africanist Congress. In fact, his evidence had been instrumental in gaining the convictions against Nelson Mandela and other members of the black resistance.

His most famous coup in the eyes of the whites had been one night in 1963 when he had blackened his skin with boot polish and infiltrated a squad of about 200 Poqo men armed with guns, cane knives and axes as they had set out to attack and kill whites in the outlying suburbs of the city. Using his eloquence in Xhosa and his appearance, he had led them into a police ambush. Eventually both the ANC and the PAC had put a price on his head and sentenced him to death.

It was at this stage that I had got to know him better through our common origins and our mutual interest in rugby – he had been coach of our regional rugby team – and I had begun to discuss his work with him. I had soon realized that although he was deeply conservative, having been raised as I was, he was neither pleased with his job in the Security Police nor deeply committed to the racial view. In fact, it seemed to me that he had developed quite a respect for many of those he had hunted down, especially Nelson Mandela and others of leadership calibre.

Like many policemen he was bitter because although they were expected to risk their lives often they were poorly paid, and he especially regretted not being able to afford to send his children to university as he had wanted, because his pay had been so low and his promotion prospects limited by his non-Afrikaner origins and his non-membership of the governing party. I was eventually able to help him find a better job at a much higher salary, and we had become friends.

Though I had never consciously tried to 'convert' him politically, he had met some black friends of mine who had impressed him, including Steve Biko, and he was soon developing his own radical-ized view of politics in South Africa – so much so that he eventually became a parliamentary candidate for the anti-apartheid Progressive Party of Helen Suzman and Colin Eglin, later known as the Democratic Party. He also went with a delegation of whites to visit the ANC leadership in exile in Lusaka, in the middle 1980s, and was profoundly moved when Oliver Tambo and other ANC leaders forgave him his Security Police past and one leader he had personally imprisoned, Steve Tshwete, welcomed him with an embrace.

In the late 1970s he had also become very committed to my well-being and that of my family, and when the Security Police had started attacking our house he had declared his own war against his former colleagues to protect us. Wendy only had to call his number if the house was being threatened and he was there, fully armed. He made a formidable foe, as they soon discovered. Whether with firearms or with his bare fists he was a lethal character, and I once had to talk him out of assaulting a police captain who was part of the threat against us.

Don Card had become very fond of our children and protective of them, and when our five-year-old daughter Mary was sent the poisoned T-shirt in 1977, he had become obsessed with hunting down the culprits. Within ten days he had identified them as Security Police Warrant Officers Van Schalkwyk and Marais, and when he had presented the evidence to the uniformed (non-politi-cal) police and they had refused to act, he had named them publicly. For this he had been summoned to Pretoria and told by the head of the Security Police, General Coetzee, that he would be 'eliminated' if he went on with the case. As a compromise, the general had had the two culprits transferred from the region and, presumably, cautioned against similar escapades.

When I had fled South Africa in 1977 I had left a note for Don, together with a gift. I had bought a riot gun for purposes of retalia-tion, and Don had immediately fallen deeply in love with it. Of American make, it was a fearsome weapon with a pump action, capable of mowing down a considerable number of assailants in one fusillade. Thank heavens I had never had to use it – I believe that news of its purchase served as a deterrent – and because Don and his wife Hetty were by now also under threat for having befriended us I left the gun for him. It must have served him well as a deterrent too, because in due course the threats against him died down and he actually became mayor of the city.

During our years in exile Don and Hetty had visited us twice, and Hetty, whose maiden name was Botha and who cooked wonderful Afrikaans food which was as delicious as it was unhealthy, would cook me *vetkoeks*, *boerewors* and other fare which would have had my American friends, with their dread of cholesterol, crossing themselves and backing away at the very sight.

We had always talked of the day we would visit them back home instead of their having to come six thousand miles to visit us in London, so it was with special pleasure that I set out to dine at their house again for the first time in many years. Don soon produced 'The Persuader', as we used to call the gun I left him, to show that he had looked after it lovingly. When I asked if he'd ever had to use it it was with real regret that he shook his head, while sighting wistfully along the barrel.

Staying with the Cards and using their house as a base I spent happy days rediscovering the city, and with old golfing friends I played three of the local courses. In between I went to shops and public buildings, seeing many signs of black upward mobility. I also witnessed the new phenomenon of blacks in executive positions over whites, experiencing this for myself when I called in at a city bank to change traveller's cheques.

The teller, a young white woman, said she couldn't change the cheques unless I had my passport with me for identification. I said I didn't have it with me, so she decided to refer the matter to her boss. He, a black man with an easy air of authority, initialled the OK without any hesitation, enabling her to make the payout. To a white South African of my generation it was a startling tableau in a South African bank.

I went with Don Card to visit Evalina Mvunelwa, who had been our housemaid for years and was now living on a pension in the township of Mdantsane. Over the years we had managed to buy her a house in Unit Eight in what had now become the second-biggest black township in the country after Soweto. Evalina had visited us in London in 1986, and had within moments resumed her role as queen of the household, managing to get the kids to tidy their rooms with an alacrity Wendy and I had never succeeded in achieving. The fact that the three boys were now all over six feet tall had had no effect on her authority over 'her babies'.

It was moving to see her pictures of our family displayed in her house as she served tea for me and other guests from her neighbourhood who had dropped in for the occasion. She was excited about Wendy and the children returning with me for our Christmas vacation, because she was coming with us to our holiday shack on the Transkei coast which we hadn't seen for so long.

CHAPTER 5

That Mighty Mountain

I spent the following week on a national flyabout, travelling back to Johannesburg, then to Cape Town, then to Durban, then back to East London, and my abiding impression of that whiparound of some 3,000 miles was of the staggering beauty of Cape Town. Not that I had forgotten this beauty, but I had forgotten the dimensions of it. In various parts of the world during my years of exile I had described Cape Town as one of the most beautiful cities in the world, others being Sydney, Rio de Janeiro, Vancouver and San Francisco. But when I saw Cape Town again I suddenly wondered how I could ever have mentioned other cities in the same breath. Seeing it anew, I realized that Cape Town stood alone. Aberrations of doubt had clearly occurred through familiarity. I had spent five years in Cape Town as a student and later as parliamentary correspondent of the *Daily Dispatch*, and had grown to take its beauty for granted. But now, after the years away, I was bowled over anew by its loveliness. It wasn't only the glorious Table Mountain with its flat top and 'tablecloth' of cloud towering over the city, the sweeping bay and the other two peaks, Lion's Head and Devil's Peak, flanking the city centre on either side – it was the whole Cape Peninsula with its inlets and bays, its series of mountains extending down the coast, as Mediterranean in atmosphere as the Mediterranean itself, except with everything on a bigger scale.

Called 'the Mother City', it had been the first white settlement in South Africa, in 1652, and older parts of the city, still cobblestoned, made it unlike all the other cities in the country. Greenmarket Square, with its Cape Dutch windows and gables, was one of many reminders of the city's history, and Sea Point was where Charles Darwin had found the spot where the granitic and dolomitic rock formations had met to form the continental coast. Further down the peninsula towards Cape Point was the naval base at Simonstown, where Admiral Horatio Nelson had been stationed for a time as a young midshipman.

I was asked to address the Cape Town Press Club, and in this speech, and a subsequent radio interview for the South African Broadcasting Corporation, I again held nothing back as one would have had to do in the old days, and it was accurately relayed and reported. It felt good to be able to communicate properly as a journalist again in my own country, after twelve years of 'non-quotable' status.

While I was roaming around Cape Town visiting my old student haunts, I received a call from *Time* magazine in New York. They were offering me two pages to describe the extent of change in South Africa, and the challenge to me was to find a way of conveying this after only a few days back in the country.

Clearly I needed a striking notion of how to measure change and it seemed to me after some reflection that the best way to do so would be to revisit the Security Police. Instead of them calling on me, as in the old days, I would call on them, and gauge by their reaction the true extent of change in South Africa.

Actually there was more to it than that. For two weeks I had been travelling around South Africa taking in all the social and political changes, but I needed some kind of touchstone – an ultimate proof to myself that change was genuine and irrevocable. And it seemed that if I could go back to the Security Police headquarters in our city, to the environment in which they had scared me so much with their interrogations and harassment, and not feel frightened any more, that would be the sure sign that change was real. There was also in this idea the notion of wanting to walk as an adult through a reputedly haunted house that had terrified one as a child.

I made the call to the Security Police office, and though there was initial mystification on the other end of the telephone line there was also a note of interest. The Security Police, it seemed, were themselves intrigued at the idea. I parked my rented car outside Security headquarters at the appointed time, sharply remembering past harassment and interrogations, and resorted to a ploy that had worked well in those days – mentally humming a reassuring piece

48

of music to ease the fear. During the last stormy session with Colonel Van der Merwe in 1977 I had mentally countered his aggression with the finale of Gershwin's Concerto in F, which has a lot of lively brass, upbeat and beneficial to the morale. Though no longer that scared, I was nevertheless sufficiently apprehensive to stay with Gershwin by resorting mentally to 'Fascinating Rhythm' as I pressed the button beside the steel grille I remembered so well. It clanked open with awful familiarity to reveal a young reception- ist who told me a Colonel Nel would be with me shortly. The furni- ture, the office, the whole atmosphere was more human than in the past. Armchairs, even, instead of those hard upright 'interrogation' chairs.

In came the dark-haired young Colonel Nel, smiling amiably. I was given a comfortable chair and a cup of tea, and wondered if this was how Russian dissidents might feel today on revisiting the Lubianka Prison. Nel looked too young to be a colonel, and I remembered the saying that one is getting old when doctors and policemen start looking like teenagers.

We discussed the changes in the country, and I said that after two weeks back my first impression was that South Africa seemed a very different place to the one I had left; that one couldn't describe as 'cosmetic' the fact that blacks were now allowed into public buildings, sports clubs, schools and other amenities previously barred to them by law, and that there were no more segregated beaches, toilets, lifts, parks or benches. Earlier in the week the governing National Party had voted to open its membership to blacks – an organizational turnaround analogous to a PLO recruit- ment drive among Jews, or a Ku Klux Klan appeal for black members.

So if not entirely dead, apartheid was nevertheless clearly in the intensive-care unit with the oxygen turned off. But what about the Security Police attitude to all this? Colonel Nel, from the start, spoke a different political language from that of his predecessors, and the more we talked the more I realized that the biggest change in Security Police thinking was the apparent death of their old obsession with the fancied power of 'international communism' and concomitant thinking – that opponents of apartheid were putative communists if not actual paid agents of the Kremlin. He agreed, saying their approach was more sophis- ticated these days, with the country facing a different set of perceived challenges embodied by the alienated black youth in the townships.

It seemed to me a great irony. Through four decades of apartheid the Afrikaner Nationalists had outlawed effective political structures in the townships and devastated black family life, creating in the process a generation of frightening teenagers ready to maim, burn and hack to pieces real or fancied enemies – kids who had never known a home with parents, had never been to school or followed any rule but the rule of survival by violence. Now, to save the whites from this Frankenstein monster of their own creation, the South African government was counting on the recently legalized African National Congress and leaders such as Nelson Mandela to bring this wild generation into some sort of discipline.

At one point in our discussion it occurred to me that I had been in the Security Police offices for half an hour without yet feeling nervous, and I accepted a refill of tea as we talked about changes in white perceptions. To me the biggest such change was in the acceptance of some measure of reality. In the South Africa I had left in 1977 only a tiny percentage of whites, probably fewer than two per cent, had supported the notion of full democratic rights for blacks, and most whites had been vociferously ready to fight to the death against the very idea. But now a great many, probably a majority in fact, seemed to me to be resigned to it, provided a democratic constitution could guarantee protection for minorities – whites, in the new code language.

Another big change among whites was that up to the late 1970s liberal white advocates for black rights had been overwhelmingly English-speaking, led by the likes of Alan Paton, Helen Suzman and Nadine Gordimer, whereas today younger Afrikaners were taking the lead among whites in the campaign for democracy and racial reconciliation, notably Frederik Van Zyl Slabbert, a gifted intellectual and charismatic leader; Max du Preez, editor of the crusading paper *Vrye Weekblad*, and Tian Van Der Merwe, campaigning to close the gap between white parliamentarians and the ANC. Then there was the remarkable story of the new President himself, F. W. De Klerk, who had been shown on television that very morning greeting blacks in Soweto with the black solidarity handshake – palm enclosing palm, thumb, and then palm again – and being applauded by black bystanders.

Colonel Nel and I discussed the Biko case, which had after all been the cause of my main conflict with the Security Police. He said he had known Steve Biko fairly well, having been stationed in King William's Town as a junior lieutenant. He had often seen him in the street and stopped to talk to him. 'He was very nice and very intelligent. He took a real interest in you as a person, and would talk about family matters and children, you know?' I said I still had many unanswered questions in that regard, and asked for telephone numbers of the Security Police headquarters in Pretoria. He supplied these readily, with details of the new chain of command, and spoke also about Biko's associates of that time and about how they had since progressed in their careers. Two, Barney Pityana and Malusi Mpumlwana, were now priests – hardly the bloodthirsty terrorists they had been regarded as in some quarters in those days.

Colonel Nel asked, as most white South Africans tended to do now, what I thought about the new South Africa and its prospects, and in the tone of the question itself was yet another change. In the old South Africa visitors had always been asked what they thought of the country, and the question had usually had undertones of defensive apprehension. Today the question was put, as Colonel Nel did, in the expectation of approbation. I used an Afrikaans idiom to describe how the more conservative whites who supported change were backing it *met lang tande* (with long teeth). In Afrikaans reference is made to how dogs eat food they don't find too appetizing – with 'long teeth' of reluctance, suspicion and distaste. In the end, I said, perhaps the biggest change of all for me was the absence of the sense of being followed everywhere, monitored and under constant threat by the Security Police (he shrugged, as if to say 'of course') and that this was so marked that here I was after only two weeks back in the country doing the unthinkable – actually walking voluntarily into the Security Police offices like this.

I asked about all my old enemies. Colonel Goosen? Dead. Colonel Van der Merwe? Retired. Captain Hansen? Transferred. Captain Schoeman? Somewhere upcountry. I already knew that those responsible for the acid-tainted T-shirt, Warrant Officers Lieutenant Jan Marais and Van Schalkwyk, were both dead.

I then asked Colonel Nel if I could have their files on me, as a souvenir. He laughed and threw up his hands, saying: 'We don't even have them any more.'

I felt irrationally aggrieved at having been forgotten so soon, I said, and he assured me again that I was no longer 'on their books'.

Then, as he walked me out to my car, he said: 'Please drop in any time. You're most welcome.'

No, I said. I had simply wanted to de-spook the place in my mind, telling him why I had had the idea. He said he understood fully, and shook hands.

As I drove off he waved and called out: 'Good luck!'

Good luck to us all, I thought. If we could bury the past, rectify decades of oppression, reclaim the lost generation, overcome the dangerous death throes of right-wing and left-wing extremists and create a true democracy in this country, there really could be a great future for South Africa.

A huge task, yes, with huge challenges and many high hurdles ahead. But a start had been made by brave leaders, and I hoped and believed they would get the support they deserved.

This had been the strangest day of my home visit so far. And though I hadn't once felt scared in that Security Police building, I had occasionally felt somewhat uncomfortable, and I was certainly a lot happier when I was outside it again. 'Fascinating Rhythm' had helped me through. Good old Gershwin.

CHAPTER 6

Crossing the Kei

On 10 September 1990 I set off on a sentimental journey back to my origins in the Transkei region. After several days in East London I felt the need to return to my original roots, to the place where I was born, to see for myself how much it had changed. For white Transkeians I'd heard that much had changed for the worse, but that was typical of displaced people, and heaven knew the white Transkeians had been displaced by the apartheid government as a sacrifice on the altar of apartheid. Their argument was that they had compulsorily moved so many blacks from their homes in order to consolidate 'whites only' areas that to placate their critics they also had to move whites from their homes to create 'blacks only' areas. So Transkei became the first 'independent homeland' for blacks. Being an exclusively Afrikaner government, of course, they took care to choose English-speaking whites for such displacement, and because Transkei had been set up before the turn of the century by the British colonial government as a sort of 'reservation' for blacks, the Afrikaner Nationalists found it convenient to justify their racial engineering in this way. Most of the token work had been done, including the beautiful old parliamentary building, the 'Bunga'.

The Transkei in which I grew up had been unique in South Africa. Because blacks had at least had some land rights and political rights there that they didn't have elsewhere, the relationship between blacks and whites had been more amiable and healthier than in the rest of South Africa. In an area the size of Denmark, with about 2 million blacks and only about 25,000 whites, there had perforce been more contact on a daily basis between black and white, and many Transkei whites had grown up speaking the Xhosa language as well as English. It was a highly feudal lifestyle in which we whites were of course the privileged ones, but indefensible though the situation was in all equity, there had been a considerable absence of the racial tension and ill-feeling so prevalent in the rest of the country. And conservative and racist though the Transkei whites were, they hadn't seemed to have that distant disdain for blacks that most whites had manifested in the other parts of South Africa.

My father had been a trader, one of about 15,000 white traders in the territory, and so had a number of our relatives. The trading stations had been located all over the territory and sited at least five miles away from each other. A trading station was like an amalgam of a farm and a store, but essentially it was also a country home. Serving each district of trading stations was a small village, and ours had been Elliotdale, or, in Xhosa, eXhora. It was only twenty-four miles from the Wild Coast – a wooded coastline with glorious beaches that had no equal anywhere that I had seen in the world, and I set off with nostalgic anticipation to drive the 150 miles or so from East London across the Kei river to the Elliotdale district.

Because of the racial madness of apartheid, this time in reverse to suit the needs of the Pretoria government, white Transkeians had been compelled to sell their trading stations to blacks – which had dealt a hammer blow to the economy and infrastructure of the whole territory because blacks hadn't had the working capital to run the stations properly and few of them had been able to succeed. Ironically, this had been claimed by the white racists in Pretoria as proof that blacks couldn't emulate whites in running such businesses, and it had also resulted in the destruction of many of the trading stations themselves because the black traders had had to put daily survival before infrastructural development for the future. So plantations of trees had been cut down to provide basic fuel, lawns and gardens had been turned over to maize crops, and even roof timbers had in some cases been used for firewood.

With the decline of the trading stations had gone the consequent decline of the villages. As the white shopkeepers, hoteliers, doctors, lawyers and teachers had had to move out, so these villages had begun to look like ghost towns, because blacks hadn't had the chance to be trained to replace them or maintain their houses. So as I drove across the Kei river into the territory I had

been warned what to expect from this unusual side-effect of territorial apartheid.

The countryside looked as beautiful as ever, the green, rolling
hills dotted with rondavels – round thatched huts – and as I turned
off the main highway on to the Elliotdale road I could hardly
believe I was going to see Elliotdale again. The nearer I got to the
coast the deeper the valleys and dales became, and I thought of my
days there as an apprentice country lawyer, aged twenty-two. After
my father's death my mother and I had bought a house in the
village, and as my brother had taken over our family trading
station, Hobeni, down near the coast, and my sister and her
husband had another station, Cwebe, near Hobeni, we had got
together during weekends for golf, cricket and various events with
the other villagers and traders of the district. There had been a regular Transkei golf circuit in those days, right up to 1957 when I had
left to become a reporter in East London, and each of the villages
had had its open tournament, cricket team and rugby team. Our
main rivals had been Willowvale, across the Bashee river.

But it had all started to unravel in 1956, when the architect of
apartheid, Dr H. F. Verwoerd, had decided the time had come to
balance those black removals with white removals. I started noticing the consequences as I entered Elliotdale. Most of the houses
looked run down, with paint peeling from roofs and walls, and the
Gordon Hotel, that had been the centre of dances and parties, now
looked like a derelict barn. The road was so badly rutted that it was
barely possible to drive on it.

The village hall was the saddest site. Here where I had seen my
first movies, following the fortunes of Andy Hardy, Shirley Temple,
Errol Flynn and Spencer Tracy, was an empty hulk with panes missing from the windows, floorboards rotting and an atmosphere of
general decay. One of my first memories had been of that hall, on a
magic day when Father Christmas in a big white beard had driven
right into the hall on special boards laid across the entrance steps,
in a small black car which had had cotton wool blobs stuck on it to
simulate snow – this in our midsummer December!

Opposite were the old tennis courts, barely recognizable as such
because of the overgrowth of weeds, and further down was the
very spot where Viv Whitfield, a trader fond of his liquid refresh-
ment, had used to park his car in reverse gear outside the pub so
that when he staggered out in the early hours he didn't have to do

too much thinking to drive away. Inevitably, one night, he parked it the other way with its back to the pub, and hours later came a rending crash as he let out the clutch and reversed violently through the wall of the saloon bar.

I drove down to the sports fields, to the former rugby ground, cricket ground and golf course I had often played on. There was little evidence that they had ever existed. I could barely pick out the outlines of where the fairways had been – all was now overgrown with thickets of wattle trees and scrub – and I thought of all the people I could remember there in those days, and the scene at one of the tournaments with the cars parked on the left and the tea and cakes being served in the small clubhouse. Of what had been the clubhouse only a few walls stood, with a tree growing up through parts of what had once been a roof. It was a hint of what to expect further down the road, on getting to the trading stations.

The first one by the roadside was Alderley, and it resembled the scene from *Gone with the Wind* when Scarlett O'Hara arrived back at Tara to see the ravages of war. Here where my sister Joan had attended garden parties on the lawns, and where there had been magnificent trees and an entire plantation extending down the hill, only tree-stumps were left. All the trees had been cut down for fuel, and the main house was a derelict hulk with windows missing, doors hanging from their hinges and weeds growing everywhere. Here had once lived my first love, named Shirley, who had looked like a fifteen-year-old Ava Gardner.

Several miles on I came to the next trading station, which while not as bad as Alderley looked pretty woebegone as well. Though fairly well maintained, it badly needed painting. The next one by the roadside was Mount Pleasant, which I was glad to see had retained some of its trees and looked at least functional.

I resolved to visit all the family stations before getting to our old home, Hobeni. First there was Uncle Ted's former place, Mbanyana, which looked in fairly good shape but again had lost a lot of trees. Then there was Granny Lawlor's place, Madwaleni, which had once had twenty-one rooms in which my mother and her twelve brothers and sisters had grown up. It was barely recognizable, but mainly because a hospital had been built there, with all its outhouses and sheds and garages. There was nothing left of what had been the croquet lawn or the orange orchard – all overgrown. The saddest of all was Uncle Arthur's place, Nkanya, which he had built so lovingly. Uncle Arthur and Aunt Ena had had a beautiful garden and a pond, with ducks, overhung by willow trees. All of this was gone, looking like a scarred battlefield, and the main house was an empty, ruined shell. I looked through broken windows into what had been the dining room, and not much was left of the floor. I remembered so many big family gatherings there, lunches and dinners, with various branches of the Lawlor and Woods clans. Uncle Pat, Uncle Arthur, Uncle Ted, all had had their own stations.

I hardly knew what to expect as we approached Hobeni. I'd always felt a special attachment to the house where I was born, and I'd always loved the way it appeared suddenly as the car crested the hill and you saw it down below, with the blue ocean in the background only three miles away. We came over the rise, and I was relieved to see that it looked as it had before – somewhat faded and in need of paint, but intact, and with all its trees.

As we got nearer I was even more glad to see that it was in the process of being repainted. The owners were away, and I was able to walk all over the place, looking through the windows at my old room, my brother's room, my sister's room, my parents' room, at all the places so full of memories, and it was wonderful to see it being so well maintained. There was the big Mtombe tree, planted when I was two years old. It now had a trunk some twenty feet in circumference, and its branches towered high above.

It was from here at Hobeni, which in Xhosa means 'place of doves', that I had gone at the age of six to boarding school because there were no adequate schools nearer than Umtata, sixty-three miles away. Then after five years to East London, to De La Salle College, then for the final six years of my high school education to Christian Brothers' College, Kimberley, more than 500 miles away. But always this was home, during the long school holidays back from all these places, back even from university in Cape Town 800 miles away.

Our seaside cottage, where we had spent most of our vacations, was further down the road at Bashee Mouth, and fortunately this too was unchanged. It was a coastal spot of rare beauty, located between the mouths of the Mbanyana and Bashee rivers.

Barely a mile below Hobeni the road fell away steeply to the right and you saw directly down to the valley and the banks of the Bashee, beside which Nelson Mandela was born. The far bank was always shadowed by a towering rocky cliff dotted with shrubs and flaming aloes, then you drove through a pretty little forest full of boxwood and yellow-wood trees said to have twenty-two varieties of wild orchids, emerging to breast a rise that suddenly revealed the great blue ocean sweeping from horizon to horizon. This was another of my favourite memories, the sudden combination of colours in the bright sunshine, as over the green grass you saw the white waves rolling in from the blue ocean, and over to the left the red dome of the Bashee Lighthouse rising out of the green forest.

Directly ahead was The Haven, a holiday resort of thatched chalets where my brother Harland and I used to spend many evenings because of the pretty girls from upcountry whose parents had had the good taste to bring them here for their vacations. Being from places as far afield as Johannesburg and Bloemfontein, the people at The Haven were regarded in some ways almost as aliens, because we Transkeians had our own resort just over the hill with, we believed, the better beach, the better accommodation and the better ambience. Ours was known as The Camps, or The Cottages, because about a dozen families each had our own cottages and access to 'our' beach. If 'the hotel people' or 'the Haven people' showed the good sense to come to our beach we had the ambivalent reaction of acknowledging their taste while resenting their intrusion. There was, every Christmas, a continuing rivalry between the people of The Haven and the people of The Camps. We played beach cricket against them, beach rugby, and even indulged for many years in an annual beer-drinking contest. It was hard to find any 'camper' who could recall 'the Havenites' ever winning any kind of contest, but in the evenings, when young men's thoughts turned to romance, such hostilities were forgotten as parties of raiders from The Camps set out resolutely for The Haven with the perpetual optimism of male teenagers the world over. By now greatly enjoying my sentimental journey, I checked into The Haven, then drove up and over the Lighthouse hill to see 'the camps'. Ours was the first, my father having chosen it because of the quality of water of the natural spring there, and walking among the thatched rondavels after so many years brought the memories rushing again.

My father had built the place the year I was born, and I had had my first birthday there. Such are the tricks memory plays that most of what I could remember of childhood was a state of perpetual happiness in seemingly perpetual vacations there.

Every morning, it seemed, one had woken up to bright sunshine streaming over the half-door of the rondavel with the loud roar of the pounding waves only yards away, and the same reassuring roar of the waves had lulled you to sleep at night. Yet it couldn't always have been that sunny, because I also remember having enjoyed the distinctive thrumming of rain on the thatched roof at night. Nor could we have spent as much time there as I now felt we had, though the Christmas vacation alone had been more than two months, and the family had often spent weekends there because Hobeni was only three miles away. The next cottage, which in the old days had belonged to the Sutton family from Darabe trading station, now belonged to my sister Joan and her husband Jim, and five cottages further had been, and still was, that of my wife Wendy's parents. She and I had met on 'our' beach, though when I was sixteen she had been only eight, one of the next-door kids I barely noticed. Then suddenly, one vacation, when I was back from my student days in Cape Town at the age of twenty-three, I noticed with increasing interest that she had grown highly attractive, apart from which she played the piano well, read a lot and had a keen sense of humour. Though she was only sixteen at the time, I had found her conversation and company more interesting than that of the Jo'burg girls over at The Haven, or that of any others, a view which was to survive my next few years in East London, including my two years as a learner-journalist in Europe and America, and to result in our marriage shortly after her twenty-first birthday. So our beach held a lot of significance and stories, many of which I recalled as I went past all the cottages on the way to the Mbanyana mouth. The Mbanyana had been 'our' river, much as the Bashee had been that of the Havenites, but it was smaller than the Bashee, having to my mind a kind of shadowy mystery as it flowed out of the Cwebe forest in a curve to the sea.

Where else in the world, I wondered, were there scenes like these? Hawaii, and parts of Australia, have some of this coastal beauty, but often at the price of high humidity – one of my pet hates. In this mile or two of forested beach between the Mbanyana and the Bashee, including the island at about the mid-point which was more of a small peninsula, becoming an island only at high tide, was for me a rare blend of natural beauty, including the placid lagoon, the Mpenzu, between the resort and our cottages.

Before returning to the hotel for dinner, I took a last look at the grassy rise where my family had been picnicking one day shortly before my sixth birthday when all the grown-ups heard something from the crackling radio that had changed the whole atmosphere, all suddenly looking stricken and using unfamiliar words like 'Hitler', 'Poland' and 'ultimatum'. Even a child could tell it had turned from a light-hearted picnic to a grim occasion, and when I asked for the second time what was wrong my father had said: 'It's war, son. World War. The Second World War.' Whatever that meant, I knew it was serious because of the way they all lost interest in the sandwiches, tea-flasks and chicken legs, which were abandoned on the picnic rug till hours later. I was thinking back to that day fifty years ago as I returned to The Haven.

I went into the cocktail bar where the manager, a black woman, said: '*Tyeni, unguZweliyanyikima!*' When my sister Joan, my brother Harland and I were born we had each been given Xhosa names by the local Bomvana elders. Joan was Nomatamsanqa ('the lucky one', being the first child to survive after my mother had had several miscarriages), Harland was Dumekude ('to be known far and wide', celebrated as the eldest son) and I was Zweliyanyikima ('Earthquake', or literally 'the world is shaking') which had intrigued my father because things like earthquakes were unknown in South Africa in recent memory.

As in the East London hotel, The Haven staff were summoned into the cocktail bar to shake hands and welcome me back, and I was glad to find that more of my Xhosa had returned to me than I had expected, including whole phrases and words I had thought I had long forgotten in the years away. I noticed that this recollection of the Xhosa language increased with each celebratory drink I had . . .

I set off next morning for Umtata, the Transkei capital sixty-three miles away, to which I had first gone to boarding school at the age of six, and as I drove back past Hobeni I remembered the time in 1943 when we had had three American sailors as guests. By that time America had entered the war and Prime Minister Smuts had appealed to South African families to take in foreign servicemen on furlough far from home. Dad had said we would take three sailors, and when they arrived and saw him they looked shocked, and passed some remarks to each other in that burring way with the slurred 'r' sounds we had heard on the movie screens. Finally one of them said: 'Sorry, Mr Woods, but we kinda got a shock – you see, you look so much like our President, Mr Roosevelt.' It wasn't the first time people had said this, and some even jokingly called him 'FDR'. Many years later a New York taxi driver thought I looked like one of Mr Roosevelt's sons, so there must have been a family resemblance.

I drove past places where I remembered having seen Bomvana axe-fights as a child. The locals now said that sort of thing hadn't happened for years, and was fortunately dying out. In fact, the ubiquitous red blanket all the Bomvanas used to wear, dyed with ochre, was now also increasingly rare, and instead I saw a number of the younger men wearing T-shirts, usually with Nelson Mandela's face on the front.

Entering Umtata it was easy to see how the town had grown, spreading in all directions, although the familiar avenue of trees leading into it was still there. My first surprise, in view of the obvious growth of the town, was to find how little had changed in the central area. The old Victorian city hall, from whose balcony my mother recalled the Boer War hero, General Louis Botha, speaking, was unchanged, and the great hall below was memorable to me for a special reason. Back in 1955 I had come in from Elliotdale to spend the weekend with my parents, who were living in Umtata since Dad had retired and turned Hobeni over to my brother Harland, and on picking up the local newspaper I had seen that the great Julius Katchen was giving a piano recital in the city hall.

I had jumped in my car and rushed down, arriving with minutes to spare, to find a crowded hall with everyone in formal dress – I was in jeans and a checked shirt – but I had been too keen to hear Katchen to bother about sartorial matters. The great American virtuoso, then only in his middle twenties, was regarded as one of the four best pianists in the world, and I already had some of his records. Fortunately his was predominantly a Chopin programme, with Fantaisie in F minor as the centrepiece, and though he had included some testing major works such as Lizst's 'Mephisto' Waltz I thought the highlight of the evening was his playing of Chopin's Ballade in A flat major. When a pianist was that good you could relax after the first few bars and enjoy the performance without tensely worrying for him, and it was hard to imagine anyone being able to play that ballade better.

My only comparable experience of a piano recital had been many years later in London when Wendy and I had been to one of Horowitz's rare concerts at the Royal Festival Hall, knowing that a Horowitz performance was a bit like Russian roulette – heavily dependent on whether the mood was on him or not. This had been one of his good days, and he had been at his inspired best. This Umtata hall had had an excellent Steinway grand on which the great Nikita Magaloff had also played, after first intimidating the chairman of the Music Society, Dr Geoffrey Airey, by waving his arms in the air and shouting: 'London, New York, Paris, Rome, Vienna – Umtata! Bah!!' Dr Airey, an eccentric man, had done his medical rounds in the hot Umtata sun as if he were in Edwardian Harley Street, complete with spats, a morning coat and monocle.

Another familiar old Umtata building was the Holy Cross Convent, which I had attended as a boarder for five years from the age of six. The old stone façade looked exactly as it had fifty years back, as did the kindergarten section which both Wendy and I had gone through at our respective stages of initial schooling. In those days it had been an all-white school, of course, but now it was non-racial. Across the street from it was the cathedral in which Wendy and I had been married back in 1962.

And nearby was the small playground where I had had my first fist-fight, at the age of eight, a protracted business involving one Dennis Brandt, another trader's son, in which we paused from time to time, panting to recover from exhaustion before getting stuck in again. The supervising nun, who was Swiss, had continued reading from her prayer book and looking the other way. Perhaps she had seen the hostility building up and felt it healthier that we should settle the matter finally. Or perhaps it was just another example of Swiss neutrality . . .

My worst conflict at that convent, however, had been with a German nun who had tried to force me to eat a piece of bread with awful mass-produced jam spread on it. I was all of seven years old and called her a 'bloody German', whereupon she dragged me off to the Mother Superior's office to be punished. There I denied the offence, claiming that I had said the jam had 'bloody germs' on it, at which the Mother Superior, an Irishwoman, could scarcely keep a straight face as she attempted to admonish me for bad language. In fact, at one stage she laughed out loud before turning her veiled head aside in the hope that the insulted nun wouldn't notice.

All in all, my five years at that convent had been reasonably happy. But most of my schooling had been at Christian Brothers College, Kimberley, and that was where I set off for my next sentimental journey.

CHAPTER 7

Diamond City Days

I had already heard from several sources that there had been major changes at the school. For many years one of the best-known private schools in South Africa, Christian Brothers' College in Kimberley had in my time been all-male and all-white – and now it was fifty per cent black and totally co-educational. Some of the venerable brothers must have been whirling in their graves at the sexual rather than the racial change. Even to me it was more of a shock to see the familiar striped green-gold-blue blazers on girls than on black pupils – a pleasant shock, but a shock none the less. I landed at Kimberley airport and rented a car, driving through the well-remembered semi-arid scrubland dotted with acacia trees towards the city. This countryside couldn't be less like the green hills and valleys of the Eastern Cape more than 500 miles away. It was utterly flat, dry and very hot indeed in summer, as was to be expected from a region bordering on the Kalahari Desert further to the north.

I had spent six years here as a boarder, along with hundreds of others from long distances away, many from what was then Rhodesia, many from Johannesburg and Cape Town and one from as far afield as the Seychelles. The reason for our being sent so far had been a combination of lack of good schools in the remote country areas most of us came from, and the high reputation of CBC academically and on the sports field. I suspect it was the latter consideration that prompted many fathers to send their sons here – the college had been noted for producing international rugby players for the national Springboks team, dedicated for ever to beating the New Zealanders, the Australians, and the Welsh, English, Scots, Irish and French in roughly that order of priority.

Kimberley was an interesting city, full of character. A hundred years back it had been the biggest city in South Africa and the wealthiest in the world, having its streets lit by electricity before even London, Paris and other European capitals, attracting to its opera house and theatres some of the world's greatest singers and actors, staging international boxing contests, upstaging today's larger metropolises of Cape Town, Durban and the then newly founded Johannesburg. The reason, in a word? Diamonds. This had been the diamond capital of the world. In its heyday, when the world's richest seams of diamonds were not only mined but marketed from here, and international prices were fixed by such young diamond magnates as Cecil Rhodes and Barney Barnato, Kimberley had called the diamond tune even over New York, Amsterdam and London, and the bustling young city had reflected this power.

It seemed an unlikely spot for a city of wealth to have sprung up, here in semi-desert hundreds of miles from other cities, where for various periods a bucket of water cost more than a bucket of whisky and where initially the only transport links were the stagecoach and the covered wagon. The surrounding aridity was what had made the green lawns around the mansions of the diamond magnates so striking. Sprinklers had had to stay on incessantly to create those lush grass verges and flowerbeds, offsetting the wrought-iron balconies and pillared verandahs of the wealthy. Because this had originally been a mining camp with its design determined by which claims yielded diamonds, much of Kimberley wasn't a pattern of squares and regular blocks as in most cities, but a hotchpotch of winding streets and odd-sized, odd-shaped properties, some large rectangles and others small triangles.

As I drove into the city I came first to the large playing fields and extensive buildings of what had been our rival school, Kimberley High School, and was so instantly transported back in my mind to a favourite day in 1951 that I parked the car and wandered over to their first-team cricket pitch to relive the magic moment. It was hard to believe it had been forty years earlier. It had been the big annual cricket match between CBC and KHS, when by tradition each school XI could include the school professional coach. The KHS pro had been a wily Welsh left-arm spin bowler named Emrys

Davies, whose deceptive curving flight through the air was compounded by the ability to disguise which way the ball would spin on hitting the turf, making footwork the key to survival against him. I had been doubly nervous because if I did well in this game I stood a chance of being selected for the regional team to play in the national Nuffield tournament, every South African schoolboy cricketer's dream. There was one place still available in the team, for an opening batsman, and my main rival for this spot was the KHS opener, a boy named Jasper Streak, so the ideal scenario was for me to do well and Streak to do badly.

Our team had batted first, and my own venture had begun disastrously. Instead of opening his attack with two fast bowlers, as usual, the KHS captain had started with his trump card, the dreaded Emrys Davies, whose first five balls had beaten me completely both in flight and off the pitch, curving one way and spinning another. This man, after all, had played for Glamorgan when they had won the county championship. When I had played for his off-break, trying to read the directions of his spinning-fingers, the result had been a leg-break, twice in succession, and the following two deliveries which I had 'read' as leg-breaks had turned out perversely to be off-breaks. To make matters worse, his fifth ball had been a googly – an off-break delivered as a leg-break out of the back of the hand with a dropped wrist. At this stage he had pitched five balls at me and I hadn't managed to lay a bat on any of them. I was, in short, starting to look downright silly.

Facing up to his next delivery, I had decided my best hope was to get at the ball before it could land and spin, and as Davies was a master of curved flight through the air this would require some nifty footwork. In fact I ran at it almost before the ball had left his hand and he, adjusting quickly to my charge, dug it in shorter. This time I 'read' it as an arm-ball, designed to continue its curve from right to left, and swung through it as it hit the turf to loft it into the deep left field on the half-volley. But he had cut it the other way again, and what started as my intended on-drive became a grotesquely sliced off-drive – not at all what I had had in mind. Still, there was enough solid bat on it to send it flying deep over the offside field to the boundary for four runs. I remember him placing a hand on my shoulder to say, and it was the first time I had ever heard the lilting Welsh accent: 'Now that shot didn't go at all where

65

yew intended, boy, did et?' Fortunately, however, all had gone well thereafter as my confidence had grown.

When it was the other team's turn to bat my rival, Jasper Streak, had had to face up to our professional, an Australian fast bowler from Melbourne called Des Fitzmaurice, who had given me a reassuring wink as he ran in some twenty paces to let fly. His first two balls had been fast outswingers, curving late from right to left, and his third, a vicious inswinger, had darted in between my rival's bat and pad to uproot his middle stump. Jasper Streak was out for nought, and I was in the Nuffield team. And forty years later, reliving the excitement, I could still see that beautiful fast inswinger from 'Des Fitz', could still hear his ripe Australian accent as he turned to me and growled: 'Y'owe me a beer for that one, son.'

The nice thing about reminiscence is that we can be selective, remembering our little triumphs and forgetting our little disasters. And songs of the time helped bring it all back. That season the big hit was 'Silver Dollar', which had bounced around in my mind throughout that game. Had it really been forty years ago? On that day, aged seventeen, I couldn't have imagined such a period of time as forty years. There had been no intimations of mortality in those days. The bright sun on the green grass, with a cloudless sky of blue overhead, had given everything the sense of permanence. I know I scored exactly 44 because on the same day, 6,000 miles away at Murrayfield in Edinburgh, the rugby Springboks had beaten Scotland 44–0, at that time a record score in international rugby. One wry old Scots fan had commented: 'Aye, and the Springboks played so weel – we wurr lucky to get the nil!'

Yet there had indeed been intimations of mortality in that place at that time, if we had bothered to look. As I had got back into my rented car I had glanced up at the huge war memorial, with names of the dead from two world wars. I had remembered there was a similar roll of names from both world wars at my own school, CBC, and set off to see the old place again with memories crowding in one after the other.

The familiar clock tower came into view, and the great old main building erected before the Boer War. When I had been at school here there had still been some oldtimers in the town with childhood memories of that conflict in the last months of the previous century, and on our playing fields we had occasionally scuffed up bullets and parts of shells from the siege of Kimberley, and once, to great excitement, the rusty remnant of an old Martini-Henry rifle. The siege of Kimberley had lasted four months, during which the townsfolk had lived mostly in fear of the Boers' biggest field gun, 'Long Tom', which had fired ninety-pound shells into the city at regular intervals – except on Sundays, which the religious Boers devoted to prayers and hymns.

Kimberley's response, ordered by Cecil Rhodes, had been a gun designed and built in Rhodes's mine workshops by an American engineer, George Labram, inevitably dubbed 'Long Cecil' by the Kimberley people, which had fired huge shells back in the general direction of 'Long Tom' to cheers from the townsfolk and the British garrison. Labram had later been killed by a shell from 'Long Tom'.

The buildings at CBC had grown since my time. Where the cricket practice nets had stood was now a theatre and assembly hall, replacing the old assembly hall near the main building, and new classrooms extended beyond what had been the old science laboratory. But the campus was largely unchanged, and around every corner and beneath every tree there was a vivid memory. All the sports fields were now grassed. In our time only the first team had got to play rugby on grass, and pupils from coastal schools had scarcely been able to believe that we had to do all our scrumming, tackling and rucking on diamondiferous gravel, which was as abrasive as it had once been profitable. Brother Elliffe used to set his tackle-bag over the roughest of it, and if you didn't go right into the tackle you risked scars from a cane to match the scratches on your knees and elbows. The Harris ground had been the roughest of all, and every scrum had churned up a cloud of dust. I remembered the incongruity of seeing one boy, Rex Hudson, then playing the role of Ralph Rackstraw in the school's production of *HMS Pinafore*, being ploughed under in one such dusty scrum, in contrast to his pristine costume as he sang: 'I know the value of a kindly chorus . . .'

He had had what South Africans called a Malmesbury bray, characteristic of a region in the Boland district of the Cape Province, where the letter 'r' was pronounced with a distinctively guttural sound like a noisy gargle in the throat, so that what emerged when he sang was: 'I know the value of a kindly chorghus, but chorghuses yield little consolation . . .' The next line, 'When we have pain . . .', had been particularly appropriate in the context of a rugby scrum on the Harris ground back in 1946, because along with the gravel was a ubiquitous little multipointed thorn with two main shafts, called the '*dubbeltjie*' in Afrikaans.

A look at all the old classrooms was like revisiting the years from 1946 up to 1951, though a couple had been remodelled, and I remembered how little impact the year of apartheid, 1948, had had on us as schoolboys. We had heard vaguely that a new government had come to power, that of the Afrikaner Nationalist Party, and that it was bringing in 'the apartheid system', but the only change we noticed was that our British-style cadet caps were altered by the new government's edict into German-style army caps more favoured by the new regime whose leaders had apparently admired Adolf Hitler and some of his ideas about 'racial purity'. To most of us at English-language schools our Afrikaner fellow-whites had been an almost unknown quantity, practically foreigners. We had encountered them occasionally on the rugby field, where they had literally spoken a different language, and their idea of rugby had been war. Our coaches had occasionally warned us before matches against Afrikaans schools such as Diamantveld, Sentraal, Vaal-Hartz, Boshof and others, that our opponents all wanted to 'refight the Boer War' and correct the injustice of a British victory in that war; that they hated to hear English spoken because they hated anything English, and that we could expect a rough time. The warning had been merited. In most cases the Afrikaners had been bigger than we were, because they had tended to be older than their class counterparts in our English-language schools, and we had also been struck by their comparative poverty. Their rugby kit had been shoddy, the jerseys thin and easily torn, and many in the junior games had played barefoot for lack of rugby boots. Most of them had had shaven heads, to avoid the cost of frequent haircuts, and in some cases winning teams had been rewarded with a tiny packet of sugar per player to take home. We weren't to know it, but we had been witnessing the final phase of one of the Afrikaners' most distressing historical periods. Although they had numbered about sixty per cent of the country's white population they had become by far the poorest sector. After defeat in the Boer War they had been a shattered people, and had seen their plight in simplistic terms as follows: the British had destroyed their farms, rounded their women and children up into concentration camps in which 26,000 had died of disease and neglect, and had handed political and economic power to the English-speaking minority, who had thereby gained control of the mines and all commerce and industry, and had monopolized the wealth of the land.

Apart from this major complaint of the Boers, or Afrikaners, as they came increasingly to be called (*Boer* simply means 'farmer' in Afrikaans) there was also the feeling among them that the British, and by extension the English-speaking white South Africans, had become 'too liberal' towards the blacks.

So the election victory of the Afrikaner National Party in 1948 had been a means not only to reverse the result of the Boer War a half-century earlier in terms of economic redistribution but to save the white race from what they saw as the increasing tendency to enfranchise blacks. That election victory, whose significance had passed right over our heads as we schoolboys had played our rugby and cricket and sung our Gilbert and Sullivan, had profoundly changed the circumstances not only of blacks, whose misery we barely noticed, but also of our shaven-headed barefoot opponents on the rugby field. The new apartheid government had taken away the votes from even those few blacks who had qualified for it under the previous system, had banned all future access to voting rights for blacks, had changed the boundaries of voting districts to nullify the English-speaking white vote further, and had embarked on a massive programme of Afrikaner economic empowerment in banking, insurance, farm grants, industry and mining which, within only two decades, had changed the economic face of the country for Afrikaners. From their point of view such change had been overdue and just, but much of it had been done at the expense of blacks and black potential in all spheres of life.

If I could have looked into the future in 1948 I would have been astonished at how quickly Afrikaner political and economic power was consolidated and at how comprehensive Afrikaner control was to become. But in those early days on those dusty rugby fields 'the Afrikaners' had been those foreign-looking, foreign-sounding 'outsiders' whose language we had had to learn for one period in the day, and which I liked, in spite of the general tendency of my fellow English-speakers to look down on it. One strange thing we had never been able to figure out about our Afrikaner rugby opponents had been the contrast, when we visited their schools to play against them, between their physical viciousness on the rugby field and their quaint, almost old-world courtesy to us as hosts after the game. They had served us sandwiches and soft drinks with elaborate consideration, had struggled to speak English, and had obviously been under orders from their teachers to extend gracious hospitality. Years later I was to experience the same strange blend of viciousness and courtesy from their security police.

Wandering over the Harris ground and the Keeley ground and other sports fields of my old school I had suddenly perceived, with a sense of awe, how swiftly human events developed and how brief, in the broad sweeps of history, periods of dominance ultimately proved to be.

It had seemed such a short time ago in the memory that the apartheid laws had been hurried into legislation, while at roughly the same time 6,000 miles away new tensions between the Soviet Union and the West had been building towards the Berlin Airlift and the slamming down of the Iron Curtain. As recently as the early 1980s both these systems, apartheid in South Africa and communism in various parts of the world, had seemed so powerfully entrenched and immovable, yet by the early 1990s the Iron Curtain had disintegrated and the granite monolith of apartheid was cracked right down the middle.

I wondered whether schoolchildren in the future would have any idea how formidable these systems had appeared in their heyday, or how mighty the Nazi military machine had seemed in 1940, only to be smashed to smithereens in 1945.

In the evening after dinner I went for a walk down Dutoitspan Road towards Jones Street in search of familiar landmarks in the city centre, noticing some strange looks from the hotel staff but not registering anything beyond their possible recognition of me from newspaper photographs. The first clue that all wasn't well was when I came to St Mary's Cathedral and found it locked, but I hadn't read any significance into it apart from wondering why it should be closed up so early in the evening. Opposite the cathedral, in the old days, had stood the Minerva Café, a favourite haunt of the CBC boys after Sunday Mass. Old George Pentopoulos, known to all as 'Mr Penny', had presided here through three generations of schoolboys and had been noted for devising the best sodas any of us had ever tasted. They had been made up to his own formula by Sullivan's mineral water factory in Kimberley and had been known simply as 'Red', 'Green' or 'Yellow'. What had made them distinctive, apart from their marvellous taste, had been the way he had blended them with aerated mineral water on tap from an old, well-worn pump. If you asked for 'Green' he'd splash about two inches of the emerald-green syrup into a big imperial pint glass, then with a small ice-pick he'd chip two blocks from a miniature iceberg at his side, plop them into the glass, wedge it under the pump and pull the lever until the full glass was fizzing with the tiniest bubbles, each barely the size of a pinhead. By the time he handed the glass to you with a curious daintiness, his little finger elevated and only the thumb and forefinger holding the glass, the action of the aerated bubbles would already have smoothed the edges of the ice blocks into the curved harmony of a Henry Moore sculpture. Mr Penny's ice was never sharp-edged, and his famous drinks were like heavenly elixir. Many were those who sought his formula, but it was never divulged, though stories were legion about the offers he received from soft-drink manufacturers. But now Mr Penny was long gone, and the Minerva Café was no more. How appropriate that this ambrosia so well remembered by the taste buds of thousands was produced by a Greek. We wouldn't have been surprised if we had heard he'd brought it down from Mount Olympus itself.

Standing there where the Minerva had been, I remembered one kindness for which I had revered the old Greek gentleman. In 1947 I had had scarlet fever and had been sent to the isolation hospital well outside the city for a two-week quarantine, and halfway through the second week a wonderful gift had arrived, two large bottles – one of Red and one of Green – specially made up and sent to me by Mr Penny. Being one of hundreds of small schoolboys wearing identical striped blazers I hadn't even been aware that he knew of my individual existence, but somehow he had heard of my illness and knew I was a special fan of the miracle drink. I'm sure it speeded my recovery.

Throughout my six years in Kimberley I came to know the Minerva Café in all its different facets according to our stages of progression year by year. As junior kids in our first years we had been regulars in the front section strictly for the wonderful soft drinks, usually on the way to the movies or on the way back. As seniors, later, we came to know the inner room with its marble-topped tables as a meeting place with the girls from the convent or the high schools, and right at the back was a final sanctum where very senior pupils with immense prestige were able to smoke, by selective and unwritten permission of Mr Penny. Mr Penny's rooms had also been the débutant locale for the privileged few who had

71

won 'colours blazers' to show these off discreetly while appearing, unsuccessfully, not to be too aware of these wondrous garments. The first-team colours blazer hadn't been simply for the glorious few who had made the first team. It was awarded for having consolidated one's place in that august side beyond all doubt, and was generally awarded by the sportsmaster only after a series of meritorious performances in the sport the colours were awarded for. I could not imagine any garment being the object of more covetous dreams by ourselves and our peers. Different from the regulation school blazer all college pupils were required to wear, which had had a repeated pattern of green, gold and blue stripes, the first-team colours blazer had been plain green edged with gold and blue checked braid. It had been made of the finest broadcloth and had been horribly expensive, and we would almost have killed for the honour of wearing it. It had been élitism of the worst kind, and we had loved it, especially those of us who had finally made it to the glorious green garment. And it was to Mr Penny's that one had ceremonially come for the unofficial inauguration of one's colours blazer, borne thence by friends as one had tried not to look too self-conscious in one's splendour.

It was on precisely such an occasion that I had had one of the most embarrassing moments of my life. I had worshipped from afar a convent girl named Denise Coqui, and on one fateful day my friends had accompanied me to Mr Penny's to be introduced to this totally perfect and stunningly attractive young lady.

Preliminary negotiations by others on both sides had arranged the great encounter and I still winced at what had happened as we had been duly introduced. There, in that front room of Mr Penny's, she had stood in her loveliness with her friends behind her, and there, confronting her, I had stood with my five friends behind me. It had been a tableau, as in a painting, and as the devastating Denise had smiled encouragingly and looked directly into my eyes I had been struck literally speechless. She had nodded encouragingly, and had said a few friendly words, whereupon I, miserably conscious that it was now my turn to smile and say something, had been able to do neither. My features had become frozen into a horrible immobility, and my voice had simply not emerged. Nor had I known what to say or do. There had been a long and agonizing silence, during which all I had managed had been a series of idiotic nods, as if agreeing to be consigned to any fate that awaited me.

Eventually the dear creature herself rescued me, asking a question to which I could manage some sort of reply, and the ice had finally been broken.

And that was how I had come to be standing in Dutoitspan Road, in front of where the Minerva Café had once stood, blushing over an incident that had occurred forty years earlier. No matter that Denise and I had got on well thereafter before going our separate ways, and that I had heard she had married a doctor in Durban and had lived happily ever after.

I turned to continue down towards Jones Street, although in the midst of my reminiscences I had begun to feel slightly uneasy and was starting to realize why. In that lighted area of the city centre I was now conscious firstly that there were relatively few people about on the pavements, although the car traffic was fairly lively, and secondly that of all the other people on foot within sight there wasn't a single white one. I was now about four blocks from my hotel, and receiving even more strange looks from the other pedestrians. I realized finally that they regarded it as unusual for any white to be walking in the city at night, and that most of those hanging about were young blacks in groups of three or four, several of whom were looking me over, as if speculatively with a view to a possible mugging. Trying to look casual and confident, I had hurried my pace as unobtrusively as possible.

About halfway back to the hotel two of the groups had started to cross the street, possibly to head me off – I by now being frankly scared – and might well have done so but for a fortunate sequence of passing cars that kept them on their side long enough for me to be past the point opposite to them. For the rest of the way back to the hotel I had done a passable imitation of those speedwalkers one saw in the Olympics, and had been ready at any time to break into a run, though I knew I could never have got away if they had seriously pursued me.

When I arrived back at the hotel the lobby porter, observing that I had been walking, told me deferentially that it hadn't been a good idea to be out on foot in the city at that time of evening. And though I had been really scared for a while, my prevailing emotion for the rest of the evening was one of sadness. It had been naive to believe that the city centres of South Africa were as safe as they had been in the old days. Today no sensible whites went abroad on foot at night in any major city in South Africa. It was also hypocritical to pine for the safe old days, which after all were so for the awful reason that blacks had simply been excluded by curfew legislation from the city centres at night. This was the new South Africa, in which along with reforms came political and economic realities, one of the latter obviously being that if a huge number of blacks were unemployed many could only survive by crime. This was true of the economically disadvantaged in most of the great cities of the world, and was now even more true of South Africa, where all problems had been compounded by the long legacy of apartheid.

The hotel itself was familiar to me. Wendy and I had stayed here in 1977 while our son Dillon was at CBC. It had been shortly before I was banned, and on that visit in the same hotel we had met an already banned person. Robert Sobukwe, leader of the Pan-Africanist Congress, had after years of imprisonment on Robben Island been moved to Kimberley and had been placed under restriction orders forbidding him to travel beyond the city or to talk to or be with more than one other person at a time. We had telephoned him and had been delighted when he had agreed to meet us at the hotel. The Security Police, who had kept him under surveillance at all times, had watched from the hotel forecourt as he had met us in the foyer and then joined us for tea in our room. Wendy and I had noticed the immense respect the black hotel staff had accorded our distinguished visitor and the obvious pride they had felt in him. Robert Sobukwe had been as charismatic in fact as he had been by repute, and had talked excitedly of his clandestine meeting with Steve Biko several months earlier. They had discussed the reunification of the PAC with the ANC and Sobukwe had been enthusiastic about this prospect. 'Steve is the man who can bring us all back together again where we belong,' he had said. Yet within a year both men were dead, Sobukwe of cancer and Biko at the hands of the Security Police.

I had gone the next morning to the Big Hole. This enormous pit, Kimberley's main tourist attraction, had held a weird fascination for me since my schooldays. When I had first seen it, in 1946, it had been an awe-inspiring sight to a twelve-year-old. Said to be the world's deepest man-made hole, it had been the largest of the old De Beers opencast diamond mines and had gone down more than half a mile. An American tourist at the observation platform had commented that you could stand two Empire State Buildings down there and not see the top of the upper one. From the observation platform you looked across the mouth of the funnel-shaped excavation about a quarter of a mile across, then down into the ominous depths where the 'stem' of the 'funnel' plunged vertically for about half a mile. It had been hard to imagine human beings digging that deeply without modern machinery, or even overcoming the fear of that awful vertical drop on the way down to dig further.

The mine, started in 1871, had finally been closed down in 1914, and most of the shaft had now filled with water. You therefore couldn't see to the bottom of the Big Hole. You could only see as far as the angle of observation from the platform allowed, to the surface of the dark green water. It had been more frightening in 1946 when the water table had been lower, because that meant you could see more of the vertical shaft, when the rocky walls of the 'stem' section seemed to plunge on to unimaginable depths. When I had seen it again in 1977 the water had been considerably higher, and now in 1990 it had come up even higher to within about seventy metres from the top of the vertical shaft.

However, facilities for tourists were now greatly improved, and included reconstruction of buildings typical of old Kimberley, with old-style saloons and barber shops and illustrated brochures with facts and figures about the Big Hole. These proclaimed that during the four decades of the mine's life twenty-two million tons of earth and rock had been excavated, yielding more than fourteen million carats of diamonds, equivalent to nearly 3,000 kilograms. I had a last look down the Big Hole, recalling the fact that during the Boer War hundreds of families had taken refuge down there from the shelling, being lowered with ropes and pulleys. I thought I would have found it more frightening than the shelling. But diamonds were still being mined at other workings in Kimberley, and as recently as 1974 the largest modern brilliant-cut diamond in the world, the Sterns Star, had been found at Dutoitspan Mine. At 223 carats it didn't rival the massive Cullinan, found at the Premier Mine near Pretoria in 1905, which at over 3,000 carats had been as big as a fist, and when cut yielded nine major gems, ninety-six small ones and ten carats of polished fragments.

South Africa's mineral wealth was astonishing, and the statistics made impressive reading. Apart from its world predominance in diamond production for more than a hundred years, South Africa was first in the world in production of gold, platinum, chromium, manganese, vanadium and alumino-silicates, and was among the world's top producers of coal, iron, lead, zinc, nickel, asbestos, phosphate, titanium and uranium. What made this particular corner of the world more wealthy in minerals than any other part of the globe was something even geologists found hard to explain. Certainly no other country of comparable size, and few countries of any size, could rival such abundance and variety of valuable minerals. And if you added the agricultural wealth in what was one of the best climates in the world to the wealth in human resources in a vigorous and diverse population, you began to see the extent of the tragedy and folly of the system that had shared so little of this wealth with the majority of people in such a richly endowed country.

The story of Kimberley, the city of diamonds, was remarkable enough. The story of Johannesburg, the city of gold, had been even more remarkable. Just as Kimberley had begun in 1867 with a man's chance discovery of a diamond, so Johannesburg had begun nineteen years later with a man's chance discovery of the world's richest seam of gold, and less than two decades after that Kimberley had lost its primacy as the country's biggest city to the incredible mushroom metropolis of Jo'burg, which in little more than a single century had grown to become the hub of the nation's biggest sprawl of conurbations totalling more than five million inhabitants.

CHAPTER 8

Mines and Monuments

Several hours outside Kimberley by road was Schmidt's Drift on the Modder River, where we schoolboys from distant places used to go on camping trips during the shorter holidays, and near the bank of this river we found one of the blockhouses from the Boer War. These were extraordinary structures, mini-fortresses built by Lord Kitchener in the latter stages of the war to try to cordon off the Boer guerrillas who were raiding across the Cape Province frontier into the Transvaal and Orange Free State. They were built in a giant chain along 3,700 miles, and by May 1902 there were more than 8,000 of them, built within rifle-fire of each other and linked by barbed-wire fence and telephone, with bells suspended from the fencing to give the alarm if the Boers tried to cut or cross the line.

The cost must have been huge. The blockhouse we found was a substantial structure three storeys high built of faced stone and iron with firing-holes for the riflemen and accommodation for several troopers on each level. According to Thomas Pakenham, historian of the Boer War, the blockhouses were guarded by a total of 50,000 white troops and 16,000 black scouts. I remember admiring the workmanship and the masonry, thinking it odd to have transported British craftsmanship of this order 6,000 miles to the hot African veld when there must have been thousands of homeless people in London at the turn of the century. But that was for me one of the mysteries of war. Considering the cost of a single battleship or fighter plane, why couldn't political leadership mobilize the same energy and productivity, not to mention money, for ordinary social goals such as housing in time of peace?

I remember also thinking what formidable foes the Boers must have been, pitted against the might of the British Empire when this empire was at the peak of its power. The Boers were, after all, not professional soldiers as the British had been. They had been amateur, if expert, cavalry and excellent marksmen, but ultimately no match for the British in numbers, weaponry or discipline.

Approximately halfway through the conflict the three-year war had changed from a relatively chivalrous, almost gentlemanly clash into a vicious and brutal precursor of all modern war, with machines playing an increasing role in the human destruction. And the change had come about primarily through cultural differences and misunderstandings.

Initially the niceties had been observed. During the siege of Ladysmith in Natal the Boers had lobbed a shell into the besieged British camp on Christmas Day, which when examined had turned out to be a dud containing a large Christmas pudding with the message 'Compliments of the Season' written on the casing. But subsequent misunderstandings were to put a stop to such civilized proceedings.

One was when the Boers, suffering from the extreme cold, took uniform tunics and greatcoats from the British dead before burying them, to wear themselves, only to be shot when captured by the British for what the latter thought to be the dastardly practice of looting from the dead or, worse, wearing enemy uniform as a policy of deceit. Another was when the British, in an attempt to prevent enteric fever from claiming the lives of more Boer women and children in the concentration camps, mixed medicinal crystals into the food and were accused of putting ground glass in the rations to murder the inmates. Then there was the belief among the Boers, on first being opposed by Scottish troops in kilts, that the cunning British were trying to trick them into believing these were women, not to be fired upon, until the highlanders were at close quarters, with bayonets drawn.

My favourite sculpture of all, though I have seen only pictures of it and never the original, is *Boer Soldier Returning from War*. It is a magnificent equestrian statue in which the theme is defeat and dejection. The slump of the Boer horseman's shoulders, the downward slope of the horse's neck, the whole composition bespeaks an unbearable pathos, but it has a moving beauty and an unusual majesty. I discovered finally that the sculptor of this striking work was the American, Gutzon Borglum, better known today for having sculpted the faces of the four presidents on Mount Rushmore in South Dakota.

Fascinated by this connection and intrigued at what sort of drive and scale of ego must have led to so enormous a concept as the carving of a mountain, I decided to travel to Rapid City in South Dakota to see Mount Rushmore for myself and to learn more about Borglum and his background. During what was to be my final lecture tour in the United States I managed to get to the scene of Borglum's mammoth effort and what I saw and learned justified the journey, because Mount Rushmore was soon revealed as one of those places that exceed the expectations, and Borglum one of the people who, like his work, loomed larger than life when researched. Born in Idaho of Danish descent, he was already fifty-eight years old when he started his megasculpture on Mount Rushmore, which was to take fourteen years to complete. He had been based in San Francisco, then London, and had already had an international reputation as a sculptor when he started carving mountains, beginning with an attempt at a giant Confederate memorial on the face of Stone Mountain in Georgia.

I found Rapid City a pleasant little town bordering the Black Hills, which didn't look black at all but shone with silver granite and were originally named for the dark shadows created by the indigenous forests there. Mount Rushmore itself had been named on a whim by a local joker guiding a New York lawyer named Charles Rushmore through the area to look at mining claims on behalf of his clients. Rushmore had pointed to a particular mountain and asked its name. ' 'Tain't got one yet, so we'll call it Mount Rushmore,' the guide had laughed.

The great thing about Mount Rushmore, for me, was the beauty of the monument itself and the taste with which tourists were catered for. The monument wasn't only a spectacular sight, sheer scale on its own account, but essentially good art, good sculpture; the likenesses strikingly convincing as well as artistically pleasing, constituting more than mere imagery, and the composition of the figures owing as much to art as to necessity of design. For me the most striking of all the images was that of Lincoln, as Borglum had managed in spite of the immensity of scale to capture the brooding sadness and nobility of spirit of the man. In the image of Lincoln, as with the other three images, the eyes looked alive because Borglum had left in the core of each pupil a shaft of granite whose shadow from the sun or from the illuminating beams at night gave the eyes the illusion of animation.

Looking at that enormous work of sculpture one was immediately struck by the immensity of it and the magnitude of the sculpted features. The eyes of the presidents are eleven feet wide, the noses twenty-one feet long, the mouths eighteen feet wide and the heads sixty feet long from the chins to the tops of the heads. Borglum had transferred the exactitude of the dimensions from his models with the aid of a lead weight on a cord, or plumb bob, on a scale of ten to one, with each point on the mountain 'portrait' marked in paint before drilling and dynamiting began. Many tons were blasted from the mountain to create, initially, the approximate dimensions of each portrait, then drilling to various depths began, carefully calculated with the holes close together so that the pieces to be removed more precisely could be chipped away by chisel. Originally only three presidents were to be depicted – Washington, Jefferson and Lincoln – and the shrewd Borglum is said to have added Teddy Roosevelt at least partly as an unspoken inducement to his cousin, Franklin Roosevelt, to authorize the completion of the Congressional funding.

It had long seemed to me that countries which appropriately celebrated and commemorated their heroes showed as confident a readiness to tackle the future as to salute the past. Many countries advanced in democracy and civilization, America and Britain eminent among them, seemed to illustrate this, and South Africa could fittingly follow suit as a new democracy with a talent for nurturing greatness, because South Africa already had a remarkable list of its own heroes.

South Africa has long been a setting for heroic deeds and it has also proved to be a place where world figures made their first public impact in their youth. Mahatma Gandhi, Winston Churchill and personalities such as Rudyard Kipling, H. G. Wells, Edgar Wallace, Conan Doyle, from Britain, and Will Rogers and Herbert Hoover, from America, were among those from outside South Africa who gave early hints here of wider prominence later.

Kipling, Wallace, Wells and Doyle were in South Africa during and after the Boer War, writing about the conflict as war correspondents or helping to edit newspapers in various parts of the country after the Boer surrender. Conan Doyle also worked as a medical doctor, having maintained his profession despite the success of his Sherlock Holmes stories. Will Rogers ran a rodeo in Natal before he became the famous cowboy philosopher, newspaper columnist and entertainer in the United States, and Herbert Hoover was one of the brightest young mining engineers in Johannesburg when the world's richest gold mines were being developed there. It was after his return to the United States that he entered politics, eventually gaining the Republican Party nomination and becoming President and immediate predecessor in the White House of Franklin Delano Roosevelt.

But the two most prominent were, of course, Gandhi and Churchill. Gandhi had come to South Africa as a young barrister, having trained in London, and it was here that he first experimented with and later perfected non-violence as a positive campaigning tool for his drive, before the turn of the twentieth century, for the emancipation of South African Indians from the earliest racial laws. He served during the Boer War, on the British side, as a stretcher-bearer and medical orderly, and after the conflict developed his Phoenix community near Durban, forerunner of his later settlements in India where whole communities worked together growing food and spinning their own cloth. Gandhi was the acknowledged leader at an early age of the South African Indian community, which eventually numbered about a million persons either recruited from India or descended from such recruits, to work in the Natal sugar plantations. The Indians came to identify strongly with the Africans and those of mixed race, classed as 'coloureds', in the development of a united front against white minority racism. Gandhi maintained his strong campaign for civil rights for all, and was imprisoned by General Jan Smuts for 'creating civil disturbance'. His response was to make a pair of sandals, in his prison cell, for Smuts. On his eventual return to India Gandhi was to apply all that he had learned, and taught, in South Africa.

Winston Churchill was only twenty-four years old when he arrived in South Africa in 1899 to cover the Boer War for the London *Morning Post*, but within days of his arrival he got involved in military activities to the extent of playing a leading role in commanding a group of soldiers isolated in a wrecked armoured train under Boer fire in Natal. He was eventually captured and made a prisoner of war in Pretoria, but within weeks he had escaped by climbing over an iron fence while the Boer sentry was turned away cupping his hands to light a cigarette. The Boers were enraged by Churchill's escape, as he had been their most prominent prisoner of war, and they issued posters offering a £25 cash reward for 'the escaped prisoner of war, Churchill, dead or alive'. For several days Churchill rode goods trains or walked the tracks eastward, making for neutral Mozambique, and was helped on the way by being hidden down the shaft of a coalmine near Witbank by some English miners, while Boer search parties checked over the area and the surface buildings of the colliery.

His helpers concealed him aboard a goods train at Witbank station, bound for Mozambique, which he reached the following day with a few nervous moments en route. Churchill became an international celebrity overnight, served with distinction for a further period of the war, and returned to Britain to a hero's welcome and a safe seat in Parliament. The rest of the Churchill story is well enough known and his fame will rightly ring down in history as the inspired leader of the Allied cause in the Second World War, and, like Abraham Lincoln, one of history's greatest writers in the English language.

Some interesting attempts were made by the Boers to discredit Churchill at the time, including the suggestion that they were about to free him anyway when he escaped, though this was hardly borne out by their poster offering a reward for him dead or alive. They also circulated the story that he had claimed in his writing to have 'swum the mighty Apies river', the tiny dry-bedded Pretoria gulch, but no research has ever been able to unearth this claim.

This attempt to destroy Churchill's credibility was of special interest to me, because I had had a similar experience at the hands of the apartheid Security Police, possibly descendants of those same Boer denigrators, more than seven decades later. When I escaped from Security Police surveillance to exile in Britain in 1978, the apartheid regime's Pretoria spin-doctors were quick to put out a story that I had claimed to have swum the Telle river, which is usually only a few yards across in various places, and that the river was 'crocodile-infested', whereas every South African knew there were no crocodiles in our rivers that far south. Interestingly enough, though the story was printed in *Time* magazine and in a number of journals, the only South Africans who had swallowed

Right: Nelson Mandela at Wembley wearing the tie given to him by Donald and Wendy Woods.

Below: In festive mood after handing over the Presidency to Thabo Mbeki.

Below right: South Africa's new President, Thabo Mbeki, relaxing near his birthplace in the Transkei region with his wife Zanele.

Above and below: The many moods of Archbishop Desmond Tutu, during the hearings of the Truth Commission.

rchbishop Tutu confronting the police with a cherubic smile at a protest march
uring the apartheid days.

The Big Hole, where families took refuge from the Boer shells in the siege of Kimberley during the Boer War. They were lowered down to hide in tunnels well below the present waterline, which has risen to its highest level during the past ninety-two years.

Donald and Wendy Woods after crossing the border into Lesotho.

The colourful waterfront of Cape Town with Table Mountain donning its 'tablecloth' of cloud.

Richard Attenborough directs a crowd scene during the filming of *Cry Freedom*. As in *Ghandi*, where he had up to 300,000 extras in one scene, Attenborough's special strength as a director was in the meticulous planning and bold execution of spectacular set pieces.

Wendy Woods, accent coach to Denzel Washington during the making of *Cry Freedom*, listens to his dialogue on every take.

Donald Woods and Kevin Kline, after the make-up department had finished changing the star's appearance to make him resemble the author.

The Woods family on the day of their arrival in Lesotho to begin their exile. From the left are Wendy, Duncan, Dillon, Jane, Gavin, Donald and, in front, Mary.

The Woods family on the day of their return to South Africa after twelve years in exile. From the left are Dillon, Duncan, Wendy, Mary, Donald, Gavin and Jane.

the fiction that I had made this claim had been the more gullible whites. The vast majority of the blacks, who knew far more about Security Police disinformation, had seen through the deception immediately and had given it no credence.

Churchill had travelled from Mozambique to Durban and then East London after his escape, and while in East London had borrowed five pounds from Will Crosby, editor of the *Daily Dispatch*. When I was editor of the *Dispatch* in 1972, on the newspaper's centenary, we came across Churchill's promissory note which was seemingly never redeemed, the *Dispatch* obviously having felt that his subsequent deeds had warranted the favour. We wholeheartedly endorsed this view, rather than claim from the Churchill family what would have been an interesting sum in compounded interest after seven decades. Also unearthed in our archives was a letter from Cecil Rhodes, agreeing to lend the paper's proprietor, Sir Charles Crewe, money to buy a new press provided he kept faithful to their agreed policy of 'a fair deal for the black people'. Few of Rhodes's critics credited him with adherence to such a policy.

Cecil Rhodes had come to South Africa at the age of eighteen, had consolidated control of much of the country's diamond and gold mining, had become Prime Minister of the Cape and had backed and secured voting rights for all blacks who could prove literacy or property ownership. He called this 'equal rights for all civilized men', and when asked to define a civilized man he replied: 'Someone who can write his name and isn't a loafer.' But he also stood accused in history of driving black farmers off their land, of massive exploitation of black labour and of cheating the inhabitants of Zimbabwe of their land, known for the period of its colonization as Rhodesia.

But good or bad or both, Rhodes had been an extraordinary man who had shaped the economic development of Southern Africa and its railways and harbours, obtained an Oxford degree while buying up diamond claims and working them between terms in Kimberley, and gained respect from warring tribesmen in the far northern territories by walking unarmed and alone between both their armies to persuade them to make peace. Rhodes, Barnato, Beit, Robinson and other mining magnates had ended up virtually running the economy of the subcontinent, and though not of the stature of Churchill and Gandhi as figures in history, they had certainly influenced the course of history in Southern Africa.

Even more remarkable were South Africa's own home-grown heroes. The first of these to make his mark on the country's history was Makana who, like Steve Biko more than a century and a half later, died at the age of only thirty having significantly altered the course of that history. Makana rejected colonial rule of his country, articulated the first elements of what became known as Africanist ideology and led the first uprising in South African history with 10,000 Xhosa men in the Battle of Grahamstown in 1819. British troops hunted him down and he was captured and imprisoned on Robben Island. He escaped and was last seen clambering on rocks near Blaawberg Strand, but was thought to have drowned as he was never heard from again.

Robben Island served as a political prison as early as 1795, and went through several phases over the next century and a half, first as a leper colony, then as a military garrison and again as a political prison from the late 1950s, serving as the top-security gaol to hold Mandela, Sobukwe and most of the leaders of the African National Congress and Pan-Africanist Congress who were to emerge in 1990 to consolidate the victory over apartheid.

My only visit to Robben Island was in 1953, when it was a military garrison and I was a law student in Cape Town. The purpose of the trip was to play cricket for Claremont against the garrison. Rain washed out play, though not before I managed to hit a ball through the window of the officers' recreation room, leaving shards of glass scattered over the green baize cloth of the snooker table.

Robben Island was the birthplace of one of the most notable white opponents of apartheid, Archbishop Denis Hurley, whose father had been the lighthouse-keeper on the little island at the time. Denis Hurley was the youngest Catholic clergyman in the world to be chosen as a bishop, being in his thirties when consecrated. A tall, handsome man of Irish descent, he was for forty years a thorn in the side of the apartheid regime because they couldn't deport him as they could those clergymen from abroad who opposed apartheid on religious grounds. Having been born on South African soil, Hurley was non-deportable, which constituted one of the supreme ironies of the South African situation. I remember his superb address to a seminar of Catholic lay people who were resisting church calls to pay their employees more. When one man got up and used the old excuse that he could afford to pay his washerwoman only R25 per week, and would rather she earned that than nothing, asking sarcastically what His Grace the Archbishop had to say about that, Hurley had replied: 'What I have to say is that obviously you can only afford her services for one day, so why not pay her the R25 for one day, freeing her to earn other wages during the rest of the week?' His reply was met with glum nods, for there were few things more gloomy than an audience whose last excuse for meanness had been removed so clinically.

Hurley was a particular monster in the regime's eyes, because the Afrikaner Nationalists had a special hatred of Catholicism, referring to it as *'die Roomse Gevaar'* ('the Roman Danger') and putting pressure on Catholic schools by barring subsidies and cutting down on clergy being allowed into the country to teach in convents and colleges.

Another clergyman who was a hero of the Xhosa people was Tiyo Soga. A convert to Christianity, he also preached an early form of Africanism or Black Consciousness and became a noted journalist, translator and composer. He translated the Bible into Xhosa and also *The Pilgrim's Progress,* and established several mission stations throughout the Transkei and Eastern Cape. He was educated at Scottish missionary schools in the Eastern Cape and began theological studies at the seminary of the Free Church of Scotland at Lovedale in 1844. His studies were interrupted by the Seventh Frontier War in 1846, so he was sent to Glasgow where he completed his studies at Scottish seminaries. After several years back in South Africa he returned to Scotland for further study and was formally ordained in 1856, becoming the first Xhosa minister. He married a Scotswoman, Janet Burnside, in 1857 and they returned to South Africa and established a mission station near King William's Town.

They had seven children, four boys and three girls. All four boys and the youngest daughter were educated in Scotland, where the Soga family felt the education system was superior and there was little or no racism. One of his sons was to become one of the most famous of the Soga family in the annals of the Xhosa people. He was John Henderson Soga, born at Mgwali, near King William's Town, in 1860, and educated in Glasgow and at the University of Edinburgh. After his ordination in 1893 he returned to South Africa with a Scottish wife and worked at Miller Mission, near Elliotdale in the Transkei territory, not far from the birthplace of Nelson Mandela. He became a distinguished author and composer, writing the first two history books by a black South African: *The South-Eastern Bantu* and *The ama-Xhosa: Life and Customs*, and his musical compositions were published in London. He retired in 1936 and went to live in Britain where he was killed during a Second World War air raid in March 1941 at the age of eighty. My parents were grief-stricken at the news, as they and the Sogas had been friends. Although they were far from liberal on racial matters – indeed they were as racist in their attitudes as the vast majority of whites of their generation – they venerated the '*Mfundis*' (short for '*Umfundisi*' or 'Reverend') because of his intellect and his advanced education, far beyond theirs or that of any whites they knew. Rev. Soga left our family three treasured possessions – two volumes of his most famous books, mentioned above, inscribed to my father, and a fine Broadwood piano upon which he had composed most of his music. Our home was only a few miles from Miller Mission, so the *Mfundis* had been a frequent visitor, and my elder brother recalls seeing him and my father sitting on the running-boards of their cars opposite each other in the yard of our home, Hobeni, sharing a bottle of whisky and talking endlessly. We still have the piano in our family, and can point out the scorch marks underneath the keyboard where the *Mfundis*'s pipe would burn the wood while he absent-mindedly played chords with his other hand.

His brother, Dr William Anderson Soga, also served at Miller Mission, and his son, Dr Lex Soga, also educated in Scotland and also married to a Scotswoman, also became a friend of my father, frequently going golfing and hunting with him. Dr Lex Soga was said by my parents to have saved my life shortly after I was born. Then – scandal in the district – he had seized the shoulders of the white doctor who had delivered me, shaking him and shouting that he deserved to be struck off the medical roll for incompetence. So I had practical reasons for being grateful to the remarkable Soga family.

Another famous leader from the Eastern Cape was Dr John Tengo Jabavu, founder of the Xhosa newspaper *Imvo Zabantsundu* (Voice of the Black People) and one of the founders of Fort Hare University, which produced most of South Africa's black leaders. One of the most gifted black writers of his time, he was a historian as well as a journalist, and was a leading member of the first black delegation to Britain to try to persuade Queen Victoria and her government not to grant the white minority control of the black majority in South Africa. As history records, the delegation was unsuccessful, and the consequences became ever more tragic over the following ninety years.

Then there was the remarkable Sol Tshekisho Plaatje, author of the first novel in English by a black South African. Writer, poet, journalist, politician, translator and interpreter, the versatile Plaatje was first secretary of the African National Congress and also played a leading role in delegations to Britain to try to reverse the decision giving the white minority control of all South Africa.

But in the final analysis the four most heroic figures in South African history were all from the Eastern Cape. They were Chris Hani, who was assassinated by a white racist fanatic shortly after the victory over apartheid; Robert Sobukwe, founder and leader of the Pan-Africanist Congress, whose mass protests against apartheid led to the Sharpeville massacre of 1960; Steve Biko, whose death in 1977 led directly to the strongest international pressures against the apartheid state; and, of course, Nelson Mandela.

The greatest recorded example of mass heroism by black South Africans occurred in a tragic incident during the First World War. When trench warfare in Europe had reached a stalemate and casualties on both sides were hitting record levels, the British government had asked the South African government to send more troops. On receiving the reply that no more white troops could be recruited they had asked for black troops who, in deference to white sensitivities, would be unarmed and would be used only in non-combat duties such as ambulance-driving, stretcher-bearing, trench-digging and general labour.

The South African government's appeal for volunteers drew an overwhelming response from many sectors of the black population, and on 21 February 1917, the troopship *Mendi*, carrying 828 men who were among the last of what was officially called the South African Native Labour Contingent to be sent to Europe, sank after colliding with another ship in fog in the English Channel, and 615 of the blacks, and ten of their white officers, were drowned.

Because of the nature of the collision some of the holds in which the men were quartered were sealed off from the upper deck, so hundreds of men knew during the half-hour it took for the ship to sink that they were going to their deaths, as did a number of those who made it to the upper deck but could neither swim nor get to one of the lifeboats or rafts that were being launched in the chaos of that night.

Only 191 blacks and twelve white officers survived to testify to the valour with which their doomed comrades met their deaths. According to these accounts the men who knew they would die were addressed by their chaplain, the Rev. Isaac Dyobha: 'Be quiet and calm, my countrymen, for what is taking place now is exactly what you came to do. You are going to die, but that is what you came to do. Brothers, we are drilling the dance of death. I, a Xhosa, say you are all my brothers – Zulus, Swazis, Basutos – so let us die like brothers. We are sons of Africa, so let us raise our voices, for though they made us leave our weapons at home we still have our voices.' They then sang and danced as the ship went down until the survivors couldn't hear them any more.

Researchers into the *Mendi* tragedy have never been able to determine whether the men addressed by Rev. Dyobha were those trapped in the hold or those stranded on the deck, or both, and there are no longer any survivors able to give the precise details that should have been recorded at the time. But a wealth of authentic research is contained in an excellent book on the subject by Norman Clothier, from which it emerges that altogether more than 20,000 blacks served in the Contingent in France, that all were volunteers, and that the *Mendi* was carrying the last detachment on its fatal voyage.

There are also some moving accounts of individual sacrifice relating to the period during and after the sinking. Few of the blacks could swim, many of them never even having seen the ocean before the voyage, and a white officer named Richardson tried to encourage a group of them to jump into the sea and make for the rafts by jumping over the side himself. He then managed to get on board again and was finally drowned after trying to reach the trapped men in the hold to rescue them.

Another white, an Afrikaner, resorted to physical blows to get the men to jump to safety, and risked his own life repeatedly to save them.

Fourth Officer Trapnell was rescued by two blacks after half an hour in the water. He was no longer able to swim, so each took an arm and kept him afloat until they reached a raft.

Another white sergeant, unnamed, was rescued by two blacks who carried him to a raft and slapped and pummelled him to keep him from dying of the cold, and a white officer named Emslie, who couldn't swim, died after giving up his place in a boat to one of the black troops.

A strange sequel to the story of the *Mendi* is that district commissioners in some far-flung rural regions of South Africa as far apart as Zululand in the north and Transkei in the south-east reported that in the early hours of 21 February 1917 the women started wailing, crying out that something terrible had happened to their men on the other side of the world, though the first news of the tragedy was telegraphed to the South African government only a day later and officially confirmed to the public only on 9 March when all the facts of the tragedy had been gleaned.

Another of South Africa's great stories of heroism at sea was that of the wreck of the *Birkenhead*, sunk off the coast of the Cape Province on 26 February 1852 in what was in some ways a mirror image of the *Mendi* story. The *Birkenhead* was also a troopship sent 6,000 miles to a distant war, but in this case the troops were white and they were being sent to fight against blacks.

At the time the British Colonial authorities were at war with the Xhosas in the Eastern Cape, and had requested more troops from England for the garrison of General Sir Harry Smith at Port Elizabeth. The *Birkenhead* had sailed from Portsmouth with 491 soldiers under the command of Colonel Alexander Seton, a crew of 142 and more than fifty women and children, all relatives of soldiers already with the garrison.

The ship struck a jagged rock off Danger Point near Cape Agulhas and, like the *Mendi*, sank within half an hour with the loss of 445 lives. In another similarity with the *Mendi* disaster, hundreds of men faced death with courage and discipline and there were many accounts of individuals sacrificing their lives for others. But the most lasting image from the *Birkenhead* story is that of hundreds of troopers drawn up in formation on the sinking deck to a regimental drum roll so that the women and children could board the few lifeboats available; the troopers holding their formation to the end. An added horror was that sharks were circling and attacking any survivors in the water who couldn't make it to the boats, and the cries of their victims could be heard by the young troopers, most of whom were in their late teens or early twenties, who therefore realized the fate awaiting them as the vessel sank.

They couldn't even hope to make for the few boats pulling away with the women and children, because Colonel Seton, addressing them in the last moments, asked them not to. 'It would swamp the cutters containing the women and children, which is why I ask you to stand fast here.' Captain Wright, one of the few to survive, said afterwards: 'Every man did as he was directed and there was not a cry or murmur among them until the vessel made her final plunge. All carried out their orders as if they were embarking instead of going to the bottom of the sea, the only difference being that I never saw any embarkation conducted with so little noise or confusion.'

Among the individual acts of courage one of the most memorable was that of Ensign Russell, in charge of one of the boats. Seeing a man struggling in the water near the boat, one of the few still alive in an area teeming with sharks, Russell dragged him aboard and gave up his own place on the already overloaded boat. Shortly after he entered the water he was taken by a shark and with a terrible scream was pulled under and never seen again.

One of the survivors, Private Boyden, had managed to clamber on to a bale of compressed hay and was eventually carried by the currents to the shore. Another, a cabin boy, found a floating door and succeeded in paddling it to shore. An officer named Sheldon-Bond managed to swim all the way to shore, and was astonished to find his own cavalry horse waiting for him there, one of five horses that had swum to safety.

Even after landing many of the women and children would not have survived the next few days if the regimental surgeon, Dr Culhane, had not secured a horse and ridden over a hundred miles to Cape Town to summon help. Dr Culhane completed the hundred-mile ride in twenty-three hours, eclipsing the feat of Paul Revere in faraway Massachusetts.

But the epic ride in South African history which makes Paul Revere's feat and Dr Culhane's seem like a casual canter by comparison is that of Dick King in 1842, who rode from Durban to Grahamstown to summon help for the besieged garrison of Captain T. C. Smith during one of the first conflicts between Boer and Briton that were to preface the Boer War at the turn of the twentieth century. Dick King completed the 500-hundred-mile ride in exactly ten days. A relieving force was immediately dispatched and the siege was lifted a month later.

Two Afrikaner heroes were also noted for their horsemanship. One was Wolraad Woltemade, who in 1773 rode his horse seven times into the raging surf of Table Bay, Cape Town, during a severe storm to rescue passengers from the wrecked ship *Jonge Thomas*. The survivors clung to his saddle girth, to the bridle, to Woltemade's boots and to lines he had attached to his saddle, and he had helped bring out fifty-three survivors when he turned for the eighth time to swim out to the wreck. This time he and his horse disappeared, sharing the fate of more than a hundred passengers still on the doomed ship.

The other Afrikaner hero on horseback earned his place in history not by riding but by dismounting from his horse. He was fifteen-year-old Dirkie Uys, who was riding in commando with his father Piet Uys during a Boer conflict with the Zulus in 1838. Dirkie and his father and seven other riders on a skirmishing patrol were ambushed by several hundred Zulu warriors at Italeni in Zululand and all but young Dirkie were unhorsed, wounded by spear and assegai. He could have ridden off to link up with other members of the commando who, seeing what was happening, were rushing to help, but he rode to his father's side, dismounted, and stood over his body to try to defend him from his attackers. It meant riding to his certain death, and he knew it.

When I was a schoolboy we learned about Dirkie Uys in our history books, and about Dick King, and the *Birkenhead*, and Wolraad Woltemade – but not about the *Mendi*. Nor about Job Masego. I came across the story of Masego in the 1970s, when I was writing a syndicated column for South African newspapers, and made it the subject of one of the columns. But to make the point to my fellow-whites that we had not been taught about black heroes, I structured the account to withhold the hero's name and race until the final paragraphs. It therefore read as follows:

One of our greatest South African war heroes was a young man who destroyed, single-handedly, a German warship in Tobruk harbour during World War Two. He was a prisoner of war, having served with the Second South African Division in Egypt when he was captured by the Germans. Sitting in a barbed-wire compound at Tobruk, absently digging his fingers into the warm sand behind him, he touched something: a cartridge. This gave him an idea, and he dug around until he had several dozen. He emptied the cordite from them into a powdered-milk can, and further search in the sand revealed some lengths of fuse which he joined together and concealed with the cordite. He was going to make a bomb and blow up an enemy ship.

Day after day he and other prisoners of war were marched to the harbour to unload the ships, and his chance to use the bomb came when he and several others were taken by barge to a ship anchored out in the bay. Their task was to load ammunition and drums of fuel, and he asked his companions to distract the German guards shortly before they were to return to the compound at sundown.

While they did so by staging a scuffle he climbed down into the hold, took out his little 'bomb' and placed it among several drums of fuel, laying the fuse to within a few feet of the hatch above his head. He opened a can of gasoline and poured it over the 'bomb' and the surrounding fuel drums, then scrambled back on deck where his friends were being cuffed with rifle-butts for 'accidentally' dropping a box of ammunition into the water. He stayed near the hatch until the guards ordered the prisoners back to the barge, then bent as if to tie a shoelace, struck a match, and touched off the fuse.

The guards and prisoners were all clear of the ship when she blew up in a huge explosion, and though all the prisoners were interrogated the Germans decided it wasn't sabotage. Several nights later the young saboteur crept through the wire and escaped from Tobruk, rejoining the South African forces near El Alamein after walking for twenty-three days. He was later awarded the Military Medal for his feat.

His name was Job Masego.

The companions who helped him by diverting the guards were Andrew Mohudi, Samuel Masiya, Jacob Shawe, Sam Polisi and Ralph Ridgard. Yes, you can tell by the names that they were of the category of South African soldiers not allowed to carry weapons, but were there to serve the white troops.

At the time it was published, in the stormy 1970s, the article created a fair amount of controversy because it made the point that here was a major hero, Job Masego, who was not only black, but buried in a pauper's grave far from Heroes' Acre in Pretoria.

The story had an interesting sequel nearly a quarter-century later. I was working in Johannesburg in 1997 helping to train

African journalists when I received a formal notification from the South African Navy stating that as I had been the journalist who had drawn attention to the Masego case so long ago during the apartheid era, I would be glad to know that the Navy of the new democratic South Africa had decided to honour Job Masego for his heroism by naming their new warship the SAS *Job Masego*.

Shortly after this good news my wife and I were on a visit to the great South African war memorial at Delville Wood, in northern France, when we noticed prominently displayed in the memorial building a portrait, in colour, of Job Masego in acknowledgement of his heroism. The Battle of Delville Wood was the greatest recorded instance of mass valour by South Africans in sustained combat. The South African Brigade, commanded by General Tim Lukin in the First World War, having been asked by the British High Command to capture from the Germans and hold until relieved the key forest of Delville Wood near the village of Longueval as part of their advance in the summer of 1916, did so against fearful odds and at a huge price in casualties. Lukin was a beloved commander. My mother as a young girl in the Transkei had known him there and had spoken of how popular he was with his men, but in battle conditions this popularity had become love because of the way in which Lukin always walked along the front line exposed to fire while visiting his vanguard troops even if it meant a full fifteen hours on his feet without rest. In this way he shared their danger and showed his concern for them, and they repaid him with total loyalty.

Delville Wood was less than a square mile in extent, and occupied by élite forces of the German army when the South Africans were ordered in. It took them two days to clear the Germans out, then they held the wood for six days under relentless shelling and machine-gun fire around the clock. The German shells came in at the rate of more than 400 per minute, and ultimately there were few trees left, and little ground uncratered throughout what had been a forest. More than 3,000 soldiers of the South African Brigade had entered the wood, and when they handed it over to a British regiment there were only 750 survivors. When this remnant of his brigade paraded before him General Lukin took the salute with tears streaming down his face, his cap removed in his own tribute to them. In his book on the First World War, the author John Buchan wrote:

The six days and five nights during which the South African Brigade held the most difficult post on the British front – a corner of death on which the enemy fire was concentrated at all hours from three sides and into which fresh German troops, vastly superior in numbers to the defence, made periodic incursions only to be broken and driven back – constitute an epoch of terror and glory scarcely equalled in the campaign. There were positions as difficult, but they were not held so long; there were cases of as protracted a defence, but the assault not so violent and continuous. The high value set upon it by the enemy is proved by the use of the best enemy troops against it – the 10th Bavarian Division, the 8th Division of the 4th Corps, and the 5th of the 3rd Corps. The South Africans measured their strength against the flower of the German army, and did not draw back from the challenge. As a feat of human daring and fortitude the Battle of Delville Wood is worthy of eternal remembrance, but no historian's pen can give that memory the sharp outline and glowing colour it deserves. Only the sight of the place in the midst of the battle, that corner of churned earth and tortured humanity, could reveal the full epic of Delville Wood.

Today the trees again cover the pretty little forest, and the magnificent memorial building is a fitting tribute to South Africa's brave soldiers in the first of the world wars in which they fought. And because so many Afrikaner Nationalists were hoping for German victory in both the First World War and the Second World War, meaning that the South African government dared not introduce conscription and had to rely on volunteers, South Africa had contributed to the Allied cause the biggest volunteer armies, including many moderate Afrikaners, of any country in either conflict.

CHAPTER 9

Patterns of Language

After only a short time back in South Africa I was amused at the many reminders of an old South African speech pattern I had almost forgotten during the years of exile. Common to all three of the main languages of the country, Nguni (Xhosa-Zulu etc.), English and Afrikaans, it was the habit of giving a positive answer by starting with a negative. Thus, in English:

'How are you?' Reply: 'No, I'm fine.'

In Afrikaans:
'*Hoe gaan dit?*' Reply: '*Nee, dit gaan goed.*'
('How goes it?' – 'No, it goes fine.')

And in Xhosa:
'*Kunjani?*' Reply: '*Hayi, kulungile.*'
('How are things?' – 'No, they're all right.')

And as '*nee*' and '*hayi*' mean 'no', perhaps the foreigner could be pardoned for thinking South Africans a negative people.

I had never come across an explanation of this strange use of the negative to introduce a positive, but my own theory was that, in all three cultures, it sprang from a wish to give an instant reassurance to the enquirer, and in all three languages it has actually been developed further to use the negative to denote extra emphasis to the positive. Thus, a young sportsman asked if he is confident of winning a race quite often conveys his confidence by saying: 'No, I feel sure I'll win.' A Springbok rugby captain, asked to comment on the other team's performance, said: 'No, they really played well. No, they gave us a really hard game.'

The stories of Afrikaans-speaking Springbok rugby captains abroad are legion, with most of the favourites centring around the gigantic forward, Boy Louw, who in the 1930s was captaining the Springboks on a tour of Europe. Louw, whose grasp of English was only rudimentary, went to Harrods to see the famous shop and decided to buy his wife a cake of soap. When he finally conveyed to the saleslady what he wanted, she asked if he would like it scented, to which he replied: 'Ach, no, miss, I'll yuss take it with me.'

Another Springbok who got lost on a tour of France was found asking directions in Afrikaans, because, in the only world he knew, if white people didn't understand English their language had to be Afrikaans.

Wendy and I had witnessed an example of this quaint belief while on a tour of Israel in 1967. We were sharing a car with a South African Member of Parliament, who had the delightful name of Brigadier Bronkhorst, when we came to a narrow gate blocked by a large tin with which an Arab boy had been playing. The brigadier leant out of the window and asked the lad several times whether he would kindly move the tin out of the way, then realizing he couldn't speak English he said: '*Jong, vat weg daardie blik!*' and looked slightly puzzled when this didn't work either.

We encountered the brigadier later on the trip, staying at the same hotel as we were on the Sea of Galilee. We went past a sort of five-star kibbutz to a landing and diving platform to dive into the lake, and were about to plunge in when one of the locals arrived in a swimsuit with similar intent. The brigadier waved him ahead courteously, remarking to me: '*Wag, laat eers hierdie Jood inspring.*' ('Wait, let this Jew jump in first.') When we had first met him in Israel he had been somewhat disconcerted by our politics, but had been courteous and mellow, if not as tolerant as he thought himself.

Earlier on the same trip we had been aboard a motor coach from Paris to Versailles when we had heard an elderly couple seated near us speaking Afrikaans, and later that day when we saw them looking for someone to take their picture I had lined them up for it and before pressing the button said: '*Glimlag, asseblief!*' ('Smile, please!') They were astonished and delighted to find compatriots so far from home, until the old man, talking to me some yards away while Wendy chatted with his wife, realized who I was and I realized who he was. He was Dominee de Beer, Chief Morals Secretary of the Dutch Reformed Church of South Africa and a supreme pain in the butt.

Whenever our newspapers carried a picture of a young woman wearing shorts or a miniskirt, or in a swimsuit at a diving contest, we editors would receive a letter from this man, for publication, to the effect that such pictures were the work of the devil, to lure young men into temptation, and that evil English-language newspapers such as ours were doing the devil's work in publishing such filth. While he was registering shock at discovering my identity ('But you are our enemy!') his wife was telling mine: 'Last night we went to the Folies Bergère – it was disgusting.'

At this I realized that I had the power to destroy Dominee de Beer and send him into a disgraceful retirement in the eyes of his strictly fundamental church. All I had to do was lift the telephone in my Paris hotel room, call the Johannesburg *Sunday Times*, and tell them the Chief Morals Secretary had spent the previous evening at the Folies Bergère. But I took pity on the old boy, on the basis that everyone was entitled to a night off occasionally. I had a hunch that he would work out for himself that the sword of Damocles was poised over his head once his wife trilled that she had spilt the beans about the nudie show, disgusting as it had been. And, strange to relate, we did indeed notice a sharp decrease thereafter in letters from the Chief Morals Secretary. But that may have been coincidence.

It was typical of the complexity of South African politics that the old man was the uncle of our good friend Dr Zac de Beer, one of the brightest of the few white politicians in those days who opposed apartheid, racism and all forms of narrow-mindedness, and of Zac's brother, who had shocked the old man even more by leaving the Dutch Reformed Church and becoming a Catholic priest. Having opposing politics within the same family was by no means rare among Afrikaners. The first Prime Minister to introduce apartheid, Dr D. F. Malan, had been related to someone who stood for everything the old man despised, feared and abhorred. Whereas Dr Malan had spearheaded the anti-black apartheid laws, had been pro-Germany in the Second World War and was against any extension of the franchise, his relative, Adolphus Gysbert Malan, had been the famous RAF Battle of Britain Spitfire pilot nicknamed 'Sailor' Malan, had returned to South Africa from the war to lead a huge mass movement against fascism called the Torch Commando, and had fought for franchise rights for blacks until his death at an early age after a long illness. Sailor Malan had had the looks of a movie star, while his uncle had resembled a snapper turtle, and the myopic old *volksleader* had been so alienated from matters non-Afrikaans that when the country's famous national cricket team, the Springboks, under their legendary captain, Dudley Nourse, had called at parliament on their way to tour England and had been introduced to Premier Malan, he had said to the astonished Nourse: 'Your team are welcome in South Africa. I hope you enjoy your visit to our country.'

A successor of his was somewhat better informed. Prime Minister B. J. Vorster was a cricket fan even though in his time South African cricket teams were largely made up of English-speaking whites, Afrikaners only coming to the fore in cricket some twenty years later. Vorster used to have the cricket scores brought in to him during parliamentary debates, and once when his secretary reported on an international match between England and South Africa as follows: 'The English have lost four wickets for 88 runs . . .' Vorster had whispered the ironic question: '*Our* English or *their* English?'

Strange that the country which had produced the heroes and heroics recorded in the previous chapter had also been capable of producing the likes of Dominee de Beer and Daniel François Malan, but there is a good old saying in Afrikaans: '*Van die os op die esel*' ('From the ox to the donkey') – a lot more earthy than 'From the sublime to the ridiculous'.

South Africa had indeed had more than its share of ridiculousness, such as when the town of Middelburg, Transvaal, banned a replica statue of Michelangelo's *David* because David's genitalia hadn't been covered by some puritanical means, or when the censors banned the children's story of a pony, *Black Beauty*, because they thought it was about inter-racial romance. And there was the joke about the Dutch Reformed Church banning intercourse while standing, because it might lead to dancing . . .

In subsequent visits back to South Africa in between my lecture tours in America and Australia, I became increasingly relieved that the country appeared to have escaped any permanent signs or symbols of these aberrational notions, including the most aberrational of all, the apartheid policy. But when I encountered the 'parktown prawn', I began to wonder whether nature might not have evolved through physical mutation a repulsive record as a symbol of apartheid's ugliness.

I saw my first parktown prawn on a garden path by a lush green lawn in Johannesburg. It looked as revolting as its prior descriptions had led me to expect, a bit like an extra-large cockroach, but so weird that I decided to investigate the phenomenon further. The name 'parktown prawn' is a nickname, of course, Parktown being an affluent north central Johannesburg suburb. It was here, and in the adjoining areas of Parkmore, Parkwood, Parkview and Parkhurst in recent years, that this horrible little creature was first seen and from which it spread to neighbouring areas such as Sandton and Bryanston. It turned out to be a large and ugly insect with several nasty habits and some unsettling characteristics. Emerging in summer, it invades gardens and homes, grows to between two and three inches in length and is very hard to kill. It is fairly aggressive and can jump up to five feet in the air, including right at you if it feels so inclined. It is, of course, not a prawn at all, but has been given that nickname because South Africans love alliteration and also have an inclination to give harmless names to appalling things. For example, the nickname 'necklacing' was given to the practice of placing a tyre around someone's neck, dousing it in petrol and setting it alight. Thus the parktown prawn is a lot worse than it sounds.

Moreover, it is a fairly new phenomenon, not seen until recent years, and so far confined to the Johannesburg area. In frivolous mood I speculated that it might, as previously suggested, have been an apartheid mutation, a revolting creature evolving from a revolting concept and sharing at least the characteristic that it was hard to stamp out. It seemed that merely stepping on it or even jumping on it had little effect, the body being armoured and hard, and that more than one assailant, looking down to see if his stamping had crushed it, had had it jump up into his face. Discounting some of the inevitable exaggerations that attend reports of most odd creatures, I decided to seek expert entomological opinion and telephoned the relevant department at the University of the Witwatersrand, where I encountered some cagey resistance to my enquiries, being passed from one faculty member to another until it began to dawn on me that these evasive academics were slightly embarrassed because, in spite of their studies, this creature apparently remained something of a puzzle to them. Eventually it transpired by a kind of telephonic consensus that the acknowledged expert on the parktown prawn was Dr R. B. Toms, of the State Museum's Department of Entomology in Pretoria, who had studied the creature, dissected it, bottled it and analysed it to a greater extent than any other scientist, so I phoned him for an appointment.

Dr Toms was waiting for me in Pretoria with a host of facts, amid dozens of specimens in bottles which did, indeed, look truly revolting. The creature, given the scientific name *Libanasidus Vittatus*, was a dark reddish-brown colour and at first glance resembled a large roach. The first specimen I was shown measured seventy millimetres from its head to what Dr Toms described as its 'scimitar-shaped ovipositor' – and it was a female. 'It is a kind of cricket, but different from the normal kind,' he said. 'It appears to belong to the family Stenopelmatidae, related to crickets and long-horned grasshoppers, with similar "ears" located, oddly enough, on their front legs. But unlike the cricket family, which "call" by rubbing their wings together, the Stenopelmatids are wingless.' But not silent, apparently. The parktown prawn gives off a kind of scream by rubbing its hind legs against its abdomen. Dr Toms was clearly fascinated by the creature. 'The largest male I have collected measures 157 millimetres from the tip of the antennae to the hind feet, and the largest female 166 millimetres, over five inches, though these are larger than the specimens normally found in Johannesburg gardens.' It was the phrase 'normally found' that made me glad, not for the first time, that I didn't live in Johannesburg. As a creature of the Cape I had always had a prejudice against the city of gold. Little did I realize that only a few years later I would live in Johannesburg for eighteen months, that my apartment would be in Parkview and my office in Parktown, and that I would fall deeply in love with that amazing city, if not with the pernicious prawn about which I was questioning Dr Toms.

He smiled at my suggestion that the creature might be an apartheid mutation. 'They do have distressing habits,' he said. 'They frequently wander into houses and have even been discovered in beds. One appeared in my bath when I pulled out the plug – it had managed to force its way through the grating in the drain. On another occasion I was sitting barefoot reading when one started nibbling at my toe.' It hadn't been painful, he said, though the parktown prawn was carnivorous as well as herbivorous, and seemed particularly fond of snails. 'The worst thing about them', he said, 'is their propensity for defecating when molested, and the odour of their faeces is particularly vile.'

As a scientist he thought one of the most interesting things about them was the massive mandibles of the males, the function of which was 'unknown as yet' (though I would have thought the inclination to nibble at toes and snails might be a clue), and whether their ears were functional or not. 'In fact, come to think of it, we still have a lot to learn about these things,' he admitted, and as this thought came from the leading expert on the subject, I felt it an aptly mysterious note on which to end my investigation of these curious creatures.

Johannesburgers told various horror stories of the parktown prawn, most of them based on the creature's habit of jumping through ground-floor windows and getting into cupboards, beds and boxes. One couple, unpacking after a flight to London from Johannesburg, had reportedly found that a parktown prawn had got into their luggage at home and had accompanied them, emerging in Mayfair. They apparently managed to kill it, after considerable difficulty. The things might even be dying off generally, because in all my eighteen months living in Parkview and working in Parktown I saw only one, and it wasn't aggressive at all. It was sunning itself on my front doorstep, and when I flicked it away with a golf wedge it departed in fairly good spirits.

In my many visits to South Africa between 1990 and the year 2000 there seemed to be fewer manifestations of the more menacing creatures I had been accustomed to see from time to time in my childhood and early youth, such as puff adders and boomslangs, or tree snakes. Perhaps building works had encroached on their natural domain, driving them back into the deeper bush, or perhaps they had grown more shy of showing themselves. There was no reason to believe there were any fewer of them, but they had definitely become more cagey and reclusive.

CHAPTER 10

Echoes from Afar

Alternating my visits to South Africa with my final lecture tours to the United States made for some interesting contrasts between a long-established democracy and a country about to become a democracy. For example, in America newspapers were allowed to publish blatant defamation, as well as the most glaring inaccuracies, on the grounds that this was freedom of speech. Americans had accepted that part of the price to be paid for freedom of the media was freedom for bad journalism as well as good. South Africans were not even near accepting that concept yet.

Still, it was exciting to see South Africans nudging ever closer to democratic ideals, and it became clear with each successive visit that democracy was getting nearer. Coming back repeatedly to witness the discarding of so many set perceptions of the past was a pleasure, and often there were reminders of ringing pronouncements that diehard politicians had made that certain things in South Africa would never, never, never be changed, when now there were no longer even the faintest traces of those things once held so sacred. The very thought that South Africa was on course to become the world's newest democracy, in the full sense of the word, was tremendously exciting, and while negotiations were still going on to this end, one had to be greatly impressed by the progress made. Time after time deadlock would ensue, and apparently insuperable difficulties would arise, and time after time the negotiators would return to the negotiating table and hammer out a formula for the future.

And it was already clear that this wasn't going to be just another democracy. This was going to be a very special democracy, heading for possibly the most enlightened, most fair, most democratic constitution in the whole world. What a turnaround that was going to be, to turn the most reviled country in the world, so long saddled with the most hated system in the world, into the model democracy.

But South Africa wasn't there yet. At that stage the world's youngest democracy was Poland, after the recent election triumph there of Solidarity under Lech Walesa. In America for one of my last lectures, I was lucky enough to witness a unique tribute from that youngest democracy in the world, Poland, to the oldest democracy in the world – the United States.

Taking a weekend off from the lecture tour I went with my friends Bob and Mary Beth Gosende from Washington, DC to a singular function at Harper's Ferry, West Virginia, famous for the raid by John Brown, depicted in history mostly as an anti-slavery fanatic with wild and staring eyes, who with his equally wild sons used to attack and hang slave-owners and who had attempted the famous raid on Harper's Ferry to gain all the guns in the arsenal there, distribute them to slaves, and intensify his religious war on slavery. The function we were attending was part of Polish Heritage Month, and was to mark the fact that the Polish poet, Cyprian Norwid, had been so moved at the story of John Brown that he had, in 1859, written a poem, translated from the original Polish as follows:

> Across the ocean's billowing waves
> I send you a song like a seagull, O John
> She will fly a long time to the land of freedom
> Doubting if she will arrive in time
> Or whether like a strand of your venerable beard
> She will fall white upon an empty scaffold
> While the son of your executioner
> Casts a stone at the visiting gull
>
> Thus, while upon your uncovered neck
> The hangman's noose will try its mettle
> Ere your heels begin to seek the earth
> To kick aside the debased planet
> This earth will run away from under your feet

Like a frightened reptile
Thus, before the crowd says: 'He is hanged!'
And looks upon itself for confirmation
So that America, having recognized her son
Would not shout out to her twelve stars:
'Extinguish the jewels of my crown
Dark night comes with the face of a black man'
Accept, O John, my song's inceptive rise
Ere Kosciusko's shade and Washington's do quake
For ere the song matures a man will die
But ere the song does die a nation will awake.

The invocation of the shade of Tadeusz Kosciusko was a reference to the fact that the latter had, sixty years earlier, willed his American estate to the welfare of oppressed black Americans, and that Poles likened their age-old struggle for freedom from foreign domination to the struggle of black Americans for equal rights.

The poem was carved in relief on an impressive sculpture, featuring the profiles of both John Brown and the poet Cyprian Norwid, rendered by Polish-American sculptor Gordon Kray, to be unveiled this day at Harper's Ferry before a large gathering of members of the American Council for Polish Culture and associated Polish-American organizations.

I relished this intensely American occasion, envying the Americans one quality we South Africans had never attained – the ability to celebrate cultural origins and ethnic diversity without this being seen as a dilution of nationhood or a betrayal of national unity. In South Africa any such attempt at cultural identification with the country of origin was looked on as virtually unpatriotic. Thus if Afrikaners invoked their Dutch heritage prior to the Dutch settlement at the Cape in 1652, this was seen in many quarters as an un-South African, un-Afrikaner yearning for inappropriate things of Europe. And if English-speaking whites formed organizations such as the Sons of England, the Caledonian Society, the Cambrian Society or the Sons of Hibernia, they were accused of forsaking their South African identity in favour of an unhealthy commitment to England, Scotland, Wales and Ireland, provoking accusations such as: 'Yes, you people have one foot in this country and one foot overseas – you are not true South Africans.'

The Americans had no such hang-ups. Indeed, they gloried in their identification with organizations celebrating Irish-American, Polish-American, Italian-American, Jewish-American and African-American heritage, seeing this not only as no dilution of their American identity but in fact an enhancement of it. It was such a healthy process, and so mature, and it was why the American melting-pot had melted so well, whereas in South Africa we had for so long managed to pickle our various heritages in aspic and contrived for many years to perpetuate division instead of fostering unity.

It was a glorious day at Harper's Ferry, fresh and springlike, as I watched the crowd assemble in the bright sunshine at the old cobbled section of the little town, with the green thickly wooded hills rising steeply from this beautiful junction of the Potomac and Shenandoah rivers.

This being a Polish occasion, it was no surprise to see up on the temporary platform a magnificent concert grand piano, and to learn that seven works of Chopin would be performed. The pianist was Camille Antoinette Budarz, and she began with the A major Polonaise. To anyone who had heard the poignant recordings of the Polish government appealing by radio for international help during the Nazi invasion of 1939, the appeals being made against the background of the A major Polonaise, it was a piece of music that would remain immortally evocative, though musically my personal favourite among the polonaises was the one in A flat. I loved the way the Poles resorted to the polonaises in times of stress, more recently under Lech Walesa during the Solidarity strikes at the Gdansk shipyard when, inevitably, a concert grand was set up at the shipyard and the strikers and government troops alike stood respectfully in silence while the Polonaise in F sharp minor was performed – another favourite of mine.

It was an extraordinary scene as Camille Budarz was striking those marvellous, challenging chords which echoed up the wooded hillsides to where parties of climbers paused to picnic high above us overlooking the little town, with the impressive new sculpture featuring the poem of Norwid to John Brown behind the grand piano and behind rows of chairs occupied by representatives of the government of recently liberated Poland. Invoking the memory of that salute from the old world to the spirit of the new world was also a salute to the oldest democracy from the newest at that time. And inevitably it started me thinking again about John Brown, and the words he addressed to his sons and their friends on the eve of the raid on Harper's Ferry:

And now, gentlemen, let me impress this one thing upon your minds. You all know how dear life is to you, and how dear life is to your friends. And, in remembering that, consider that the lives of others are as dear to them as yours are to you. Do not, therefore, take the life of any one, if you can possibly avoid it; but if it is necessary to take life in order to save your own, then make sure work of it.

He repeated that the main purpose of the raid on Harper's Ferry was to capture the rifles at the national arsenal there, to take them into the mountains from which, operating as a guerrilla group, he and his band would commence a series of raids on slave plantations, freeing slaves either to flee to Canada if they wished or to augment his forces to free further slaves.

Another reason for the raid was symbolic, to show black Americans that whites were prepared to risk their lives for the liberty of blacks, and Brown obviously hoped that success in the raid would inspire other whites to show equal commitment. In his raiding party of about twenty were seven blacks, and among the whites were three of his own sons and two of his nephews.

From a military point of view the raid failed. Ten of the raiders were killed – including Brown's sons Oliver and Watson – in the fight that followed the discovery of the plan and the raising of the alarm. Seven, including Brown himself, who was seriously wounded, were captured and hanged, and the others got away.

From a political point of view, however, the raid precipitated the civil war which ended slavery and preserved the union. In that sense John Brown had certainly succeeded in his aim of hastening the end of slavery. Interestingly, people who hadn't known him had thought him mad, and at his trial some had tried to plead insanity on his behalf. This had angered Brown, who told the court: 'I look upon this as a miserable artifice and view it with contempt more than otherwise. I am perfectly unconscious of insanity and I reject any attempts to interfere in my behalf on that score.' When the judge asked if he had anything to say before sentence of death was passed, Brown said:

I deny everything but what I have all along admitted, the design on my part to free the slaves. I intended certainly to have made a clean thing of that matter as I did last winter, when I went into Missouri and there took slaves without the snapping of a gun on either side, moved them through the country and finally left them in Canada. I designed to have done the same thing again, on a larger scale. That is all I intended. I never did intend murder, or treason, or the destruction of property, or to incite slaves to rebellion, or to make insurrection. I have another objection – had I interfered in behalf of the rich, the powerful, the so-called great, it would have been all right, and every man in this court would have deemed it an act worthy of reward rather than punishment. I believe that to have interfered as I have done, in behalf of the despised poor, was not wrong but right. If it is deemed necessary that I should forfeit my life for the furtherance of justice, I submit. So let it be done.

Whether or not one agreed now with the methods John Brown chose then, it interested me how readily such persons were either morally condemned or simply dismissed as crazy, and it was with similar patterns of irrationality that some in Britain and America used selective morality in condemnation of violence. In America, the same people who condemned the African National Congress for turning to violence to gain their freedom in South Africa saw nothing wrong in George Washington having turned to violence to secure American freedom from the British Crown.

In Britain at one stage Margaret Thatcher was urging the ANC to pursue only non-violent methods at precisely the time she was sending a powerful fleet of warships to retake, as violently as necessary, the Falkland Islands from Argentina.

Steve Biko used to respond to such arguments by putting the perspective of the victim. The victims of Nazi tyranny were glad that the British opted to resort to violence against Hitler. The victims of the bombing raid on Pearl Harbor were glad that the Americans opted to resort to violence against Japan. The victims of apartheid were glad that the ANC and PAC opted to resort to violence against it, and the victims of slavery at the time of the raid on Harper's Ferry were glad that John Brown had launched his raid. Hence their singing of:

> John Brown's body lies a-mouldering in the grave
> But his soul goes marching on!

As the lovely strains of Chopin's Nocturne in E minor filled the bright morning air at Harper's Ferry, I thought of the time I had heard that earlier vocal salute to John Brown at an extraordinary musical occasion. It had been during the two years I had spent abroad in my early twenties, out of South Africa for the first time. While working on a newspaper in Cardiff, Wales, I had gone to a unique concert in Ebbw Vale, in one of the mining valleys, and had heard this stirring song sung by Paul Robeson, with the chorus 'Glory, Glory Hallelujah!' sung by 8,000 Welsh miners.

The miners had rigged up a microphone stand for Robeson, but as he stood there towering over them on the platform his voice had soared so mightily above their chorus that he had casually lifted the entire microphone stand with one hand and passed it to someone behind him – he didn't need it. And then, unforgettably, his great voice and theirs in their thousands blended in the old refrain:

> John Brown's body lies a-mouldering in the grave
> But his soul goes marching on!

What a pity John Brown couldn't have been there in that Welsh mining valley to hear that song . . . and what a pity he couldn't be here at Harper's Ferry for this Polish tribute.

For me the best part of the Chopin programme had been Camille Budarz's performance of the final item, the same lovely Ballade in A flat major that I had heard Julius Katchen play in Umtata, Transkei, and that I had loved so much ever since. Like the Sonata in B minor it is in itself such a satisfying anthology of all the great gifts of Chopin, and I hoped the climbers high above us across the Shenandoah could hear it as we could, and be as moved by it as we were. This day in West Virginia had reminded me so much of what I loved about American history, ideals and generosity of spirit. They were hard to live up to – and seldom lived up to – but every now and then they were touched upon or illuminated by such an event which affirmed what is great in the human spirit and in the concept of freedom and democracy.

I hoped so much, in remembering this, that we South Africans could one day mature enough to emulate the Americans in their most generous and most enlightened traditions. I wondered how long it would take before we might see, in South Africa, an event as complex and evocative as that multicultural ceremony at Harper's Ferry.

CHAPTER 11

Time Machine Time

South Africa is a land of many surprises, and one of the most pleasant is the discovery of a pair of charming villages preserved as they had been, or almost as they had been, a century ago. You come upon the first just off the main highway out of Cape Town as you enter the wilds of the Karoo, that vast plain that was once under water and is today the great inland vastness of the Cape Province. Nearly a century ago the Karoo had become internationally famous when South Africa's equivalent of Emily Brontë had produced South Africa's equivalent of *Wuthering Heights*. Olive Schreiner, who had never ventured out of her Karoo wilderness, wrote at the age of only eighteen a novel of such towering brilliance, set in her own environment, that London publishers could not believe it when she arrived to be lionized for her international success. For a start, she was a woman, which many hadn't known because she wrote under the name Ralph Iron, and secondly she was a teenager, which people reading her book, *Story of an African Farm*, could scarcely credit because of its passion and maturity. As had happened with Emily Brontë, Olive's talent had enabled her to write of things far beyond the direct experience of most young women brought up in remote rural areas, whether in the Yorkshire Moors or the Great Karoo.

That Olive Schreiner was unusual was undeniable. On her arrival in London she stayed at the home of Havelock Ellis, who took so little notice of her as a woman that when she came down the stairs one morning without a stitch of clothing on, he – orientated as he was sexually – is said to have scarcely noticed.

Anyway, my timeless little village in the Karoo, Matjiesfontein, is a small wayside railway station which, through the preservation of its buildings, lets you step back a century to see and feel how our predecessors lived. As you drive along the main highway to the north you have to keep a careful lookout, or you will miss Matjiesfontein. But once you spot it, about a mile off the road, you see what looks at first like an oasis in the harsh veld of the Karoo, a white-washed townlet with date palms and well-tended gardens, solid, thick walls shimmering in the heat. As you enter it you sense you are in one of the charmed spots of the world.

The centrepiece is a fine hotel, the Lord Milner, which is famous not only for its splendid rooms and four-poster beds but for its multi-course meals in the imposing dining room which is the only place in the world apart from Buckingham Palace with a huge wrought-iron column holding up the ceiling and the next storey.

Matjiesfontein was an ordinary little railway siding until 1883, when an enterprising young Scot named Jimmy Logan bought it and brought it to fame far beyond the Cape Colony, and indeed South Africa. Logan was the son of a minor Scottish railway official and was born in Reston, Berwickshire, in 1857.

After leaving school he went to sea, and when his Australia-bound sailing vessel, the *Rockhampton*, put into Simonstown water-logged as a result of a severe storm round the Cape, he decided to leave the ship and get a job with the Cape Colonial Railways. He started as a porter but at the age of only twenty had become station-master of the newly completed Cape Town Station. He soon saw the potential for development and wealth in the wayside stations along the great rail route north, as there were as yet no dining cars on the trains and passengers had to alight at way stations to eat and drink. Logan noticed that streams of travellers poured through Matjiesfontein by ox-wagon, train, cart, and stagecoach on their way to the riches of the Kimberley diamond fields and, later, the gold fields of Johannesburg. Accommodation and food were at a premium, and the sort of living to be made by supplying both would far outstrip any railwayman's earnings. Logan moved permanently to Matjiesfontein with his wife and two children in 1883, and between then and the Boer War at the turn of the century he developed his village into a delightful Victorian health and holiday resort to which the rich and famous began to come. Olive Schreiner herself returned many times, and the place she always stayed in is well preserved and called the Olive Schreiner Cottage. Logan's own gracious home in the village is also well preserved, with wide verandahs and stained-glass windows set in large gardens with broad lawns. Cecil Rhodes was a frequent visitor and governors, premiers and members of the British aristocracy were guests at Logan's house, Tweedside Lodge.

During the Boer War a vast remount camp with 10,000 troops and 20,000 horses was established on the outskirts of Matjiesfontein, and the veld around is still littered with rusty old bully beef tins and biscuit tins. I went walking there and saw the remains of the cricket field where the first international match was said to have been played in South Africa, although there is dispute about this because the only scorecards from the period show a match at Matjiesfontein in 1887 between '11 of England and 18 of the Colony' – hardly an even contest. But one of the greatest cricketers in all history is buried near Matjiesfontein, the great George Lohmann, who died of enteric fever a century ago, with some of the best bowling analyses in international cricket for England against Australia.

Logan himself died in 1920 at the age of sixty-three, and Matjiesfontein went into decline until it was bought by David Rawdon in 1968 and restored to its present splendid condition. Next door to the Lord Milner Hotel is the Laird's Arms, a typical Victorian country pub, and then a trio of semi-detached buildings of which the post office is the centre. To the left of it is the Olive Schreiner Cottage and to the right the Marie Rawdon Museum, which houses a fine collection of domestic Victoriana. What used to be Logan's General Store has been completely restored as a coffee house. There is also a smaller hotel, the old courthouse, the original church and police station.

The only other place in the world which reminds me of Matjiesfontein in its well-preserved atmosphere of a century ago is Tombstone, Arizona, one of those small towns that seem a long way from anywhere. It flourished in the last century because of the silver mines there but ultimately became famous because of its unusual cemetery, Boot Hill, and the gunfight at the OK Corral, fabled in song and story. On a recent visit to Tucson I had driven the eighty or so miles to Tombstone on a day so blazing hot that I wondered how the early cowboys and miners had survived without air-conditioning. Fortunately the heat was dry, reminiscent of Kimberley as was the countryside, and the highway was strewn at intervals with shreds of tyre from numerous blow-outs. The historical features of Tombstone are well preserved, even to the old Wells Fargo office and the Bird Cage Theater, built in 1881, still with its original wallpaper, where Wyatt Earp had an early clash with a group of outlaws. The OK Corral is also lovingly preserved, and details of the gunfight are comprehensively kept in old files of the town's newspaper of the time, the *Epitaph*. From contemporary reports it appears that the Clanton gang – Ike Clanton, his brother Billy, and the two McLowry brothers – had a vendetta against Wyatt Earp and his brothers Virgil and Morgan, and had come to town from their ranch armed with rifles and revolvers for a showdown. Virgil Earp was Marshal of Tombstone at the time and Wyatt, who had earned fame through his exploits as Marshal of Dodge City in Kansas, had been deputized along with Morgan to stop the Clantons rustling cattle. The Earps had with them Wyatt's disreputable friend, a consumptive dentist known as Doc Holliday, who always wore a long coat and invariably carried a knife and a six-shooter. On this occasion he had a rifle with him as well when the two parties confronted each other at the Corral on 26 October 1881.

From evidence at the court hearing which followed, Virgil Earp had called on the Clantons to raise their hands and give up their arms, whereupon they had reached for their guns and there had been an exchange of fire at a distance of only a few feet. Morgan and Virgil Earp were both wounded, as was Doc Holliday, and Billy Clanton and the McLowry brothers were shot dead. Also with the Clantons shortly before the shooting was their friend William Claiborne, known as Billy the Kid, but he had left before the shooting began.

The dead were buried in Boot Hill cemetery, where many of the graves are still marked with the most cryptic of epitaphs. It took me about twenty minutes to find the best known, and certainly the most poetic:

> Here lies Lester Moore
> Four slugs from a .44
> No Les, no more.

It was recorded elsewhere that Moore had been a Wells Fargo agent shot in a dispute over a package.

Some epitaphs had simply recorded the deceased's name with the single word 'hanged' or 'shot' under it. There was one James

Hickey, buried in 1881, having been shot by Claiborne in the left temple for his over-insistence that they drink together. Claiborne had been buried here too, having been shot in 1882 by one Frank Leslie in a saloon fight.

There was John Hicks, 1879, shot by Jeremiah McCormick of the Lucky Cuss Mine in a saloon brawl; John Heath, taken from the county jail and lynched by a mob in 1884, and George Johnson, whose inscription was 'Hanged by Mistake'. Apparently he was thought to have stolen a horse, and then it was discovered, too late, that he had bought it. Billy Kinsman had been shot by a jealous woman in 1883, and 'Three-fingered Jack' Dunlap had been 'shot by Jeff Milton'. One epitaph simply read 'Killeen – shot by Frank Leslie', and local records revealed that the dead man had found his wife in bed with Leslie, who had married the widow after shooting her husband. One Hancock, undignified by name or initials, had been shot by Johnny Ringo for insulting a woman. Ringo, whose full name was Jonathan Ringgold, was described in a contemporary report as 'a well-educated and cultured man when sober, but a pitiless despot when drinking'.

Boot Hill was discontinued as a cemetery in 1884. The townsfolk must have thought it was filling up too fast. I was interested to see it had a Jewish section with quite a lot of graves.

Tombstone, in fact, was more than just a Wild Western town, there having been repeated attempts by its inhabitants to bring in culture through theatre and music, and there are records of several performances of Shakespeare's *As You Like It*. At the time of the gunfight at the OK Corral there was a current performance by the Theatre Comique followed by farce, melodrama and vaudeville. There were also performances by Eddie Foy and the Seven Little Foys, and Gilbert and Sullivan operettas such as *HMS Pinafore*.

Lack of water had been a major problem from the beginning of Tombstone's history, as the town grew with the growth of silver mining, and a twenty-eight-mile-long pipeline was laid to bring water from springs in the Huachuca Mountains in 1881, but within a few months of its completion Tombstone had such an abundance of water that it ended the mining boom – the miners struck water at 500 feet which flooded the mines. After initially pumping out 7 million gallons of water a day the miners eventually gave up.

Yet Tombstone had never become a ghost town as so many of the other old mining towns had. It maintained and still maintains a vigorous chamber of commerce and now generates most of its income through tourism. There is an Episcopal church in Tombstone, St Paul's, built in 1881 – the same year as the gunfight at the OK Corral – by Endicott Peabody before he went to Massachusetts to found the famous Groton School of which he was headmaster for fifty-four years, counting among his many famous pupils the likes of John F. Kennedy. Peabody returned on a visit to Tombstone in 1941 to walk on the same flooring he had laid in the church fifty-nine years before, and told of how cowboys, miners and gamblers had contributed the money to build his church. Of all the Western towns I have visited in the United States, including Laramie, Cheyenne, Durango, Tucson, Pecos and El Paso, none evokes the atmosphere of the old West better than Tombstone, and none reveals more accurately through its records the contrast between the myths built up by the movies, of gunmen not firing until the other man drew, and the reality of those times, in which men were frequently blasted by shotgun and usually from behind.

It also evokes the surprisingly persistent aspirations of those times, in the most out-of-the-way places, towards culture and civilized standards. During my lecture tours in the United States I have often been astonished on arrival at the most obscure places to find they were visited on lecture tours in the nineteenth century by the likes of Charles Dickens and Oscar Wilde. How Dickens and Wilde managed their trips without the help of modern airlines, Greyhound coaches, cars and air-conditioning is an intriguing thought.

One of my favourite hotels in the world, the Parker House in Boston, was usually the base from which Charles Dickens launched his tours, and stories still abound of how he and Emerson spent convivial evenings there discussing the new wonder of the age in that famous hostelry – the en suite bathroom in an era when there were entire hotels in various parts of the world without a single bathtub. It is part of the Parker House legend that Dickens and Emerson had been drinking so much when Dickens took the great poet to show him his bathtub filled to the brim that Emerson staggered, tripped, and fell into the bathtub.

Small towns in America often boast a single characteristic which sets them apart, either as birthplaces of some famous personage or as possessors of some unique object. In one of them, I forget which, is what is claimed to be the world's largest ball of string. In Wichita, Kansas, is the world's first Pizza Hut. Ripon, Wisconsin, is the birthplace of Gordon Selfridge, founder of London's famous store. Oshkosh is where the famous overalls come from, and so forth. But for one of the most gracious of such claims we return again to Tombstone, Arizona – and what is said to be the world's biggest rosebush. It grows in the patio of the Rose Tree Inn. In 1885 a rooted shoot of an old English rose, The Lady Banksia, was sent to a girl who had come from Scotland, Mary Gee, to live in Tombstone. She planted and cared for it so lovingly that it grew to a great size, and after her death it was tended for longer than sixty years by a woman called Ethel Robertson, so that today it spreads over a trellis covering more than 7,000 square feet. It is a strange and beautiful legacy for a town otherwise more famous for gunplay, mayhem and frontier violence in an earlier age.

South Africa's other place where time stands still is, in my opinion, the picturesque village of Rhodes, in the north-east corner of the Eastern Cape by the Lesotho border. It is a long drive from anywhere, but the effort is worth it. You climb steadily and steeply and the scenery gets more dramatic the nearer you come to the village, as clear trout streams run through craggy mountains and bright green valleys fringed with giant poplars and cypresses.

The village at first seems like a film set – too good to be true. It has quaint houses in architectural styles of the nineteenth century, with ogee roofs over the verandahs and the occasional porch roofed in the bullnose fashion, curving downward to the drainage gutter. The houses are in a variety of colours and are referred to by colour – the yellow house, the blue house, the red house – because there are so few of them. When I was last there Rhodes had more houses than people, there being thirty-seven people but about fifty houses. The unoccupied ones belonged to people as far afield as Johannesburg and Cape Town who had stumbled on the place, fallen in love with it and wanted to own a piece of it for occasional holidays.

The main attractions are trout fishing in summer and skiing in winter, but I thought the village itself had a mysterious charm, a little like Brigadoon. Rhodes is distinctive for its massive and numerous trees, including the biggest weeping willow I've ever seen. The leading citizen I met there was Meneer Buytendag, an old gentleman with a variety of civic roles. He was acting mayor, acting tourism officer, acting real estate agent and chief trout spotter, with all the information you needed to know about the village, past and present, at his fingertips. It was unthinkable to call him Mister

Buytendag, or to speak to him in English. You would have been missing an authentic experience of the old Afrikaner courtliness that recalled a more gracious age.

Many years ago a certain Van den Horst came to the village and boarded with a bearded patriarch and his five sons. There being nothing to do in the evenings, the old man and his sons would sit around the sitting room after supper, smoking and saying nothing. Well, almost nothing, because every now and then the old man would take the pipe out of his mouth, sigh deeply and say: '*Ja, nee.*' Whereupon one of his sons would respectfully respond: '*Ja, Pa!*' Somehow the Afrikaans phrase 'Yes, no' is far more eloquent than its tame English equivalent 'Ho-hum'.

One Christmas a friend was shocked out of his sleep by what sounded like a shouting horde of invaders from Lesotho, but it was only a party of local mummers singing carols from house to house. Suddenly it could have been an old-time village in Wessex, with the tranter and the chandler in the choir. But in spite of his rude awakening my friend said Rhodes was usually so quiet that he could hear the stars.

Without quite hearing the music of the spheres, I once spent a week in this enchanted village and didn't have a moment of boredom. Who could be bored in Brigadoon?

In some respects Rhodes, Tombstone and Matjiesfontein were all very different one from the other. But in all three I strongly felt this sense of what it must have been like to live a century ago. All three should be linked as at least three places in the world – and there must be many – which can most convincingly transport us back in time a hundred years, and charm us totally in the process. But while Rhodes and Tombstone are well off the beaten track, Matjiesfontein is easy to visit in total comfort. What Matjiesfontein has that Tombstone and Rhodes do not is a railway station serviced by one of the most luxurious trains in the world, the Blue Train.

The Blue Train runs from Pretoria to Cape Town and back, or from Victoria Falls in Zimbabwe to Cape Town and back, and though I have travelled on some of the world's fanciest trains nothing quite matches the Blue Train. The Orient Express may rival the cuisine but cannot match the décor, space and spectacular scenery, the transAustralia hasn't quite the elegance and the scenery is mostly boring, and the great transcontinental trains of Canada and the United States don't have the quality of food and wines to go with the more majestic mountain vistas of the Rockies. But again, apart from the Rockies, these trains have little more to offer on the long runs than rather boring prairie.

The Blue Train has it all. With the luxurious appointments and a superb observation lounge go the finest wines and foods along with a wide variety of great scenery. Its timing is good, too, because on its southward run especially its progress along the flatter parts of the Karoo is at nightfall, and the southbound traveller awakens to some of the greatest mountain and valley views in Africa.

While on the subject of trains, I must say that I was equally impressed, though for different reasons, with a very different train from the Blue Train, but one that is a shining example of the best of the new South Africa. The Phelopepha, literally 'bringer of health', is a train of sixteen coaches containing medical students, nurses, dentists, oculists, eye specialists and dieticians that travels all over the country to rural areas short of medical services, stopping for several days at agreed points planned well in advance with local headmen and administrators. It turns nobody away, and the patients give what they feel they can afford, to help finance the train. It also brings to the rural areas teachers of basic health practices, to train local people in setting up primary health clinics. All the students are volunteers, working for nothing apart from a bunk on the train to sleep on and daily food, and many return for further journeys, not only because they admire the idealism of the venture but because it is valuable practical experience for them.

The woman who runs the train, Lillian Cingo, is a highly qualified administrator and she is the train's best advertisement, because when she travels abroad to speak, financial support pours in to keep the wonderful health train going. She says the most rewarding experience of all is to see the long lines of patients waiting at the rural stops, most of them people who have never seen a doctor in their lives, never having been able to afford medical treatment and in some cases never even having been near any place of medical treatment.

The health train brings not only health but hope, and it adds a new smiling face to the rural reaches of South Africa. It could not have happened in the apartheid era; but, as the new millennium began, it was, fittingly, in full swing.

CHAPTER 12

Some Related Questions

As apartheid began to be dismantled, so too did my long-sustained project of international lobbying for economic and diplomatic pressures to end it, a project which had ridden on the back of my many lecture tours. During twelve years in exile I had gone on lecture tours to the United States, speaking at 462 universities, many of which had had apartheid-related investments which they disposed of, and I had also addressed many other audiences including state legislatures, public affairs forums and community colleges while giving newspaper, radio and television interviews in each city or region. Now, with Mandela's emergence from prison, it was time to wind down and end the campaign.

I had asked my New York lecture agent, Carlton Sedgeley, who over the years had become a good friend, to help me to end with a lecture in the 50th state, Alaska. I had lectured in all the other forty-nine, and in some of them many times, but had yet to lecture in Alaska, so Carlton was glad to secure me a final engagement in Fairbanks, in the heartland of the great arctic state. He was also able to indulge another long-held ambition of mine, to see the homes of my four favourite United States Presidents – Lincoln, Jefferson, Washington and Franklin Roosevelt, all four of whose lives, I felt, held important lessons for our new South Africa. As my tour took me to speak at the beautiful University of Virginia, founded and designed by Jefferson, I started with a visit to his home, Monticello.

This fine mansion, also designed by Jefferson and built at the heart of a 5,000-acre plantation, is full of interesting ideas and gadgetry typical of that versatile soul. Though formal in appearance the great house is characterized by comfort and convenience many years ahead of its time. Jefferson had his bed built as part of the junction of his bedroom and study, so that he could get out of either side depending on his mood on awakening, whether for reading or for dressing. He had a gadget for holding big heavy books he wished to read, and another multiple-pen device he rigged up to save time in making copies of manuscripts. He built a seven-day calendar clock into the entrance hall, single-acting double doors into the parlour and dumbwaiters and a revolving serving-door into the dining room so that servants did not need to enter, as Jefferson didn't like dinner conversations to be interrupted.

The dumbwaiters on either side of the dining room fireplace were connected to the wine cellars below, and I liked Jefferson's notion of placing small four-tiered tables between guests from which they could serve themselves, again to avoid disruption of conversation.

But Monticello was more than a gracious home. It was also an experimental farm and forestry, with many species of trees planted and herbs grown. The graveyard was laid out by Jefferson in 1773 and is still reserved as the family burial ground for his descendants. His own grave bears an obelisk inscribed:

Here was buried Thomas Jefferson
Author of the Declaration of American Independence
Of the Statute of Virginia for Religious Freedom
And Father of the University of Virginia

Obviously as far as the good people of the great state of Virginia and its distinguished citizen himself were concerned, the fact that Jefferson was also one of the country's greatest presidents was deemed superfluous to the other Virginian virtues listed on the above inscription. I had long felt that if South African leaders could show the gifts of motivation of their legislators that Jefferson did in getting Congress to approve the Louisiana Purchase, similar miracles of consensus financing might be possible in our new democracy.

My next stop was Mount Vernon, the stately home of George Washington, on the crest of a broad hill overlooking the wooded banks of the Potomac River, with several thousands of acres of estate given over, as in the Jefferson house, to forest plantations, experimental farm crops and dependent buildings to serve the manor house.

George Washington was, in my opinion, underestimated by historians. Without self-promotion in his personality yet with the love and respect of most who met him, he was at the age of only eighteen voted by forty-two veteran soldiers as their commander in the Virginia militia, an astonishing tribute to his early stature as a natural leader. Unusually tall and of commanding presence and character, he became during most of his life the logical choice of his countrymen in Virginia and later throughout the United States as leader at various levels up to and including President. But he first achieved fame as commanding general of the American forces rebelling against the British armies of King George the Third, and proved himself a great military leader. Well read and a good writer, as his letters and notes attest, he was also a versatile man who, like Jefferson, designed his own home at Mount Vernon.

At Mount Vernon the eight big pillars fronting the two-and-a-half-storey mansion were made of hardwood shaped and textured to look like masonry, as were the exterior finishes of the mansion, which had the sidings bevelled to give an appearance of stone, with sand applied to the freshly painted surface. Washington called this treatment 'rusticated boards' and used it more extensively than any other builder had up to that time, and it had the double virtue of looking good and costing little. Washington was a thrifty but generous man, and wrote to his estate manager while he was away in 1775:

> Let the hospitality of the house, with respect to the poor, be kept up; let no one go hungry away. If any be in want of corn, supply their necessities, provided it does not encourage them in idleness, and I have no objection to your giving my money in charity, to the amount of forty or fifty pounds a year, when you think it well bestowed.

The interior of the house was as interesting as that of Jefferson's Monticello, and, like his illustrious successor, Washington was also buried on his own property, with no inscribed allusion to his presidency but simply the words: 'Within this enclosure rest the remains of General George Washington.'

If South African leaders could find out and emulate how Washington had succeeded in getting so many of his countrymen to put their own material interests aside to sacrifice money and comfort for the national good, great deeds might be possible on the same scale in the new South Africa.

Franklin Roosevelt's house at Hyde Park was a grand old mansion overlooking the Hudson River north-west of New York. It had ramps for FDR's wheelchairs, and a recording facility from which he broadcast one of his famous 'fireside chats' to the nation on 1 September 1941. His greatest achievement was to transmit in times of economic terror during the Great Depression the total confidence that alone could lift the nation out of its trough of despair, and to preside over what became not only a recovered economy but the most powerful economy in the world.

If South African leadership could emulate how Franklin Roosevelt had reversed the national mood of his country from despair during the Depression to new hope, many of the daunting problems now facing South Africa could be tackled more confidently, and it seemed to me that Rooseveltian use of radio would be appropriate in a country where many rural dwellers are still illiterate.

I travelled finally to Springfield, Illinois, to see the former home of my favourite of all the presidents, Abraham Lincoln. I had lectured the previous evening on a campus near Chicago, after dining with Kevin Kline, the actor who had played me in *Cry Freedom*. Kevin, who had become a good friend and generous supporter of our educational projects in South Africa, was a versatile man, not only an Oscar-winning actor but a fine musician who could conduct an orchestra or play the piano to a virtuoso level. I enjoyed going with him to restaurants in New York, Los Angeles and other American cities, basking in the reflected celebrity, because the other diners always fell silent and then whispered behind their hands the question, wasn't this, bygahd, Kevin Kline? Once at an Italian restaurant in Chicago the same thing happened, except that whereas usually the other diners accorded him privacy, on this occasion a man came straight to the table and said he didn't usually do this kinda thing but that he and his wife Harriet thought Kevin wuz the greatest actor ever and that that wunnerful film wuz the best they had ever seen.

'Which film?' asked Kevin politely. '*Sophie's Choice*? *A Fish Called Wanda*? *The Big Chill*?'

'Naw!' said the bold one. 'The one about South Africa. *Cry Freedom*. You played a South African guy called Dennis Woods, and it wuz just wunnerful,' he said.

'Well,' said Kevin mischievously, 'meet Dennis Woods!'

The man stared and said in an awed whisper: 'Are you really Dennis Woods?' and I responded with what I hoped was a modest inclination of the head, whereupon the man turned and called out across the whole restaurant to his wife: 'Harriet! Harriet! Y'aint gunna believe this. Come on over! This here's Dennis Woods!' And so I became for a few moments, so as not to spoil the occasion, Dennis instead of Donald, as we shook hands all round and agreed that, bygahd, *Cry Freedom* was indeed a great movie, a view with which it was easy for me to concur.

The next morning the train moved smoothly across the Illinois prairie, which stretched flat as a table as far as the eye could see. I was heading from Chicago to Springfield, and as the hours rolled by on the southward run I was struck as so often before by the vastness of the United States. Though born in South Africa, a big country by any standards, and accustomed to wide horizons, I found that the scale of things there paled by comparison with the United States. The state of Illinois alone, economically or geographically, would if separate be a considerable country in its own right.

I was travelling on the same railroad that Lincoln had travelled so often more than 100 years before, and wondered how it could have been that in those days, without the marvels of air travel, mass communication and varied media, Americans were able to find and elect to their presidency persons of the calibre of Lincoln, Washington and Jefferson, whereas in the last stage of the twentieth century the American voters had chosen a criminal, Richard Nixon, a bribe-taker, Spiro Agnew, an ill-informed actor, Ronald Reagan, and, at one stage a heartbeat away from the presidency, a Dan Quayle. These, remember, were supposed to be leaders of our free world with the power to unleash nuclear war. It put one in mind of the story of the Duke of Wellington, who, inspecting his troops on the eve of the Battle of Waterloo and finding them to be under-age, ill-equipped, under-trained and inadequately uniformed, said: 'Well, I don't know if you'll frighten the enemy, but by God you frighten me!'

Reagan, defeating Carter by successfully blaming him for an 'intolerable' deficit of $80 billion, had then presided over an escalation of this same deficit to more than $300 billion! And the thought of Dan Quayle being within reach of such authority had been scary. It was Quayle, after all, who had said, seriously, in a public speech: 'We love our families! We love the Indiana National Guard!'

One could hardly go about the United States, enjoying American hospitality and friendliness, while telling them that most of the world thought they had a tendency to elect idiots to high office from time to time, though I did try to convey this message in many speeches in which I pointed out that their choices occasionally caused the rest of us to quail with fear . . .

But in Lincoln's day the American people had got it remarkably right. Here was a country farmboy with no formal schooling, who had learned to read only late in life compared with most city boys of his age, who became, with Shakespeare and Dickens and Scott, one of the greatest writers of English prose and who massively changed the course of American history for the better, abolishing slavery and holding the Union together when it was under the greatest onslaught.

As the train pulled into Springfield station I thought of Lincoln's letters to his friends Joshua Speed and Billy Herndon, of their anecdotes about him and of Lincoln's last words spoken in Illinois as he departed to take occupancy of the White House in 1861. It was at the same little red-brick depot, still standing today, that he had said on the eve of the Civil War: 'I now leave, not knowing when or whether ever I may return, with a task before me greater than that which rested upon Washington.'

A task greater than Washington's indeed – of greater scope, scale and complexity. Fewer than 10,000 Americans had died in the War of Independence, and more than 600,000 were to die in the Civil War – more than were later to die in Vietnam, Korea, and both World Wars combined. And Lincoln was assuming the presidency of a country deeply divided not only between North and South on the issue of slavery but in the North itself about how to respond to the secession of the South.

I checked into a hotel several blocks from the Lincoln home and went to New Salem, less than an hour away by car, to find a small village of log cabins preserved and restored to how Lincoln had seen and served it as postmaster, storekeeper and land surveyor while he taught himself grammar and law through borrowed books. Young Abe had carried the letters in his tall hat as he went about delivering them, and sometimes as he sprawled beneath a tree studying his law books the villagers would ask if he had any mail for them in his hat.

Moving to Springfield, Lincoln had shared a law office with his friend Billy Herndon, and it was interesting to walk through these small offices recalling the many anecdotes and incidents described as having occurred there, and seeing the corner where Lincoln had spent many hours lying his long frame down on a couch as he chatted when work was slack. I went from the offices to the Lincoln house, bought by Abraham and Mary Todd Lincoln in 1844, and while it was different from and smaller than the homes of Jefferson, Washington and Roosevelt it was to me more moving and immediate an evocation of its one-time incumbent than any of the other three.

While there had been early indications of Lincoln's unusual gifts of intellect and personality, it had been after his departure from Springfield, on his accession to the White House in Washington, that his greatness had progressively emerged. He had been noted for self-deprecation – the opposite of that quality in one later aspirant to the White House, George Bush, who had said the following words without a blush or stammer: 'This election is about character. I have character, so elect me as your President.' Instead of being embarrassed and repelled by such conceit, voters had actually elected Bush to the White House.

It had also been Bush who, condemning black South Africans for turning to armed struggle to end apartheid, had betrayed a dazzling ignorance of American history and the American War of Independence by saying: 'We Americans do not believe violence is an answer to oppression.' George Washington would certainly have been puzzled by this odd assertion.

Another great quality of Lincoln's had been his sense of humour. He had praised General Grant to his cabinet for winning battles while most of the generals sat tight in their defensive encampments, and when members of the cabinet protested that Grant drank a bottle of whisky a day, Lincoln said to his secretary: 'Have a case of whisky delivered to all the generals.'

The question about Lincoln whose answer could, I thought, best help South Africa in planning its economy, had to do with the financing of the Civil War at a time when the Union coffers where virtually empty. How had Lincoln raised the money to pay the Union soldiers year after year, when their pay for three months came to more than the total funds of money in the entire US treasury? Had the North simply printed notes, trusting success would result in the confidence of the people that would keep the currency strong? The opposite had happened to the Confederate currency, which was worthless by the time the war ended. How could the new South African government keep its currency valuable and respected? Could it be done, as in Lincoln's case, mostly by power of charismatic leadership?

Some cynics maintained that national leaders, even United States presidents, were basically powerless and that real power resided in their legislators and economists, with the presidents unable even to influence foreign policy against trade interests. But I had personal reasons for knowing this simply wasn't true.

Only days after I had escaped from South Africa I had been invited to New York to address the United Nations Security Council, then to Washington to testify before the Senate Foreign Relations Committee, and finally to the White House, where I was taken into the Oval Office to meet President Carter. He had started by welcoming me to the United States and arranging for a picture to be taken of me with himself and Vice-President Walter Mondale, to show the South African government that I had the support of the United States in the campaign against apartheid.

Then President Carter had said: 'Mr Woods, what should we be doing about South Africa?' and I replied: 'Mr President, I would need about three hours to tell you, and that's not practical, but I can sum up the main points.' The President turned to Vice-President Mondale and said: 'Fritz, call Cy Vance [then Secretary of State] and see that Mr Woods gets to brief all senior State Department staff involved with South Africa policy. He is to get at least three hours to tell us what we should be doing about South Africa.' He smiled broadly and said in his Southern accent: 'Tell them ever'thaing you like 'bout what we should do.'

I made use of my three hours firstly to brief the officials on just how bad things had become in South Africa, and to urge a range of specific actions against the Pretoria regime, including immediate revocation of all visa facilities for South African Security Police officers, some of whom had been regular visitors to the CIA; refusal of entry to the most notorious apartheid officials, many of whom I named; cancellation of 'exim' bank credits, export and import bank credits facilitating financial dealings between the US and South Africa; legislation to prohibit investment by Americans in the apartheid economy and to impose punitive taxes on corporations trading with South Africa; prohibition of bank loans to South Africa and withdrawal of investment benefits related to South Africa; encouragement of divestiture of all South Africa-related shares in state and city pension funds; intensification of the oil embargo and weapons embargo against South Africa, with stiffer penalties for breaches of these embargoes; scaling down and eventual cancellation of military collaboration between US and South African military agencies; closer monitoring of US businesses engaged in South Africa; pressures for disengagement from the South African economy generally, and ultimately the final and most valuable prize – removal of the veto against mandatory international economic sanctions against Pretoria.

Though some of these measures took time to implement, several of them were adopted within days by the Carter administration, notably when General Hendrik van den Bergh, head of South Africa's Bureau of State Security, was abruptly refused entry, and he and other security chiefs on my suggested list were never to enter the United States again. Export–import bank credits were also cancelled shortly after, with considerable and immediate effect, and new guidelines were issued which helped to lead eventually to effective legislation restricting investment in and loans to South Africa. The oil and weapons embargoes were more strictly applied, and notice served that the Carter administration would prosecute any US citizen breaking them.

Although this was due to the dedicated staff of the State Department, it had been made possible by the leadership and influence of a principled President Carter. He showed, just as Abe Lincoln and other principled presidents had shown, that the personality and purpose of the President counted for far more in terms of influence, and therefore power, than the cynics liked to suggest.

Returning to my hotel in Springfield from visiting the Lincoln sites, I hoped the new South Africa would produce its own geniuses as leaders. There was already evidence that black South Africans had a high rate of intellectually gifted children, and our history showed that even the smaller white group had produced unusually gifted prodigies.

South Africa had produced its white political geniuses in the early part of the twentieth century, though their achievements had no modern relevance to the nation's future as a democracy and had been flawed by the conditions of white privilege so entrenched during their careers. Geniuses, however, they had been, and worthy of note for their academic brilliance alone.

Both had been Afrikaners and both had shown their brilliance at an early age. The first, Jan Christian Smuts, as a country boy had started school only at the age of twelve, and only at the age of sixteen began speaking English in addition to Afrikaans, yet he was to set the all-time record at Cambridge University, England, in the speed with which he passed both parts of the Law Tripos concurrently, with honours in both, and the examination of the Inns of Court in 1894. Many years later this remarkable Afrikaner was to be elected Chancellor of Cambridge University.

He was appointed State Attorney of the South African Republic by President Kruger while still in his twenties, and when the Boer War broke out he became one of the most successful field commanders of the guerrilla war, eventually becoming a general while in his early thirties. He used to ride with Greek and Latin classics in his saddle-bags.

After the war he played a leading role in the reconciliation between Boer and Briton, during the National Convention that formed the Union of South Africa out of the two former Boer republics of Transvaal and Free State and the two English colonies of Natal and Cape Colony, leading to the granting of independence by Britain to the new Union – over the strong objections of black delegations who naturally resented Britain's grant of control to the white minority over the black majority.

Smuts did a great deal for the Allied causes in both world wars, being appointed Field Marshal in the Second World War, and played a major role in drafting the preamble to the United Nations Charter. Also a leading botanist and philosopher, through his treatise on Holism, Smuts was defeated in 1948 by the apartheid Afrikaner National Party, which successfully convinced white voters that Smuts was going to extend the franchise to blacks and that this would lead inevitably to black majority rule. Though less extreme than his opponents on the matter of black rights, Smuts never saw such rights as the practical politics of his time and paid the electoral price for frequent absences on the world stage while the apartheidists carefully canvassed the rural areas and played on white prejudice and bigotry.

For a towering intellect who was acclaimed in many parts of the world as an international statesman, Jan Smuts had few pretensions in his lifestyle, as typified by his farmhouse at Irene, near Pretoria.

Nothing like the Jefferson, Washington, Roosevelt or Lincoln homes, Irene was a rambling corrugated-iron farmhouse where Smuts and his wife delighted in entertaining their children and grandchildren as well as, on occasion, the King and Queen of England or famous statesmen of the day from foreign lands.

Jan Smuts had been known affectionately by his supporters as 'Oubaas' ('Old Master') and Mrs Smuts as 'Ouma' ('Granny') and the old lady was particularly loved by South African soldiers because of the Ouma Gifts and Comforts Fund, which had millions of women throughout the country knitting socks, sweaters and scarves for our fighting men and sending them foodstuffs to the front in Egypt, Libya and Ethiopia, and later in Italy, France and Germany during the Second World War. At one stage, as a reward for helping to defeat Rommel's Afrika Korps, South African soldiers were granted furlough in Palestine, and in Jerusalem were taken to what the guide referred to as the Mosque of Omar. One young Afrikaans soldier asked his sergeant: 'Wat maak Ouma dan met 'n mosque?' (What is Ouma doing with a mosque?)

The other Afrikaner genius, with even greater intellectual gifts than Jan Smuts, was Jan Hendrik Hofmeyr, who became Smuts's protégé and deputy in parliament during the Second World War. Hofmeyr was known to be a genius from the age of five, when his elders were astonished to hear him reading aloud from books in English and Afrikaans. In junior school he was promoted in grades with amazing rapidity and he matriculated out of high school at the age of eleven, his marks placing him third in the entire Cape Colony. As a reward his mother offered him a trip to Robben Island (at that time a pleasure excursion), a box of chocolates or three tins of condensed milk (which most young South Africans enjoyed in those days) and young Jan settled for the last of these rewards.

Allowed into university at the age of twelve, Hofmeyr had two degrees by the age of sixteen, his MA at seventeen, was a Rhodes

Scholar at Oxford at eighteen, and returned to South Africa as a Professor at twenty-two. At twenty-four he became Principal (President or Vice-Chancellor) of the University of the Witwatersrand and at twenty-nine Administrator of the Transvaal by appointment of the then Prime Minister, Jan Smuts.

Smuts then appointed Hofmeyr to his cabinet, where he proved a brilliant Minister of Finance, and was reputed to have delivered one budget speech without reference to notes, having had a genuinely photographic memory.

At one time during the war absences of Smuts Hofmeyr held as many as five cabinet portfolios, and had parliament smiling when he said: 'As Minister of Finance I would not have presumed to introduce this Bill were I not assured of the support of the Minister of Mines, the Minister of the Interior, the Minister . . .' (reeling off his remaining portfolios) and when, shortly after the end of the Second World War, Hofmeyr died comparatively young, in his early fifties, Smuts was devastated because he had looked on him as a son as well as a successor.

But the worst aspect of the loss of Hofmeyr was that he had increasingly been voicing his opposition to policies of racial unfairness, serving notice that under his leadership the United Party would adopt a more liberal line. This had been used by the Afrikaner Nationalists to frighten the white electorate further.

So Smuts and Hofmeyr were the two towering geniuses of Afrikanerdom, and they hadn't backed the racial extremes of policy which were to follow for the next four decades in South Africa, yet in spite of their intellectual brilliance their stories prompted no questions which could even begin to compare with the pertinent questions the stories of the great four American Presidents posed for the future of our new South Africa, and I was aware of this as I prepared to leave Springfield, Illinois.

On the morning of my departure I was startled to be served breakfast in the hotel breakfast room by a nun in a full habit and veil, with three teeth blacked out, and served coffee by a witch, complete with broomstick, and to see other strangely attired waiters moving about like characters in some horror film, until I realized this was Hallowe'en, which the Americans pronounce Hollowe'en, and that weird costumes, grinning pumpkins and trick-or-treaters would be the order of the day.

Before leaving the United States to return to South Africa, I had

had to deliver my Fairbanks lecture and couldn't have ordered a greater climatic contrast between my country and Alaska. The only similarity was in the magnitude of the mountains and valleys. The snow-covered peaks and plains in Alaska were high and vast indeed, and it was quite a relief when the aircraft reached the heartland and the relative flatlands of the Yukon River region. The city of Fairbanks was fascinating to a South African who had never seen snow in his own country. Here it was everywhere, and at near midwinter most of the days were as dark as night.

During the only few hours of light I visited the university campus and was surprised to see a new cricket ball on one of the lecturers' shelves. Though American he was a lover of the great game, but he had few chances to play in Alaska except when Indian, Pakistani or Jamaican visitors called by.

One of the lecturers, a young woman named Deborah Wells, asked if I would like a dogsled ride, and I accepted keenly, with visions of a gentle swishing over the level snow as she stood behind me urging on her dogs with 'Mush! Mush!' But the first signs that a dogsled ride was usually something more than a gentle swishing over the level snow and a few cries of 'Mush!' came within the next few hours as I met various professors and faculty members on the Fairbanks campus. 'I hear you're going on a dogsled ride,' said one. 'Good for you!' Another said: 'Hey, so you're going on a dogsled ride – you're a sport!'

I began to feel a trifle apprehensive, asking if there was anything daunting about a dogsled ride, and was not reassured by the too-hasty denials and the way the would-be reassurers didn't look me in the eye. Eventually some basic facts of dogsledding began to emerge, such as that while it was a fairly gentle business if you were being pulled by two or maybe four dogs, it was a far livelier matter with a full team of frisky runners. And I began to realize from my dogsled host Deborah that she was planning to hook us up behind a really fast team of ten or twelve huskies, and that we were taking one of the speedier trails. I had a macho reluctance to demur, being unwilling to seem a wimp, and so the whole business began.

We went out to her country place where she kept her dogs, and there I was dressed in layers of warm clothing covered by caribou hide, with a hood called a parka, and huge mittens so that I resembled Captain Scott when he was only a few miles from the South Pole. Then we went out to the dog quarters, and I met my first huskies and was immediately charmed by them. They are beautiful dogs, with ghostly pale blue eyes, and they are super-friendly and hyperactive. That is to say they are constantly jumping around as if to say: 'C'mon! C'mon! Let's go! We wanna drag something!' Debbie said they were the greatest athletes in the animal world, pound for pound, and she clearly loved and admired them, and judging by the zeal with which they kept jumping up to lick her face they obviously felt the same way about her.

First she lashed the sled to a sturdy young tree, then strapped me into it and began to inspan the dogs two by two. I noticed immediately that the more dogs formed the team, the more the sturdy young tree to which we were tied began to bend like a longbow with the power of unleashed dogforce that was building up. When the whole team was inspanned (and the young tree beginning to resemble a fishing rod after a major strike) Debbie climbed to stand behind me and issued some last-minute instructions. 'If I should come off,' she said, 'stay with the sled and don't leave the trail, there may be grizzlies about out there. Oh, and throw out this anchor if you can,' she said, handing me a large, heavy and ominously sharp metal thing for which there was no space on the sled other than on my lap.

I have yet to meet a male who travels happily at speed with a large, heavy sharp object in the vicinity of his groin, but not wanting to be a spoilsport I didn't mention this awkward fact as Debbie began to untie us from the young tree. As we cast free we didn't so much shoot forward as fly through the air for several yards at a shocking speed, hitting the trail fortunately the right way up and going almost immediately into a long curve to the right, with the sled leaning over with the camber of the trail so that the bottom of the trail was whizzing by only inches below my face. It was instantly terrifying and then almost as instantly exhilarating, as we straightened up again and positively rocketed along through the crisp snow.

Ahead at eye level I had a snow-flurried vision of dozens of pounding paws sending little jets of snow back over my head as the dogs positively galloped ahead. The trail itself was a defined track through the snow, with snowbanks on either side, and as we occasionally came to a fork Debbie would tell the dogs which way to go with an appropriate monosyllabic yell which they instantly, and apparently joyously, obeyed. She spoke again about what wonderful

131

athletes the huskies were, and let them have a good gallop for several miles before giving them a pause for a breather. 'Okay, guys,' she said. 'Have a drink, now,' and the huskies turned to bite off a bit of snowbank and dissolve it in their mouths, as this was their water supply. But they were soon champing at the bit to get going again, and Debbie gave them a good gallop for a long stretch of trail at full speed for thirty minutes. Altogether we sledded for more than an hour, covering around twenty miles or so (which when one is seated two inches above the surface feels very fast indeed) and Debbie didn't fall off and I didn't get the ice anchor stabbed into my vitals and we weren't menaced by grizzlies, and apart from the first few seconds of fright it was a great experience.

I learned many interesting things about the remarkable huskies, and found most appealing the fact that when you are out on the trail, or on one of the long-distance endurance races such as the Iditarod, the way to locate your huskies the following morning is to look for the little vapour-trails from their nostrils as they lie embedded in the snow for warmth. They were wonderfully friendly animals, and when we got back to Debbie's base I got a personal farewell lick in the face from every one of them.

It was already growing dark in the early afternoon as we headed back to town, and the snow was impacted everywhere, even on the road. I noticed that in the early gloom passing cars flashed their lights and motorists acknowledged each other far more than in most places. It was explained to me that in Alaska, where the elements are such a powerful factor in daily life, cars acknowledge each other as a reassurance in case someone should go missing, and that there is more sense of community because people have to depend on each other more.

A blizzard was building up as I prepared to leave Alaska, and as the aircraft took off to bank over the frozen Yukon, conditions could not have been less like those in my next destination as I returned to the warm and sunny South African veld of limitless skies and infinite horizons.

Back in South Africa, as I prepared to travel to the main cities to look at how living patterns were changing in the new era, I was reminded again of how precipitate the final days of inflexible apartheid had been once the grim determination to uphold it for ever had gone.

Clearly the major pressures had been twofold – growing military challenge by the armed wing of the African National Congress not only on the borders of the country but within South African territory – and sometimes deep inside it – and the inexorable turning off of the international money supply, the bank loans and investments which had been the economic oxygen of the apartheid state.

Because of the censorship of the media many South Africans had been unaware of the scale and scope of the military challenge, so that in the late 1980s of the more than ninety significant ANC attacks within South Africa, not one was reported and therefore few were known to the general public beyond a limited number of soldiers and police involved in the actions. But what other influences had contributed to the decision to release Mandela and begin public negotiations?

One major development 6,000 miles away and only two months before Mandela's release which undoubtedly had had some contributory effect on the decision had been the fall of the Berlin Wall on 8 November 1989. The final stage of the collapse of international communism had started in Poland in June of that year with Solidarity's triumph, which had sparked off Hungary's decision to open its border with Austria, allowing East Germans to begin a stampede that led to the breaching of the wall, Czechoslovakia's 'Velvet Revolution', the end of Nicolae Ceauşescu's reign in Romania in December and the subsequent unravelling of the Soviet Union itself as the whole myth of united communist power came apart.

It was the fall of the Berlin Wall that made the greatest impact. After its decades as a symbol of death to all who sought to escape the grim circumstances of life behind the Iron Curtain, the will of the German people, from both sides of the wall, had challenged the communist guards to open fire as usual on those defying the wall, and the guards had failed to do so.

From the moment that even a few climbed up on it with impunity, the wall was doomed, and the delighted Germans had started literally tearing it apart, smashing it down, then bulldozing it away, in one of those great defining moments in world history.

I remembered seeing the wall in 1967, not only at Checkpoint Charlie but at various other points, and being horrified at the amount of money and manpower being wasted on enforcement of this awful quarantine. Wendy and I had climbed up on an observation platform, whereupon two East German guards had ostentatiously photographed us and flourished their automatic rifles menacingly. Like our South African Security Police, they had obviously seen too many cheap movies, and were doubly dangerous because of their limited intelligence.

Our own South African version of the Berlin Wall, the strict apartheid prohibition against whites entering black townships without documentary permission, and vice versa, were also now departed, and as with the wall it seemed hard to comprehend how so senseless a prohibition could have lasted so long. The answer, of course, was firepower and police and military support. As in Russia, as in the whole Soviet Union, so in South Africa a crazy system opposed by more than nine-tenths of the people had stayed in place because the minority regimes in both countries had controlled the armies and police forces to buttress the control of the minorities. And, again in both places, the moment the will to impose by force of firearms the rule of the minority on the majority had lost its strength, that previously powerful will had become unenforceable.

Travelling to many black townships in South Africa during the early 1990s, I saw much to lift up the spirits in the dying days of apartheid, but also much to worry about. The destruction of the Berlin Wall was, however, highly pertinent to the post-apartheid townships and hugely symbolic of the new order in South Africa, and so its importance to our own unfolding new history could not be discounted. Not only did the fall of the Berlin Wall and the subsequent collapse of international communism remove one of the central planks of the racist platform – that any concession to blacks would leave South Africa vulnerable to the international bolshevik conspirators just waiting to exploit such a weakening of resolve – but it also showed how quickly mighty monoliths of ideology, whether symbolic of communism or of the unshakeable will of the Afrikaner Nationalists to fight to the last drop of blood for apartheid, could crumble at the hands of large majorities.

And the removal of the wall served as a reminder of how the bureaucratic walls of apartheid, the paperwork and police patrols needed to stop whites getting into black townships or blacks getting out of them, had also been torn down. We had no more Checkpoint Charlies to go through now to enter a township. We just drove in, and there were no Security Police to check our papers, follow us or otherwise monitor our visits there.

I went back to the biggest and smallest townships I had known. After one of the biggest in the country, Mdantsane, and Duncan Village, both adjoining East London, there came massive New Brighton, Port Elizabeth, Langa and Nyanga and Khayelitsha, Cape Town and the biggest of all, Soweto, whose name had come from the first two letters of the general term SOuth WEstern TOwnships.

These were all what had been called 'Bantu' townships, for what had also been called 'blacks' or 'Africans'; then there were the 'coloured' townships, for those of 'mixed' blood and 'Indian' townships, for descendants of the Indians originally brought to South Africa to work in the sugar plantations, because the Zulus hadn't liked the work of cane-cutting or the proliferation of deadly mamba snakes in the hot sugar-fields of Natal.

As I had found on my first day back, when visiting Duncan Village, there was still tension in the air when whites went into townships. Although the bureaucratic laws were gone or going, there was still a residue of resentment understandably lingering after all the years of racial extremism. Still-angry blacks in the townships didn't bother to enquire into the political credentials of whites when they first saw them, as there was still an initial assumption that all whites had been the enemy.

But I was surprised to find that the 'coloured' townships were scarier than the black townships. I was interviewing youngsters in the Cape Flats, in Hanover Square and neighbouring townships when I realized that these kids, averaging twelve or thirteen years of age, were not only perpetually high on a combination of crack cocaine and mandrax, but were members of killer gangs that dominated the region. What chance had these children? They knew no other world than the drugs and crime scene, and life to them was cheap. There was in their culture and their consciousness no thought of any kind of education or personal progress, their eyes had a dead expression, and by the time they were fourteen they were lost to the world.

One sunny day in 1992 I had a sudden vision of the immensity of the challenge facing the African National Congress. It was one thing to know you would certainly win the first democratic election in your country, but it was entirely another to realize that your voters expected you to change their entire lives. There was Nelson Mandela, hero of most of the nation, committed to improving every South African's circumstances of living, and there were many of his supporters who believed that when he came to power he would find them all jobs, houses, cars and, at last, a sense of security.

How could this be done? While apartheid lasted, one small fraction of the nation, the whites, had had all the best of everything, the best areas to live in, the best education, the best jobs, the best opportunities in life, the best medical treatment. But with the end of apartheid, all this was changed. Now the expectation was that nine times as many people would have the best medical treatment, the best education, the best jobs, the best housing, and so forth. Imagine being Mandela! Acclaimed by nine-tenths of the nation, who now expected that everything would improve almost overnight, where could he find the money to provide even simply fair educational and medical services for all?

A country like Britain, one of the leaders of the world in the calibre of its health care for all citizens, and with more than ten times the gross national wealth of South Africa, could not afford to pay for ten times the health and educational services it provided. How, then, could South Africa, with far fewer resources than Britain, provide health and educational services for nine times as many South Africans as the original group, the whites?

This was the enormity of the task facing Mandela, Mbeki and the other ANC leaders in the early years of the post-apartheid era. Where would the money come from to make South Africa a fairer society?

Although South Africa was, on the face of it, a wealthy country, rich in mineral resources, it now became painfully obvious that such wealth was superficial. Real wealth lies in the calibre of productivity and education of a nation's people, and in this respect South Africa was poverty-stricken.

What I couldn't work out was how the majority of inhabitants of the townships survived. Unemployment was up to forty per cent, which in the absence of a South African equivalent of the British social safety net meant no income at all for almost half the people, yet, as in Nigeria and other African countries, they somehow survived. Part of the reason was the traditional generosity of Africans, who as a matter of course shared their food with those less fortunate. But for so long? And for so many people?

In 1992 South Africa had around 40 million people, of whom only about half had any sort of job or income, and I knew that all African National Congress leaders would be required by many of their supporters to find the shortfall in employment and income. But from where? There had for years been a belief among many blacks that somewhere in the world, somehow, was a big box full of money for the victims of apartheid.

Some trainees from South Africa who wanted special treatment in Britain were asked why they thought they should get better food than British students and they replied: 'Because we are from apartheid.' So although the non-governmental organizations and embassies of supportive countries, such as the Nordic nations, were immensely generous in helping victims of apartheid, they had unwittingly created the impression in the minds of some of these victims that the world was full of guilt over apartheid, and that all that was necessary to release this conscience money was to demand it.

And adding to the burden of South Africa's new government was the fact that even the most generous countries, such as Denmark, Norway, Sweden, Finland and Holland, would soon be concluding that with apartheid over South Africa was now on its own, and that relief should in future be directed at countries worse off than South Africa, such as Mozambique, East Timor, Sudan and other places the plight of whose peoples would be occupying the disaster headlines henceforth.

CHAPTER 13

Changes, Changes, Everywhere

Everywhere I was going in South Africa, and I was covering as much territory as fast as I could, I saw the most staggering changes on all sides. I saw blacks staying at hotels in the Free State as registered guests, not waiters, and I saw Indian businessmen drumming up orders in that same province, from which Indians had been barred for generations unless they were travelling through in transit, in which case they had, anyway, to be over the border within twenty-four hours.

In Bloemfontein, capital and heart of the Free State, I saw my first white townships, with poor whites living in row after row of identical dwellings just as the blacks had during apartheid, and I spoke to a number of them, including some white women who now worked as domestic servants for black families. The consensus seemed to be that apartheid had failed them, that they somehow understood and accepted philosophically, if reluctantly, that it was now the turn of the blacks to be in charge. The great reality of life to these people was economic survival, on a day-to-day basis, and past obsessions about racial pecking orders seemed to have no relevance to them.

I stopped and spoke to people in a line waiting for soup and basic provisions funded by a voluntary organization, and both those in the queue and the voluntary staff were of all races. The whites had no problems about being in a line with blacks, and several chuckled when I asked about this. 'Hunger makes us all equal,' said one old white man in Afrikaans. A white woman three places back, who was leading some others in prayer, said: 'Poverty makes us all brothers and sisters', and an elderly black woman chimed in emphatically, in English: 'People is people.'

A white Afrikaans woman who worked as a domestic servant for blacks was equally philosophical. 'Ach, in the apartheid time it couldn't happen, but to me it's a job. The people I work for treat me well and pay me fair. No, it isn't good money but it's money, and I'm glad to have a job. Lots of people haven't got a job.'

To any South African well acquainted with all the implications and nuances of the four decades of apartheid, the changes throughout the country varied from the startling to the staggering, and they were comprehensive. The dumping of apartheid was no surface matter of window-dressing. Some of the visiting foreign journalists wrote rather superficially that there had been little real change in the country and that apartheid lived on. This showed the extent of their ignorance of what had been here from 1948 to 1990, because in most major respects nowadays it was like being in a totally different country from the one I had left at the end of 1977.

To see blacks in restaurants, clubs, cinemas and theatres; in executive positions at banks and businesses; in the same sports teams as whites, in the armed sections of the army, navy and police as well as in the senior ranks of the security services; and to see courting couples of different races openly going out together and acting affectionately in public – to see these things was to witness real radical change in South Africa and to deny this was churlish as well as insulting to those who had given their lives to achieve such change.

And this was only the beginning. These changes were being consolidated and developed by negotiation at the highest level, with delegates of all races and interests debating and evolving a national democracy with a national constitution.

Each time I went back to Britain from South Africa, or for that matter anywhere abroad, I found that while there was good coverage of developments in South Africa, there was inadequate perception internationally of the scale and scope of the miracle that was taking shape there. This, however, was understandable, given that for people in the rest of the world things were hardly standing still. In fact, changes and evolution were to be seen in many parts of the globe, as momentous events were succeeded by momentous developments that had also been believed unthinkable by many only a few years before.

Operation Desert Storm was now concluded, and the Iraqis expelled from Kuwait, though I felt a wonderful opportunity had been squandered in the process. The Iraqis, all of them, could have been given their first-ever opportunity to choose their own government at the conclusion of that conflict, and the massed air forces of the victors could have been used to build on the Kuwait–Iraq border a gigantic pyramid of burnt-out tanks, assembled and put in place by helicopter, as a permanent memorial of what had happened and as a symbol of international commitment to oppose all violent invasion anywhere.

Hard on the heels of the conclusion of Desert Storm was the escalation of the downfall of autocratic states in many parts of the world: in the former Soviet Union, in Eastern Europe, in South America, Asia and Africa, as the long-suffering people of the world increasingly demanded democracy.

There was material change, too, to be seen, including such spectacular feats of engineering as the Channel Tunnel, linking Britain to Europe. After two hundred years of argument and controversy, on both sides of the Channel, over the desirability or necessity of such a link or lack thereof, the British and French diggers met each other under the Channel waters in November 1990, and within four years the project was completed with the aid of gigantic digging 'worms' that chewed their way through earth and rock and cycled the excavated debris back through their vitals to each respective shoreline. When it was completed I couldn't wait to try out the journey, and Wendy and I set off for Paris, enjoying the unusual treat of a champagne lunch under the Channel and emerging, with cognac and coffee, into the French sunshine to cruise steadily to Paris at around 200 miles an hour.

All that was missing, I felt, was Japan's ingenious arrangement whereby if you get a ticket for the bullet train from Tokyo to Osaka you wait at a precise point on the Tokyo platform marked to indicate where the coach with your seat will be stopping. The same procedure is observed on arrival at Osaka, so that people meeting you on the platform know to within inches where you will be stepping out from your coach. I felt it was a pity such common-sense precision wasn't followed by rail services elsewhere.

Back in South Africa, Wendy and I decided to do what we'd long spoken of during the years of exile abroad – rent a car and drive to all the parts of our own country that we'd never been to before, and visit those places we felt we hadn't seen enough of in the old days. We flew into Johannesburg and set off in a lively rental BMW for the Eastern Transvaal, spending most of the day driving until we reached the Kruger National Park and checking into a rest camp near the entrance gate as night fell. For the next three days we drove all over the Park, which is bigger than Belgium, and saw a wide variety of game including, excitingly and rather alarmingly, a vicious fight between two huge elephants near where our car was parked. I kept my hand by the ignition in case we had to beat a hasty automotive retreat, provided the warring elephants were considerate enough to leave the road open to us . . .

After enjoying the remarkably cheap accommodation and facilities of the Kruger National Park we decided to treat ourselves to a day and night in one of the horribly expensive but highly luxurious private game reserves, where you are virtually guaranteed to see all the seriously glamorous animals without waiting for many hours. The accommodation was magnificent, and we got a five-star treehouse to ourselves, with haute cuisine and a six-hour safari in an open vehicle, during which we were brought even closer to the scariest animals than we particularly cared to be.

Of the two of us, Wendy is the wildlife enthusiast. Her favourite television viewing is usually about lion cubs or bears or other denizens of the wild animal kingdom, and when the two of us are viewing real-life wild animals she is usually the one who wants to get closest and to watch for longest. Once at Etosha in Namibia she persuaded me to park near a group of elephants at a watering hole, and although the little ones were very cute as they played at the feet of the big ones, the big ones were very big indeed. In fact, the Etosha elephants are a good six to eight inches taller at the shoulder than the biggest African elephants, which is how they evolved over many centuries in order to reach the highest foliage and trees in arid conditions. Well, after about twenty minutes of elephant watching I was a combination of bored and apprehensive, but my charmed spouse could have stayed parked there for hours.

It wasn't quite like that with the lions we saw at the fancy game park adjoining the Kruger. In fact, Wendy started regretting that she was sitting on the lion side of our open Land Rover as soon as our driver/ranger nonchalantly switched off his engine and sat with his back to his rifle as he pointed to some nearby lions. There were three of them, three big males lying dozing in the grass within ten

141

yards of us, and they looked like big boulders matching the grass, at first, until we saw the great manes and the big open eyes as they looked up and around occasionally. One kept giving a great yawn, as if he were the MGM lion. At this stage we recalled a number of stories about careless game-watchers. Only months before, at the same game park, a Korean tourist had ignored a warning not to get out of the vehicle. He had asked his friend to photograph him standing near a sleeping lion, which had woken up and attacked him in a flash, dragging away most of him as the game ranger fired to drive him off, and all that was left of the tourist at the site of the attack was part of his left arm, still with a wrist-watch on, and quite a lot of blood. These disturbing thoughts were going through our minds as we pondered the ranger's next words, to the effect that we would be amazed at how fast these lions could move if they resolved to attack us. I asked why, in view of that fact, he had his back to his rifle, and he said reassuringly that he could see that the three lions had recently fed. What I didn't ask but nevertheless wondered was – what if the lions, or even just one of them, felt like dessert?

After a few minutes all three lions got up and started walking towards our vehicle, and we were asked to keep absolutely still (no problem there as we were too petrified with fear to move anyway), then they walked along the side of our open Land Rover, and as all three ambled past with their bushy-tipped tails flicking away flies Wendy was horrified to feel one of the bushy tail-ends brush the side of her bare knee.

Although she didn't cry out, she did shudder comprehensively. After thirty-seven years of marriage I could sense her shuddering across a crowded room, let alone right next to me as we both cowered back towards the lionless side of the vehicle. Back at the luxury *boma*, sipping high tea as we watched a friendly rhinoceros trying to menace a brace of buffaloes just across the river from our balcony restaurant, we agreed that close-up film shots of lions were infinitely preferable to actual proximity to them as they breathed and got up and turned their yellow-brown eyes on you.

We returned to Johannesburg via the sort of stunning Eastern Transvaal scenery that I hadn't known existed. We of the Cape Province and Natal had tended to be scenic snobs when people mentioned the Free State and Transvaal, and now I could see what nonsense that had been. The Blyde River Canyon alone was obviously one of South Africa's scenic wonders, and driving through the surrounding mountains was a treat. It shouldn't have been a surprise, of course, since the canyon was part of the Great Rift Valley of Africa which continued through Natal via the Valley of a Thousand Hills and ended only a few miles from our own birthplace in the Transkei region.

Our next marathon drive was through Transkei, from Umtata, where Wendy was born, to Cofimvaba, and southwards to Elliotdale district, where I was born, to the Bashee Mouth, where we had first met, and then to various coastal resorts such as Hole-in-the-Wall, where a giant rock dominated a beautiful little bay and the waves poured through a forty-yard hole in the great rock, and Xhora Mouth, where my mother's family had had a cottage on the ridge between a Rhineland-type wooded cliff and the ocean, with a beautiful lagoon with a mangrove island in the middle. When we were teenagers there had been a huge ship's helm, barnacled fast to the beachside rocks for decades until the force of the waves finally removed it. The helm had been from the sailing ship *Circassia*, one of the many wrecked on that notorious coast, and in my granny's cottage up on the ridge was a lovely antique corner cupboard with glazed doors salvaged from the *Circassia* many years earlier. Most families living along that coast had a memento from some shipwreck, and Wendy and I have to this day a small round table with heavy cast-iron legs washed ashore near Bashee Mouth from a ship called the *Clan Lindsay*.

From Bashee Mouth Wendy and I drove to East London, then along the south coast road via Port Alfred and Bathurst, where my 1820 settler ancestors had come to from England 172 years earlier, to Port Elizabeth where we visited relatives and friends.

On the coast road out of East London we passed Fort Glamorgan Prison, the notorious old jail established in 1832, and Wendy recalled her visit there in 1976 when Steve Biko had been inside during one of his frequent imprisonments. She had recorded her impressions at the time, writing:

I drove through the prison gates, past cottages and blocks of offices, past vivid green lawns and obedient garden beds, and eventually found what I assumed to be the actual jail – a dark redbrick building, double-storeyed, old and forbidding. There were no welcome signs for visitors, no obvious parking places, no helpful arrows pointing anywhere – not even a sign saying 'Jail'. I stopped the engine and stared and listened. There was an enormous wooden double door in the middle of the building and the only other apertures were many small windows at regular intervals covered by thick wire mesh. From these windows came singing, shouting and laughing. I began to feel nervous as if by now someone would have come up to me, demanded to know what I was doing there, and said that I should move my car and that I should have applied four months ago to the Department of the Interior to be there in the first place. Nothing happened, so I scanned the building again, trying to decide how to get inside. Those doors looked ridiculous. They were reinforced with crossbeams; they had huge studs in them and, best of all, at their centre were two cast-iron door-knockers. I couldn't bring myself to walk across the gravel, raise the knockers and bang them down without dissolving into hysterical giggles. Then I noticed that one of the windows on the left was slightly larger than the others and had a sign 'Blankes' (whites) above it. I went over, peered through the mesh and saw two young men walking around in an office. They both had guns at their hips.

'How do I get inside to see a prisoner?'

'Just bang on the door, lady.'

So there it was – I banged the knockers and, to my delight, a small panel slid open and an eye stared at me.

'I want to see a prisoner,' I said to the eye.

The panel slid closed and there was a lot of vigorous and hollow clanking. The doors were being unlocked. One side opened. I stepped inside and found myself in a caged vestibule. The turnkey was locking the door again. He was white and middle-aged. He had a gun at his side and attached to his belt was a chain on which hung several huge keys. He was good-natured and friendly and stupid. I looked around and found the office with the two young men.

'I want to see the man in charge.'

'You can't, lady, he's in court.'

'Well, can I see the person under him, then?'

One of them came into the vestibule and motioned to the turnkey, who loped forward to unlock a gate in the cage which separated the vestibule from the main body of the prison. The

144

young man disappeared and I waited, looking up and down the corridor. It was very noisy in there. Prisoners, black and white, walked past looking surprisingly cheerful. It reminded me of a hospital – the only apparent difference being the lack of wheelchairs and trolleys and the fact that there was more rowdiness. An official-looking white man walked slowly up to me and stared at me curiously. Determined not to state my case with my face pressed to bars I said as imperiously as I could: 'I'd like to see you in your office, please.' He nodded and again we had the turnkey letting me out of the cage into the corridor. In the official's office, which was not his office but the office of three people, I said: 'I've come about a prisoner called Steve Biko. I believe he is an awaiting-trial prisoner and I'd like to know what his privileges are.'

'Oh, yes, lady, he is allowed to have letters,' he said. 'He is allowed visitors. He is allowed to read newspapers and books. He is allowed to receive food and cigarettes and he is allowed to receive money.'

I wrote all this down and thanked him and then asked if I could see the prisoner. He was about to say yes when one of his colleagues who had wandered in during our talk said very quickly: 'No, lady. Whites are not allowed to visit Bantus (blacks) in this jail.'

My official and I looked at each other, shocked – he because it had never occurred to him that I could possibly be visiting a black man, and I because I hadn't realized that he had misunderstood me.

'But don't you ever have whites visiting blacks in this jail?'

'Never, lady.' They were emphatic, but embarrassed.

'But don't blacks ever have white doctors or priests visit them?'

'No, lady, they have their own people to do that.'

'But I have visited blacks in the King William's Town jail.'

'Yes, well, they have the facilities there, lady. That's a new jail.'

'But don't you have facilities here?'

'No, lady, there's no facilities here for that.'

By now they were both very uncomfortable, avoiding my eyes and moving about awkwardly. I gave up and let them escort me to the turnkey, who locked me out. Outside on the gravel, my frustration surged forward, took hold of me and propelled me back to the 'Blankes' window and the two young men in the office.

'Who's in charge of this whole place?' I asked.

They told me: 'The commandant.'

'Where can I find him?'

'Down the road in the main office.'

I walked down and came to what was obviously the main office, because it had a flagpole with the South African flag flying at the top of it in the surrounding garden.

Two important-looking uniformed policemen stood on the verandah. I introduced myself and asked to see the commandant. They were both charming and one stepped forward, identified himself as the commandant and asked me into his office. He had a large desk, a picture of Vorster hung on the wall, and the floor was thickly carpeted. Before I could start talking his genteel secretary walked in, was introduced to me and said in Afrikaans to him that she had all the invitations to the coming performance in East London of the Orange Free State Police Band, and seeing that 'the editor' and his wife were getting one, and seeing that the editor's wife was here in person now, could she not hand it to her? Yes she could, said the commandant, and expressed the hope that the editor and his wife would come to the performance. Being prepared to endure even this, provided he would let her see the prisoner, the editor's wife accepted graciously. I looked at the secretary. Her reality was here with this carpet and desk and picture, and not thirty yards away was the world I had just left, the world of the inmates, which she had probably never seen. The commandant and I got on with our negotiations, and to my amazement he agreed to let me see the prisoner. He called his second-in-command to escort me back to the jail and organize the visit. Back again to the turnkey and the vestibule, but this time with the second-in-command hurrying things up. The prisoner Biko was called. I heard the imperious shouts, 'Biko, Biko', getting fainter down the passage. He was a long time coming and, as I waited, I noticed a young black prisoner in regulation prison khaki shorts and overshirt standing a little way down the passage. He looked anxious and submissive, the look I have seen on a thousand black faces in the country, the look of someone waiting to accommodate the mood or whim of the white 'Baas'. He stood there as if he had been told to stand there and wait. A white, fat, sleek warder appeared, and as he strolled past him suddenly made a threatening lunge at him and started shouting at him in Afrikaans. There was no anger in this warder – he was merely teasing, having some fun. The man's arms lifted at once to shield his body from the expected blows. One arm curved around the stomach and the other rose to the head, and the man stammered out answers to the questions and taunts being thrown at him. Then the warder strolled on, walking towards me. He saw me staring at him and, as he looked at me, I realized that not only was there no shame or even defiance in his bearing, but that, in his eyes, my white skin made me an implicit and automatic collaborator in what he had just done. He strolled past, bored, disappeared for a few moments and then came back towards the black man. As he got near, the black man started cringing, his arms taking their positions again in what was now a conditioned reflex action. The warder was enjoying himself hugely. The audience (me) was making it that much more pleasurable.

But this time he only shouted something and then disappeared around the corner. The black man dropped his arms and continued his anxious vigil.

I heard noise from the other direction and pressed my face to the bars to catch sight of Steve. I couldn't see him, but I could see a group of warders and policemen and I knew he must be in there somewhere. And then I saw his face and, with a slight sense of shock, I realized that I had never seen him look like that before. He was looking down, his expression sullen, withdrawn and angry. If he was curious as to why he was being summoned, he didn't show it, and then as he got closer I suppose curiosity did get the better of him because he looked up and peered round one of the heads and caught my eye. I will never forget the change that took place in his expression. It seemed to take place in slow motion, starting from total withdrawal to reluctant curiosity, to intense curiosity and then a huge, naked smile of recognition. But that did not last long. He had been caught unprepared, and as they let me through the cage he had collected himself and the old reserve had taken over. We shook hands stiffly, like two strangers, and mouthed social platitudes with all those people milling around. We were shown into a visiting room with a long bench along one wall, a small table near it and one steel kitchen chair with a blue seat drawn up to the table. This was obviously the visitor's chair – it looked like a throne in that dingy room. The bench was meant for the visitee. I avoided the kitchen chair and went around the table to sit on the bench. So did Steve. The second-in-command stayed in the room to listen and took up his position near the door, facing slightly away from us and trying to retain some dignity while playing the role of eaves-dropper. So there we were – three awkward people trying to be normal in a bizarre situation. I think I asked Steve about five times how he was and didn't listen to any of the answers. He told me that he didn't expect to be there long (as it turned out he wasn't) and that I should tell his mother that he was all right. We talked about his 'privileges' as an awaiting-trial pris-oner and arranged for me to bring some reading matter and food. At one point he asked the second-in-command a ques-tion about visiting hours, and his tone was so rude and abrupt that it shocked me. The second-in-command answered politely. It was only afterwards that Steve told me the reason for this. He knew that, while I was there, he could speak like that and get away with it. It was his way of scoring some points in the psychological warfare. He knew that when I left, the second-in-command and all the others would drop their pretence and treat him the same way they treated all the other 'Kaffirs' in the jail. His sullen expression was another defence. At the inquest much mention was made by the Security Police of the way he drew a veil between himself and his interroga-tors. This is what I had seen. He shut them out. They didn't exist for him and they could not get at him. They could hurt him, they could even kill him, but they could not get at him and this is what must have driven them mad.

I said goodbye and left after about twenty minutes. The visit had not really been a success in terms of proper commu-nication. I had been ill at ease and Steve had sensed this and had kept talking. I hadn't listened to half of what he said and felt dissatisfied at the end of it all. I felt as if I hadn't used the time well, but looking back now I realize that in spite of the clumsiness it succeeded in terms of sheer human contact, and that is all that matters. Some time afterwards I told Steve about my impressions of the jail and he laughed gently and said: 'Yes, it's one of the old ones.' And that was all. No anger, no bitterness – only an acceptance of things as they were.

This written recollection of Wendy's was published after Steve's death.

I had also been intrigued to see Fort Glamorgan again because I had had my own Fort Glamorgan adventure. It was in 1976, when I was sentenced to six months' imprisonment for refusing to disclose the identity of a witness to a break-in by Security Police officers when they vandalized a black community centre Steve Biko had set up in King William's Town. Before I was sentenced the Security Police had made all sorts of dire threats over the telephone, and they had had me interrogated by two colonels, one of whom had kept shouting in my face: 'You're going to prison!' Thanks to my mentor and former law lecturer, Harold Levy, who came all the way from Cape Town to defend me, the sentence was delayed while the state had to grapple with some imaginative technicality Harold had discovered. In fact, it so stymied the actual procedure that the government had to change the wording of the statute to get me into prison – but by the time they had managed that I was already out of the country in exile.

At the time, however, I was able to make a muted comment about it all in my weekly syndicated column, as follows:

A funny thing happened to me on my way to Christmas. Within 24 hours I was (a) appointed to the Board of Sponsors of NICRO, the National Institute for Crime Prevention and Rehabilitation of Offenders, and (2) sentenced to six months' imprisonment under Section 83 of the Criminal Procedure Act. The sentence, which is suspended pending appeal, was imposed for refusal to reveal the identity of a person who stated that he had witnessed criminal actions by the Security Police. Because the appeal is pending, nothing may be published about the merits of the case, but several general observations can be made. One is that if the appeal fails I'll be in a position to observe prison conditions from both sides of the bars, so to speak. In my capacity as a NICRO official I'll inspect prison facilities from the outside looking in, then in my capacity as a prisoner I'll compare these impressions with the view from the inside looking out. There's in-depth reporting for you. Later I'll co-opt other ex-prisoners, such as Prime Minister Balthazar Johannes Vorster and the Head of the Bureau of State Security, General Hendrik van den Berg, so that we veterans of the cells will be able to advise NICRO from practical and personal experience.

The prison to which I am provisionally consigned is the region's main penitentiary, Fort Glamorgan. It is a forbidding-looking redoubt high above the wooded banks of the Buffalo River. Last Christmas I donated a chess set to Fort Glamorgan for the prisoners, little suspecting I might one day have cause to be grateful for my own generosity. I've already inspected the accommodation and it leaves a lot to be desired. And that, of course, is the section for whites. The section for blacks is even more medieval. Fortunately the outfit with stripes or little arrows is now out of fashion. The garb now features a sort of off-white tunic. I had coffee with the head warder, after making an appointment to check out the facilities, and he was apologetic about the condition of the cells and the plumbing. Fort Glamorgan is one of the oldest prisons in South Africa, not a slick five-star set-up like Pretoria Central. But there are possibilities. Oscar Wilde wrote some of his best stuff in Reading Gaol, and maybe I'll be able to turn out something along the lines of 'The Ballad of Fort Glamorgan' in between the library duties to which I understand I might be assigned.

Anyway, there are several months to go yet before my appeal can be heard, so the authorities at Fort Glamorgan mustn't be surprised if a more than usually zealous NICRO official keeps calling to check on the standard of food the prisoners are getting. And I'm prepared to be generous about the whole thing. If the leading lights of our government ensure that I'm not too badly treated if I have to go inside, I promise to put in a good word for them one day when the tribunals begin in South Africa.

It was soon conveyed to me that this column, appearing in newspapers all over the country, had enraged members of the Vorster cabinet, which, in those scary times, provided some light entertainment amid the encircling gloom.

Once beyond grim Fort Glamorgan, we doubly enjoyed the rest of the drive along the coast past Chalumna Beach, where the first coelacanth had been netted by Skipper Hendrik Goosen, whose son Peter was a reporter on the *Daily Dispatch*, and then identified aboard his trawler by Marjorie Courtenay-Latimer, of the East London Museum, and famed icthyologist Professor J. L. B. Smith of Rhodes University, Grahamstown, creating a scientific sensation around the world. The famed fish, long thought extinct, was officially named *Latimeria chalumnae* J. L. B. Smith, and would go on to receive such nicknames as 'Old Fourlegs' and, from the *Reader's Digest*, 'A Fish Called Smith'.

We stopped for lunch in pretty Port Alfred with its fine marina and attractive Cowie River, then headed on to the Big Pineapple, P.E. or, more correctly, Port Elizabeth.

We East Londoners hated to admit that Port Elizabeth was the biggest of the developed cities in the Eastern Cape, and that it was about twice the size of East London, but I was inordinately proud that our East London-based newspaper, the *Daily Dispatch*, which I had had the honour to edit from 1965 to 1977, had had a higher circulation than either of the two big Port Elizabeth newspapers, the *Herald* and the *Post*, and that it still maintained the advantage fourteen years later.

From Port Elizabeth we headed for some of the finest scenery in all South Africa, after our own Transkei Wild Coast. Near Port Elizabeth was the Addo Bush, famous for its elephants and other big game including the kudu, which to me is one of the most amazing animals in terms of sheer athleticism. An enormous buck, one of the biggest, heaviest antelopes on earth, the kudu is nevertheless able apparently to defy gravity when it jumps vertically. I have seen one grazing within two feet of a high fence, taller than the great buck itself, then suddenly appear to levitate over the fence to land lightly and start grazing on the other side. The kudu must have the springiest heels in all creation, to achieve that helicopter effect with so little exertion. I mean, the kudu doesn't gather himself or appear to make any great effort. He just looks as if he is floating straight up, and comes down as if on an invisible parachute. It was in Addo Bush that the most notorious Catholic priest in South Africa, Father Matthew McManus, was arrested for poaching kudu.

Born in Kilkenny, in Ireland, Father Mac, as he was known generally, had been a heavyweight boxer and hell-raiser in his younger days, and although by the time of the kudu-poaching he was in his early sixties, he was still fit, big and strong, looking somewhat like a larger Spencer Tracey, with a shock of white hair. Before he was fined for the poaching the magistrate asked if he had anything to say and he replied: 'Yes, your honour, this is a case of much kudu about nothing.' His fellow priests believed it was more for the pun than the poaching that the bishop expelled him to the edge of the diocese, but in fact he had for some time been a problem for the bishop. Like the time he beat up three young men one evening at a beachside hamburger stand in Port Elizabeth. According to an eyewitness Father Mac was quietly sipping coffee when the aggressive young men started jeering at his clerical clothing and priest's collar, and when one of them actually hooked a finger into his collar Father Mac knocked him and his nearest friend out cold and was seen pursuing the third into the night, kicking at him as he ran.

Given a probationary parish on the distant edge of the Karoo, he was well liked there until the bishop heard how he was dealing with wife-beaters – he was beating them up. The victims felt a lot safer with him around, but complaints from the men eventually spread to Port Elizabeth, and the bishop had to act when one of the complainants turned out to be a minister of the Dutch Reformed Church whose deacon had been on the receiving end of the McManus wife-protection ministry.

He was given a spell in one of the toughest capitals of crime in the country, one of the Port Elizabeth black townships where stabbings, assaults and murders were so commonplace that even the police stayed away. Father McManus became a popular vigilante, patrolling the township armed only with a club, and emerging each night with a collection of confiscated knives and guns. The residents used to recount how he would stitch up stab wounds on the spot with ordinary cotton, using a coin to push in the needle. When an epidemic of bubonic plague raged through the township he was the only volunteer prepared to enter the stricken area to tend the sick and bury the dead. He moved in and lived there throughout the epidemic and never caught the disease, but his courage made such an impression on all at the time that he was given an illuminated scroll by the Port Elizabeth Municipality and the blacks insisted on renaming one of the main streets in the township after him.

When we met him he had been exiled, again for fighting, this

152

time to remote Komga, the furthest point of the diocese. But he had had some comfort in his exile. Pope John XXIII heard of the 'wild priest' from South Africa while Father Mac was on a pilgrimage to Rome and sent for him. The Pope embraced him, thanking him for his good work during the township plague. I asked if the Pope had been critical of his behaviour in any way. 'Ah, not at all,' he said. 'Thanks be to Jesus he obviously hadn't heard about that bloody kudu.'

Not long before Father Mac died, his friend Father John McVeagh told me of a trip the two old priests had planned on a cruise liner from Durban to Cape Town. They had embarked excitedly and gone straight up to the first-class lounge, to which their cheaper tickets didn't entitle them, to order a drink in style. But the snooty chief steward steadfastly avoided their upraised hands, preferring to serve the wealthy British and American passengers who seemed likely to tip more than the two impecunious-looking old clergymen. As he walked past them several times to take orders from other passengers, Father McVeagh lamented: 'The fella's ignorin' us, Mac, and me dyin' of the thirst.' Father Mac's eyes glinted dangerously. 'I'll fix him,' he said.

After several more attempts he managed to catch the chief steward's eye at last, and he reluctantly walked over to stand before them. Father McManus said nothing, but on his face was the look of a gentle, kindly old priest as he diffidently beckoned the chief steward closer. The steward finally realized that the kindly old clergyman wanted to say something confidential, so he bent his ear down attentively.

And into his ear Father McManus said quietly but distinctly: 'Fuck off!'

We were laughing and reminiscing about McManus anedotes as we left the Addo area and drove along the grandeur of the famous Garden Route, through the great lagoons and forests beside the coastal mountains, then up from Knysna and Wilderness, the beautiful spot where the old crocodile, P. W. Botha, was sulking in deposed retirement.

We set off for Oudtshoorn, with its neighbouring Cango Caves, one of the world's most extraordinary underground dripstone caverns with their vast halls and towering formations. We had visited the famous Carlsbad Caverns in New Mexico, USA, where the Hollywood film *Journey to the Centre of the Earth* had been filmed, with James Mason and Pat Boone, but the Cango Caves were, to my mind, even more spectacular, constituting a world with its own unique scenery of calcite masterpieces created over centuries by gently dripping water. It had taken 20 million years to form the wonderful caves and the result was unforgettable.

Discovered in 1780, the caves are in a low limestone ridge parallel to the Great Swartberg Mountains, and they extend below the earth in an amazing series of giant caves, stairways and walkways with a variety of pastel colours and formation designs. There are more than twenty consecutive chambers of varying size and majesty.

The entire region is a scenic wonderland, whether underground or above ground, and I had a strange adventure while showing Wendy the route to the north. I had twice in the past driven over the Swartberg Pass and been terrified in the process. I have no head for heights, and the Swartberg Pass is very high, very beautiful and very scary, with hairpin bends and sheer drops from cliff-edge roads. While wondering at its beauty I had shivered with fear both times I had negotiated it. It was for me almost as scary as the Chapman's Peak drive at Hout Bay near Cape Town – sensational and mind-freezingly frightening. If you steered wrongly by only a couple of feet and went over the edge, you could plunge hundreds of feet down into the beautiful bay below. But, while terrified by the Swartberg Pass I still wanted Wendy to experience it, as she was a lot braver than me at heights and a better driver besides, and I knew she would enjoy the scenery. But at breakfast the next morning in our Oudtshoorn hotel we were told that the Swartberg Pass was closed on account of road repairs at high altitude, and it was suggested to us that we should reach the northern route we were aiming for by an alternative road through Meiringspoort. It sounded dull and I was disappointed for her, but in the event this led us to one of the most amazing drives on the face of the earth, and at the end of it I was forced to admit that it had been even more spectacular than the Swartberg Pass, if very different indeed in character. In fact, it was the opposite.

To go over the Swartberg Pass you had to keep driving up and up at a steep incline, and each time you thought it wasn't possible to go higher you reached a turn which led you into another sharp upward slope, then another, then another, until you thought you'd soon need oxygen. But to go through Meiringspoort ('*poort*' means

154

'gate' in Afrikaans) you drove steadily down – towards the same high mountains but this time downwards – until you thought this was getting ridiculous and you couldn't go down further without coming to the hotter regions of the centre of the earth. The only reassuring thing as you descended ever further apparently to burrow below the foothills of the great mountains was the magnificent road, which wound and meandered through bend after bend, always downwards into the bowels of the earth, and the gigantic cliffs that towered overhead as if ready to fall on you when you got too close were a vivid orange-red, stretching up high towards where the sky presumably was if you could see that far up. The cliffs were formed of jagged red rock, and they appeared to close over you as you drove down further until, at last, you bottomed out and started following an enchanted tarred road that wound and turned, crossing and re-crossing a river, as you realized that you were penetrating deeper and deeper into the great mountain chain, through a narrow gorge that went on for another hour until you gradually started climbing again, stopping from time to time to admire the Disneyland look of the orange-red cliffs towering above on both sides until you emerged at last on the other side of the mountains.

We realized that just as the Swartberg Pass takes you scarily over the mountains by the highest route possible, so the Meiringspoort route takes you under and through them thanks to an enterprising *trekboer* named Meiring more than a century ago. While enthusing to friends in Johannesburg about this experience I learned from devotees of Afrikaans literature that one of our great national poets, C. J. Langenhoven, had written a children's story about Meiringspoort. I found it, read it and enjoyed it – a charming account of a fanciful elephant walk through the magic portal under the mountains. While the elephant was slowly progressing through the narrow opening, all traffic on the other side had to reverse out of the way.

We reached Matjiesfontein where I enjoyed showing Wendy the village from 100 years ago, and we had a drink in the Victorian pub before driving on north. The barman, however, was concerned that we were taking the due north road into the least populated part of South Africa, the Northern Cape Emptiness as it is sometimes called. 'Nobody goes there,' he said, mopping the counter, and I began to feel as if we were embarking on a Gothic horror story, like

155

Brad and Janet in the *Rocky Horror Picture Show* or any other naïve couple being warned by the locals not to venture where no one else goes. Transylvania and all that, with horses whinnying . . .

But we were determined, and after filling up we set off directly to the north. Within the hour we knew what the barman at Matjiesfontein had meant by 'Nobody goes there!' If not quite true the phrase was almost true, because in an hour we saw only two other cars on that lonely gravel road, and as we drove on for hour after hour that rate became even lower, so that by late afternoon we were driving for more than an hour without seeing a single car or human being, or even animal. It was increasingly looking like a lunar landscape as we progressed through the tiny hamlet of Sutherland, then Fraserburg, and we made a slight detour to take in the small town of Williston in the far northern Cape, in honour of my great friend and mentor, Harold Levy, who was now a distinguished judge and whose advocacy during the apartheid days had twice kept me out of prison. Harold was born in Williston, and his grandfather, an immigrant from Lithuania, had built there the first double-storey hotel in the entire *platteland*, which was how that great emptiness was called. At the time of this unique building, which Wendy and I found without any trouble because there wasn't much of Williston anyway and only one double-storey hotel, Harold's grandfather had been somewhat embarrassed on completion of the second storey, because there was no stairway and thus no way of getting to the second floor. Oy vay! The builder had been asked to add the necessary stairs, I think on the outside and at the back of the building in those days, and all was well. The building is now of more orthodox design.

It was said among his friends that the eminent Judge Levy now made it a rule, when delivering important judgments, to wear a pair of gold cufflinks I had given him when he repeatedly refused to take any fee for defending me in the Supreme Court in the bad old days. Each of the gold cufflinks had four capital letters engraved on it, because once, when I asked Harold his opinion of the case put by the opposing barristers, he replied with the story of little Hymie who, when asked by the teacher to spell a four-letter word, had said F.U.C.M., and when she asked what it meant he had said: 'Fuckem'. So I had had engraved on each of the gold cufflinks F.U.C.M.

As my lecturer, Harold had had a profound influence on me. When I was eighteen he had asked me before all the class in Cape

Town what my solution to the racial question was, and how I, as a person from the distant Transkei reserve, thought blacks should be treated. I had replied: 'They should all be sent back to the reserves, where they belong. They're happier there. It's no good educating them and bringing them to the cities. It's either send them back to the reserves or shoot them – it's them or us.'

There had been a shocked silence, my fellow students all being sophisticated city dwellers, and Harold Levy had looked at me silently for a long time. 'Do you really believe that? Is that really how you feel?' was all he said, and though I said I did and it was, I felt increasingly uneasy about my answer in the days that followed, and later realized that with such occasional questions, devoid of any expressed judgement or censure, he was putting me through a kind of juristic psychoanalysis from which my inherited views received a severe and lasting jolt of reality and logic. Imagining his childhood in Williston, and thanking my lucky stars that he had been my mentor all those years ago, I felt he was more responsible than any other person, until my encounter finally with Steve Biko, for educating me about the realities of my own country.

Having rendered our salute to Judge Levy's ancestral home, we said farewell to remote Williston and drove directly north for even more remote parts. The next village was Kenhardt, and it took about two hours to reach, which was quick going because in the virtually total absence of other traffic Wendy drove like a rally driver along the arrow-straight dirt road, sending up long plumes of dust behind us. I tried not to think of what would happen if we broke down in that remote wilderness, and as early evening fell and we found the road between Kenhardt and Upington fringed by light pampas grass, which was like a dead-straight landing-strip indicator, Wendy was by now driving so fast that the ten-kilometre indicators were almost flashing by in a blur. We relished finding ourselves on tar again as we approached Upington, into which we fairly screeched with scorching tyres at about 9 p.m. Upington was the biggest town we had seen since leaving Oudtshoorn early that morning, but it hadn't much to offer at that time of night, and the best we could do for dinner was steak and chips and some regrettably chilled red wine.

The following morning we headed for the Aughrabies Falls on the Orange River, where we found a well-planned national park and good amenities for tourists, with the only disappointment the fact that there was no frontal view of the big falls. While we were able to get within yards of the mighty eruption of water, it was to the side of the falls, on the shoulder as it were, and while the volume and force of the falls were impressive, the surrounding cliffs made it impossible to get a full overview of the whole phenomenon. Somehow, we felt, the Americans would have contrived, perhaps with a footbridge downstream, to show these impressive falls from the front. Nevertheless I was not disappointed, and felt they were like a big brother to the falls in New Zealand's North Island, near Lake Taupo, where the Waikato River bursts thickly from a cleft in the rock in the same way as Aughrabies, only Aughrabies has many more times the volume.

From Aughrabies we drove to the joke village of every South African, Pofadder. *Pofadder* is the Afrikaans word for 'puff adder', so presumably some *trekboer* must have been bitten by the deadly snake here at some stage, but over the years it had come to stand for the ultimate in the 'hicks from the sticks' – the ultimate opposite of the sophisticated city. Wendy took a picture of me posing next to the sign: 'Welcome to Pofadder; *Welkom in Pofadder*'. The village was fairly clean and neat, with at least one other sign we had to photograph, about *Oom Frikkie se winkel* (Uncle Fred's shop) having been established in the year something or other.

Filling up with petrol in the famous hickstown, we drove on to Springbok, and between these two towns came upon one of the most striking wildernesses either of us had seen. It was a gigantic basin in the red earth, crossed by the magnificent tarred highway we were driving on, and it extended for several miles, ringed by huge red-rocked mountains on all sides. It was like being on the surface of the moon, driving in an air-conditioned BMW with no other sign of human or plant life for many miles. It was a unique and awe-inspiring experience, except for a flash of anger I experienced over the fact that in these remote parts of what had been designated 'white' South Africa during the apartheid era, these roads with so little traffic had been given top-grade paved excellence, whereas the highly populated areas of the Transkei and Zululand interiors, designated black areas, had been starved of good highways and still had to make do with inferior dirt roads. Springbok was a pleasant, colourful town where we had a good restaurant lunch, reflecting on the fact that we were now in possibly the most remote rural area of all South Africa, near the Namibia border and the cold Atlantic coast – the top left-hand corner, as it were, in South Africa – and we now turned south for the first time in thousands of kilometres to drive down the west coast of the northern Cape Province. The next thousand kilometres were a real eye-opener for me, because since my early schooldays I had imagined this part of the country to be flat, boring semi-desert. On the contrary, we drove beside and through huge mountain chains, deep enchanting valleys, and always beside colourful grassland and vegetation which, at certain times of year, exploded into colour because this was Namaqualand, the home of the brilliant Namaqualand daisy.

For hundreds of miles we drove southwards, calling at Lambert Bay, where a friend of ours was born, and noticed the totally different character of these beaches, with their snow-white sand and cold water, from those of our Transkei Wild Coast nearly a thousand miles away with their yellow sands and indigenous coastal forests.

The following morning, after overnighting at Clanwilliam, we headed on down the coast to Cape Town, and found it as spectacular as the road further north. Here too were big valleys bathed in the pink light of dawn, breathtaking mountain passes, and misty saddles between the ranges where it was like being isolated in an inland lake of fog until the morning sun burnt away the vapour and revealed the magic of the great sunbathed vistas all the way south to Cape Town.

As we entered the world's most beautiful city for the first time from the north-west, it seemed again that we South Africans had undervalued our greatest national treasure, the metropolis with unparalleled gifts of shoreline, mountains, valleys and sands, reminding us again of Sir Francis Drake's description hundreds of years before: 'The fairest cape we saw in all our circumference of the Earth'.

Of course Cape Town was the most beautiful city of all on the face of the earth – how could this ever have been doubted? And though its closest rival, in my opinion, Rio de Janeiro, was obviously more blessed than all other rivals with its beautiful bay, Sugar Loaf Mountain, islands and glorious beaches, it couldn't quite match the mother city of South Africa. Arriving in Cape Town was a wonderful climax to a marvellous motoring trip of thousands of kilometres through some of the greatest scenery on our planet.

Yet it wasn't enough, because our next motoring marathon took us even further along highways we had never travelled before, starting again from Johannesburg but this time heading west beyond Potchefstroom and fabled Mafeking, now spelt Mafikeng. This small town had once been world-famous under its old spelling for its heroic defiance under siege during the Boer War, when the Boers had kept it surrounded and cut off from the British supply lines for seven months. But even more memorable was the fact that this dusty little hamlet in what was then the Western Transvaal was the birthplace of a remarkable institution that was to touch the lives of many millions of young people all over the world – the Boy Scouts and Girl Guides, the latter being called Girl Scouts in America.

The defending commander of the British garrison, Colonel Baden-Powell, seeking something to keep the young people of the besieged town from boredom, had devised the ethos and idea of Scouting there and then, and after the siege was lifted and the war was ended Scouting spread all over the world.

Beyond Mafikeng lay our destination for the night, Vryburg, which we reached in the early evening darkness after driving since dawn. Vryburg, literally Free City, boasted an International Hotel whose restaurant served some of the finest meat one could encounter anywhere, whether beefsteak, lamb chop, *Boerewors* (Afrikaans sausage), venison or game. It also presented the most excruciatingly bad cabaret turn, and provided the most eccentrically situated television set in our bedroom – we had to lie with our heads where our feet should have been, gazing upwards into a corner of the room where the set was sited.

Vryburg was so far the only town which had produced a major racial row because of school integration, for a time preventing black pupils from attending the high school until the authorities had compelled immediate compliance. Here again, interestingly, indications were that such incidents originated more from older people and parents of the white pupils than from the pupils themselves.The next morning, our necks slightly stiff from the strange television-watching angle, we drove on to Kuruman where we visited the famous Moffatt Mission with its well-preserved church and mission house, and the garden in which Dr Livingstone had proposed, successfully, to Mary Moffatt, under a certain tree many years before the explorer was so famously greeted by Stanley with: 'Dr Livingstone, I presume?' It was strange to reflect, in the hot little country town, that thanks to the Moffatt family and Livingstone, Kuruman had probably proved as significant to the spread of Christianity in southern and central Africa as the island of Iona had been to the spread of Christianity throughout the British Isles.

From Kuruman to the Namibian border at Nakop was another long haul, made seemingly longer by the worry that on this barren frontier with so little traffic there might not be a filling station before we ran dry of fuel. Although we kept seeing the names of places on our detailed road map, these names were either of abandoned sheds or derelict farmhouses – certainly devoid of fuel pumps. Beyond the border at Nakop this strange dearth of petrol pumps continued, and according to our fuel gauge we were totally out of petrol a good twenty kilometres before our next place of any size, named Karasburg. It was now getting near nightfall again, and we could see neither lights nor traffic nor any sign of human habitation beyond the straight and seemingly endless tarred road. Then we glimpsed in the distance a clump of trees, and just beyond that a roof or two, and actual walls, and as we drove into Karasburg we soon saw, with a rush of excitement, a garage complete with petrol pumps, attendants in overalls, and other signs of cheer, such as toilets, washbasins and refrigerated drinks. Refuelled now to bursting, as the pump attendant chuckled at how empty our tank had been, we sped on to our scheduled overnight stopping point at The White House, near Grunau.

While unlike its namesake in Pennsylvania Avenue, Washington, this Namibian version of The White House was nevertheless impressive. Overlooking its own vast wilderness of prairie-like infinity, it was a big house with high ceilings, a gabled roof and wide verandahs, built many years before by an eccentric German to impress his new bride, and we sat out on the front verandah sipping wine and looking up at the gigantic and seemingly nearby stars, while our innkeeper prepared our dinner of excellent beef – this still being one of the best regions for cattle-ranching in all Southern Africa.

There were other guests, no doubt in equally large apartments, but we sensed rather than saw them because those who motor for endless hours through empty vistas for entire days have little zest for socializing at night, and we simply wanted to drink, eat, bath and sleep, in that order.

The following morning, after a Namibian breakfast of spectacular proportions, we set off to drive to the Fish River Canyon on the southern border of Namibia, a vast chasm in the earth more than a hundred miles long and about half a mile deep at its deepest. Many years before we had been to see the Grand Canyon in the United States, but the Fish River Canyon in Namibia was a very different experience. The Grand Canyon was well prepared to cater for tourists: it was easy to get to by aircraft, bus or car, and the main features were well signposted and indicated. The Fish River Canyon was far wilder and less easy to reach. Although the impression the signposts from Grunau created led us to believe that the canyon was only an hour or so away, along a well-surfaced road, this was not the case. Not that the signposts actually lied about the distance, just that they gave no distance at all, but showed a bold arrow with big letters saying TO THE CANYON, and our expectations were of a reasonable immediacy, canyonwise.

The first disappointment was that the tar gave out soon, and we were on a pretty basic gravel road for the next four hours, during which we neither passed nor encountered another vehicle, and the terrain being similar to a bleak moonscape we began to feel like the last couple on earth after a universal nuclear cataclysm. On the one hand, it was disconcerting that there was not another signpost making any kind of allusion to the canyon; on the other, there was no evidence of any alternative road which might call for fresh directional information beyond that first basic arrow and sign, so there was no alternative but to drive on with a sort of Christopher Columbus philosophy that we were surely headed somewhere, this thought varied with the hope that wherever we were going to would end up having water to drink and petrol to fill up the car.

Occasionally the bare lunar landscape would be varied with a hill here and there, or even a mountain, but seldom with a tree or field of grass. Stubble and rock were the norm, and there was no sign of civilization or habitation to either side of the bare, straight, endless gravel road. It was therefore something of a shock to see, a mile or so away, a dwelling, a house with a door and windows, and what looked like an orchard of date palms. I suggested it might be a mirage, an apparent oasis which would vanish when we approached, but no. It was there, and it was with a spring in my step that I leapt out of the car to ask this country dweller whether we were indeed still on the road to the Fish River Canyon.

But there was no country dweller. There was only this house,

First day back in the Eastern Cape after all the years of banning.

Left: The author puts flowers on the grave of Steve Biko.

Below: The author sits at his old desk at the *Daily Dispatch* where he was Editor-in-Chief from 1965 until his arrest and banning in 1977.

With Nelson Mandela before filming an interview for the BBC in late 1990.

Celebrating in Boston with Andrew Young and Ted Kennedy on 19 October 1982, after the South African government decided to extend the author's banning period by a further five years. Friends took this to mean that the author's years in exile were proving a successful nuisance to Pretoria.

n the Oval Office in 1978 with President Carter and Vice-President Mondale, who oth supported the campaign to intensify pressures against the apartheid government.

t a White House dinner in March 2000 with President Clinton, who has strongly upported development in South Africa since the overthrow of apartheid.

Above: Long lines
of first-time voters
in South Africa's
first-ever democratic
election in 1994.

Left: Nelson
Mandela and Thabo
Mbeki at a victory
party after the
election.

Nelson Mandela, in a Springbok rugby jersey and cap, presents the Rugby World Cup to Springbok captain Francois Pienaar in June 1995 after South Africa's victory over New Zealand in the final at Johannesburg's Ellis Park stadium to the cheers of 80,000 spectators there – and forty million supporters nationwide.

Left: The luxurious Blue Train, with its famous cuisine and sumptuous accommodation designed for the pleasure of passengers and the profit of the South African tourist industry.

Left and below: The Phelopepha health train, which travels to remote parts of South Africa to serve the health needs of the rural people, many of whom never had medical, dental or ocular treatment during the days of apartheid.

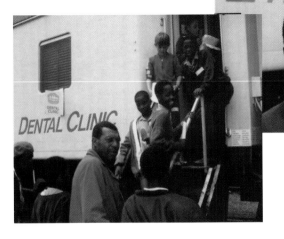

Decorated by the Queen in May 2000, by appointment as a CBE
(Commander of the Order of the British Empire).

With the family at the gate of Buckingham Palace after the ceremony. From the left
are Wendy, Donald, Duncan, Graham Tuckwell (son-in-law), Dillon, Jane, Gavin
and Mary, with Graham and Jane holding their twin daughters Katie and Sophie.

The author shows off his CBE decoration (and rented formal suit) in the courtyard of Buckingham Palace shortly after the investiture. The royal citation was: 'For Service to Human Rights'.

locked, and a sort of date plantation, deserted, with one gate swung open in the heat and dust and no sign of any kind of life – animal, vegetable or mineral. In fact it was so creepy that I backed away and got in the car and drove on quickly, as if I had glimpsed that ghostly ship the *Mary Celeste*.

Just when we were calculating what might be the point of no return with regard to fuel needs, we saw an actual sign pointing towards the actual canyon, with an actual road veering off from our perpetual gravel track. From that point things developed quickly and dramatically, and we were soon at an awe-inspiring observation point looking down into the canyon. That is to say, Wendy looked down into it while I stood back somewhat and looked less directly down into it. Then, satisfied that the footing wouldn't crumble, I sneaked forward and hazarded a directly downward look. It was like looking down from an aircraft, as the Fish River meandered below with several islands in midstream. From there we drove to several other observation points, though the roads left a lot to be desired and there was no paving like that of the Bright Angel point above the Colorado. Then, having had our fill of awe, we set off in search of the road to Luderitz.

This, too, turned out to be a fairly ambitious project, because not only did we go through the whole desolate business of negotiating endless gravel track, but again there was a dearth of explicit sign-posting until we arrived at a definite fork in the road. Given at last a direct clue, we looked for the next likely filling station, encouraged this time by at least an occasional passing vehicle and its consequent trail of dust for many a mile in the still air.

According to our map we were due to encounter the main highway to Luderitz at a town called Seeheim. We were now in what had in the nineteenth century been a German colony, administered incidentally by a governor who had been the father of the late unlamented Hermann Goering, but though Seeheim seemed to mean Seahome, suggesting we were on the right road to the ocean and the port of Luderitz, all we could see was a deserted clump of sad-looking sheds without a trace of a petrol station.

But eventually we found a human being lurking in the shade of one of the derelict sheds, and he ventured the belief that there would be a garage at Bethanie, some fifty kilometres away and therefore just about reachable on our current last few dregs of petrol.

Again, as at Karasburg, we made it with a dry tank to Bethanie, where we filled it up to overflowing and managed to buy, in a poor little grocery shop, the best hamburgers we had yet experienced in this world – yet another tribute to prime Namibian beef. This fortified us for the last mad dash across the Namib Desert to the Atlantic port of Luderitz.

As the late afternoon sun started to mellow and dim, we began to be aware that we were driving along a magnificent highway with apparently no traffic at all beyond a very occasional car every half-hour or so, through scenes of surpassing beauty unlike any we had seen before. All around us were big mountain ranges and deep valleys with a bare beauty in many subtle pastel shades, with increasingly rosy pink backgrounds of what seemed at first to be rich grassland in the fading light but was, we soon realized, sand – mile upon mile upon mile of sand. These were the sandy valleys and dunes of the mighty Namib Desert, one of the oldest deserts in the world. And as the black tarred highway cut straight across between the high ranges of dunes and occasional craggy mountains, it appeared more and more as if it also cut through a lovely rose-pink carpet spread for many miles around, a carpet of Namib sand. The next hours had been exciting as we had driven on through the enchanting landscape, sometimes feeling we could be on another planet. Then, with almost shocking suddenness, we saw the ocean, the cold blue Atlantic which sometimes produced monumental mists when meeting the hot sand of the Namib Desert at noon.

Then came the strange sensation of emerging from an African wilderness into a little town in Bavaria, a little port with Germanic roofs and street names like Kaiserstrasse, with its own excellent lager brew, Hansa Beer, and quaint little alleys with quaint little streetlights. We found our hotel, which overlooked the bay, provided excellent accommodation and served us up some of the finest seafood, including rock lobster, that we could recall, in spite of our coming from the Transkei Wild Coast with its own famous rock lobster. The prices, too, were amazingly modest, and we reflected that once the tourism industry saw what Southern Africa had to offer, at how little money compared to dollars, pounds and euros, there would be a large invasion of international pleasure-seekers.

The following morning we embarked on the longest drive of all our mighty motorings through South and Southern Africa – from Luderitz on the south coast all the way to Windhoek, the Namibian capital. This was a very long haul indeed, and we started early.

One of the nice things about going on a very long motoring expedition with only one companion was the total privacy and opportunity for uninterrupted conversation. There were no ringing telephones, knocks on doors by salesmen or market researchers, or other distractions, and subjects could be explored to the ultimate. There was also the boon of the music cassette, so that we could have our Namib Desert enhanced by Beethoven, the Great Karoo by Bach, and the misty coasts by Chopin nocturnes. This time we had the magic of the Namib Desert drive between Luderitz and Seeheim in early morning sunshine, which gave it a totally different character from the same drive in the late afternoon sun, and we wondered why film-makers didn't make more use of Namibia's sensational scenery for their dramatic productions. Wendy handed over the wheel to me at Keetmanshoop, a pleasant town in southern Namibia where the main highway to Windhoek made a direct turn left to the north, and after filling up we headed for the far distant capital. The road surface was excellent and we made good time through pleasant scenery which though flat was never dull. It reminded me of driving in the American Midwest, in states such as Iowa and Nebraska which also had arrow-straight roads. But Namibia was more pleasant because here they didn't impose such slow speed limits as the Americans did.

We stopped for lunch in Mariental, where we found a sleepy hotel with a sleepy restaurant and no staff visible at all, until a little boy saw us and shouted to his mother in Afrikaans: *'Mammie! Daar's mense!'* ('Mummy! There are people!') They served us a lunch of fine beef, inevitably, but terrible red wine which had vinegarized with a vengeance, reminding us of the worst of what used to be Rhodesian wine. In those days, when the Rhodesians under Ian Smith had been trying to defy international sanctions, they had brought in a French wine expert to help them to upgrade their wine, which we South Africans, with lofty pride in our superior vintages, used to refer to as Château Execrable, or Vin Horrible. They took the French wine expert to the Mazoe Valley, where the best Rhodesian red was made, and gave him a glass to sample. He rolled it around his mouth before swallowing it, then asked where it had been made. 'Right here,' they said. 'There is the entrance of the vineyard, fifty yards away.' He took another sip, looked into the distance, swallowed, and said with a strong French accent: 'It does not travel well.'

Wendy took over the wheel at Mariental, which meant our speed increased considerably, and we screeched through Rehoboth and points north while I tightened my seat-belt. It was early evening as we entered the suburbs of the attractive city of Windhoek.

I had a vivid recollection of the dramatic circumstances of my first visit to Windhoek, thirty years earlier, in 1961. I had been a young parliamentary correspondent, aged twenty-seven, at what we irreverently called 'the Reichstag' in Cape Town, and my editor back in East London had assigned me to go to Windhoek to do some articles about Namibia – as some radicals were already calling South West Africa – and to try to find members of SWAPO, the South West Africa People's Organisation, which we had heard was leading the campaign against Pretoria's attempt to incorporate the territory into South Africa to impose apartheid there as well. I had spent ten days travelling all over the territory in search of SWAPO, ten frustrating days because although I interviewed many locals, black and white, and researched a lot of background material on the territory, enough to send my paper, the *Daily Dispatch*, six feature articles on the issue, I couldn't find any trace of SWAPO. Whenever I mentioned this to whites they would scoff. 'There's no SWAPO,' they would say. 'It's an invention of the foreign press and interfering clerics. Blacks want nothing to do with SWAPO.'

Near the end of my stay, I had returned to my hotel and got into the lift to go to my room. I was alone in the lift with the attendant, a dull-looking Ovambo tribesman, and burst out irritably: 'Where the hell is SWAPO? *Is* there such a thing?' He ignored me, letting me out at my floor without even turning his head. About twenty minutes later I was typing in my room when a hotel cleaner entered, carrying a bucket and mop. I wondered why he was there because the room had been cleaned earlier, when he asked if I wanted to meet SWAPO. I nodded, stupefied, and he told me to wait a half-hour exactly then to go to the lift and accompany the attendant to 'SWAPO people'.

I did so and the same lift attendant, still without looking at me or speaking, took the lift right down to the basement of the hotel. He beckoned me to follow and led me to the living quarters of the black staff of the hotel, a big dormitory with multi-tiered bunks. About forty of the black hotel staff were there, among whom I recognized several waiters and a barman, and my 'room cleaner', who was a sort of secretary, sitting with the chairman at a packing case serving as a desk, beside which was a chair for me. The chairman explained that they were all off-duty for ninety minutes, and a number of them spoke eloquently of the injustices in the country, begging me to 'write about these things to the world'.

I asked if I could meet local leaders of SWAPO, and the chairman told me to be at a certain address in the Kaiserstrasse at 3 p.m. the following day, and to get immediately into a big black car which would stop next to me.

At exactly the appointed time the following day I was at the meeting place. The car drew up and a tall black man in an elegant suit got out, holding the door open for me.

I got into the back seat, next to another tall black man, and the first one got in after me, so that I was sitting between these two silent men. 'Where are we going?' I asked nervously, and the man on my left held his hand up for silence. About twenty miles out of Windhoek we came upon a strange scene on a dry riverbed: three dining-room chairs, on one of which sat a very old black man dressed in formal clothes of half a century earlier, with a watch-chain across his waistcoat. He was introduced as Chief Hosea Kotako, King of the Hereroes, who was then ninety-two years old. One of my 'minders' led me to another of the chairs, and he took the other, while about thirty Herero councillors sat on both banks of the dry riverbed. Chief Kotako spoke at length about the injustices the whites had inflicted on his people, first the Germans, then the South Africans, and he asked me to write about their grievances. I asked lots of questions, was assured that SWAPO had large-scale support, and said I would do what I could at least to put their side of a case that had hardly been heard by people in South Africa or abroad, except for the courageous campaigns of the Rev. Michael Scott.

I was driven back to the hotel, and that night as I walked in to dinner the string orchestra was playing a selection from the *Merry Widow* by Lehár and the *Gypsy Princess* by Emmerich Kalmann. The fellow diners at my table asked if I had 'found SWAPO yet'. They were greatly amused when I shook my head, and one of them said: 'We told you, man, there's no SWAPO.' I then noticed that the waiter serving us, and listening to the conversation, was one of the men who had been at the meeting in the basement, and we acted as if we had never set eyes on each other.

I think I realized that evening, for the first time in my life, that we whites didn't really know our own country, that black resistance to apartheid was far greater and more organized than most whites realized, whether in Namibia or South Africa itself, and that white ignorance of these facts would one day bring apartheid to its knees.

Now here I was, back in Windhoek with apartheid dead and buried, relishing the realities of free and independent Namibia as a close friend and partner of free and independent South Africa.

It wasn't only the completion of our longest-ever spell of driving that made that evening's dinner so memorable, it was the standard of cuisine provided by the restaurant, which would not have failed any capital city in the world.

Awaiting us at the hotel was word from our friend, Randolph Vigne, that we were invited to breakfast the next morning with the Namibian President, Sam Nujoma. Randolph had kindly arranged this from London, where his house had for more than twenty years served as a sort of SWAPO embassy during the long war against apartheid. Born in South Africa, Randolph had been a leading member of the Liberal Party in Cape Town and had also joined an organization committed to sabotaging symbols of apartheid. But an informer had ratted to the Security Police and, when they raided the homes of Randolph and his friends, most had been caught and were given long terms of imprisonment under harsh conditions. Randolph had managed to escape, stowing away aboard a Danish ship in Cape Town harbour and only emerging to inform the captain once the ship was beyond South African territorial waters.

In exile in London he had worked with organizations from the African National Congress and the Pan-Africanist Congress, but had eventually settled on SWAPO as the group most likely to succeed first. When I asked him once why he had made this judgement he had replied, only half jokingly, that the ANC and PAC had often been irritatingly unpunctual, whereas SWAPO had not. 'SWAPO wear watches,' he had said. When Wendy and I breakfasted with Sam Nujoma at his official residence the next morning in Windhoek I told him this story, which amused him greatly. 'I can just hear Randolph saying that,' he said.

The President was upbeat about Namibia's first years as a democracy, but didn't play down the problems ahead, one of which was the grudgingly low aid from the United States, despite the huge profits American mines had taken out of Namibia for more than a quarter of a century. It was a sad fact that the United States gave more aid to one country, Israel, than to Africa's fifty-two countries as a whole. We spent the day sightseeing in the attractive capital, which was built on a series of hills, and were kindly shown around by Randolph's son, who lived there.

The following morning we set off early for the north, making good time via Okahandja, Otjikango and Tsumeb, reaching our exotic destination at Etosha in the late afternoon. We had quarters in the famous old former fort of Namutoni, built by the German colonial troops and now adapted as comfortable tourist apartments from which to sally forth and watch game in the Etosha reserve. Before dinner that night we drove around Etosha until we found a group of elephants at a waterhole for Wendy to stare at for what seemed to me an inordinate length of time, from far too close for comfort in my opinion, though I kept fairly quiet about this.

There were other varieties of wildlife to be watched on the following day as we drove through the great salt pan of Etosha, emerging at the southern exit to head for Swakopmund on the coast. Leaving the Etosha national park at Okaukuejo, we drove via Outjo and Otjiwarongo before being seduced off the main road by signs indicating dinosaur tracks. Up to now we had been pretty good about not falling for diversionary sensations, such as the 80-million-year-old meteorite near Grootfontein, or the deep lake further on from there with its mouth-breeding fish, both of which phenomena would have needed a considerable detour off the main route for little reward, but the promise of dinosaur tracks seemed irresistible.

As for the Fish River Canyon, here, too, we had a long search indeed for the dinosaur tracks, with the route becoming less and less prepossessing and ultimately passing through a remote farm, where we would have had to leave the car and climb into the hot and rocky hills for who knows how long, past how many more less-than-explicit signs, so we gave up and headed back to the main highway having lost no more than three or four hours. They would probably have been only the faintest of jurassic traces, anyway.

But the charming city of Swakopmund made up for all that. With Walvis Bay to its south, this was the second city of Namibia and the main port settlement of the German colonists. Germanic roofs, street names and areas abounded, and our hotel turned out to be one of the best we had stayed in anywhere. Formerly the old Victorian railway station building, it had been adapted through some imaginative and tasteful architecture featuring grey-and-white marble and grey-and-white carpeting into a really good hotel with luxurious apartments and fine service. We stayed two days, using it as a base to explore from, starting with a drive to Walvis Bay. The highway, which runs along the seashore, also went by some resort homes which struck us as eccentrically peculiar to the region, because they were set in enclosed yards of pure sand. The houses themselves were substantial and attractive, and their surrounding fences were wood or brick-built and sturdy, but the yards, instead of the usual lawns or gardens that would have featured in an area with a better water supply, were nothing but fine-grained white sea sand. It looked very strange indeed.

In Walvis Bay we saw the building of the *Namib Times* newspaper, and I suddenly felt I was stepping into a time capsule to go back instantly some thirty years or so back to 1961, when I had come to Walvis Bay as part of my search for SWAPO.

On that trip I had come from Windhoek by light plane, a four-seater, whose radio had informed us of a ship lost up on the Skeleton Coast, and I had asked the pilot what he would charge to fly me up the Skeleton Coast for an hour to look for the missing ship. His fee had been ten pounds, it being still a year before South Africa's change to rands and cents, so off we had set on our search.

The Skeleton Coast was one of the most forbidding coastlines in the world, not only because the treacherous currents and misty conditions had caused many shipwrecks, but also because the survivors couldn't hope to find water on that bare shore. It was Namib Desert all the way up to the northern border of Namibia, the Kunene River, and if survivors weren't rescued quickly by airlift they were usually doomed.

We had flown low over the beach to the north and it had looked nothing like our friendly beaches back in the Eastern Cape. The sand was dark, the mist kept swirling up as the cold Atlantic met the hot desert, and the rocks were black, sharp-edged and menacing. In all that flight I had seen only one manifestation of startling beauty. Suddenly, from out of nowhere, there had been a flock of flamingos, and as they made their turn beside the aircraft I saw this flash of red from their bright underfeathers before they straightened out again and flew in a new formation back in their darker mode.

My pilot had been growing nervous about our search and was muttering about turning back when, through a sudden parting of the mist, we saw our missing ship, flew low over it to identify the name, were hysterically cheered by the crew and waggled our wings to let them know we would radio their exact position to the ocean rescue vessel still searching for them. On landing at Walvis Bay I had seen the office of the tiny newspaper, the *Namib Times*, which fortunately had at least one telex machine as well as one reporter, one editor, one telex operator, one advertising salesman – all the same man, a genial young journalist named Paul Vincent. Paul had sent my telex through to the *Daily Dispatch*, which had become a front-page scoop as I had described how the *Dispatch* had 'chartered a plane to find a lost trawler off the Skeleton Coast'. It had been heady stuff, which had earned me a salary increase.

And now, three decades later, I asked to see the editor of the *Namib Times*. Paul Vincent came walking out, with hair as grey as mine but still recognizable as my co-opted telex operator of long ago. He hadn't recognised me, of course, though a light began to dawn in his eyes when I said: 'I've found a lost ship off the Skeleton Coast and want to telex my paper, the *Daily Dispatch*.' He burst out laughing as he remembered, saying: 'Telex! I had forgotten about telex!' Technology changes had overtaken us all.

Recalling the incident, which had occurred a year before we were married, Wendy and I resolved to try a similar flight up the Skeleton Coast. Such flights were advertised all over Swakopmund, so it was easy to arrange, and we took off with a young American couple as the other passengers. Our pilot flew us directly to the Brandberg mountains, turning for a hectic and bumpy ride along the tops of many mountains until we reached the ocean, then he flew us, very low indeed, back to Swakopmund along the Skeleton Coast. When I say he flew us very low I mean we were only just above the waves on the beach, and when I asked him what altitude he was flying at he indicated the gauge with a laugh: 'Ten feet! But don't worry, I do it often.'

Which was all very well, but what if he had had a heart attack? Oh, well, I thought, what if he had had a heart attack over those turbulent mountains we had been skimming a short while before? That was the snag with a tiny plane. You depended on the health and consciousness of only one other person. I remembered once on a lecture tour having flown from Toronto to Dayton, Ohio, in such a plane. You always knew if the flight number on your next ticket ran to many figures that you would be on a rinky dink little four-seater. What concerned me, however, was that the uniformed airline official who checked me in, a very slim young woman who looked about eighteen, was also the one who carried my suitcase out to the tiny little plane, was also the one who handed me into the passenger seat, and was also the one who then climbed into the pilot's seat and taxied to take off. Her narrow little shoulders were just ahead of me as we climbed up into a somewhat turbulent sky, which worried me. I didn't like the notion of being in the same compartment as the pilot, and I didn't even like to see the pilot during a flight. Then to my horror we hit the worst storm I had ever experienced in a light plane. We were tossed and jerked all over the sky, as I stared fascinated at the slight figure that now controlled my destiny. Not a word was spoken between the two of us as we shared that violent cockpit, and the violence had gone on for more than twenty minutes before we finally emerged into calming sunshine and somewhat steadier air. After our landing at Dayton she had climbed out from the cockpit, put the steps down for me, removed my suitcase from the plane and handed it to me back in the airport terminal. It had been an absolutely terrifying experience, far worse than wave-skimming along the Skeleton Coast back to Swakopmund, and I had needed an immediate double whisky to recover.

One thing that struck me as completely different from that flight of more than three decades before was the absence of those menacing, sharp black rocks I recalled so clearly. Sand movement had apparently covered these up, though the pilot said that from time to time strong tides did uncover the rocks. It was a reminder of how powerful those coastal currents were, and how fierce the gales that blew periodically along the Skeleton Coast.

We headed back to Windhoek for a couple of days before returning to our Johannesburg base, deciding to drive along the recently opened TransKalahari Highway. Again, in this process, we had naive expectations about the facilities *en route*. The highway itself was magnificent, newly surfaced and well made. We reached it via Gobabis and the Namibian border, crossing over into Botswana as we began the long drive along the new highway. We had thought that given the prominence of this road and the volume of traffic it carried there would be plenty of refuelling points along it, but no. In fact there weren't any filling stations at all on the highway, and the only two in more than 1,000 kilometres were both off it, one by several miles, and both were only grudgingly signposted. Nevertheless the surface was so good that we were able to make good progress when I was driving, and sensational and possibly record-breaking progress when Wendy was at the wheel, so that we covered three-quarters of the way to our overnight destination, Gaborone, before dusk fell. This was just as well, because once the light went our speed dropped to downright slow, on account of the animals on the road. During the day you could see them well ahead, but at night you simply couldn't work up any speed for fear of running into a herd of cattle, horses, buck or other beasts. The other surprise for us was the nature of the Kalahari Desert, which wasn't at all like the Namib Desert. Whereas the Namib was sand and nothing but sand, the Kalahari was covered with shrubs, scrub and trees.

After staying overnight in Gaborone, we set off next morning for the South African border, which was geographically close, according to all the maps, but almost impossible to find because of the total lack of reliable signposting. After four false trails we finally managed to beat the system and find the right unidentified road, crossing over in the early afternoon and reaching Johannesburg before nightfall. Having seen signs on the way to Sun City, and having been there shortly before, I offered to show Wendy the place but she said she would rather get back to Jo'burg to see our friends.

To me Sun City, now that apartheid was over and it could no longer be used to lure performers such as Frank Sinatra on the basis that it was a 'homeland' exempt from the apartheid rules, was no longer a sort of 'sanction-buster'.

Nor did I see it as intrinsically bad for being a place of opulence amid an area of great poverty, since people of wealth came there from abroad and presumably this created jobs for local people and opportunities for earnings through provision of services, food and supplies. Nor was it particularly ugly; in fact it had a sort of kitsch fascination, and now that the new hotel complex called the 'Lost City' was opened, I regarded it as one of the three most interesting examples in the world of architectural extravagance in remote settings.

The other two, William Randolph Hearst's Californian castle, San Simeon, and the Neuschwanstein castle of King Ludwig of Bavaria, were both to my mind more impressive architecturally, Ludwig's a sort of mad rhapsody of turrets and colours. Most surprising of the three, for me, had been San Simeon, which I had been to see in the expectation that it would be an offensive monument to excess, but I had come away charmed by the setting, the concept and the taste Hearst and his architect had shown in the construction.

At Lost City you got extravagance, bold concepts, genuine marble and bronze and brass, but not much in the way of taste. Still, I rather liked the chutzpah of the originator, Sol Kerzner, who in this remote part of the bush had created a kind of wild dream with elements of Lake Havasu – where, in the middle of nowhere in the American West, London Bridge has been reassembled stone by stone – and touches of Disneyland. The similarity with Lost City is that at Lost City you also get waves. There, amidst all that aridity, you see people surfing in to a white beach as successions of waves are wafted shorewards by a gigantic wave-making machine. Then you can stroll on to a nearby bridge and experience your very own earthquake as the bridge smokes and rumbles, rattles and roars every so often. In the magnificent, if improbable, dining room I listened to a good Russian pianist playing on a Steinway grand while guests sipped afternoon tea, then he poured out his heart to me during his break, about being required to play 'ryubbish music' for people who simply 'dyid not cyare' about real music really. But he was the only employee at Lost City who seemed to have a legitimate grievance or that I could feel sorry for, the rest being compensated fairly well and appearing reasonably pleased with their lot.

Near the fantastic hotel was the famous golf course where the Sun City million-dollar challenge tournament was played each year, and as if golf were not already a hard enough game, certain parts of the course were stocked with crocodiles, so that if you went off line the penalty was not only a loss of strokes but, if you couldn't bear in addition loss of a golf ball and tried to retrieve it, possible loss of limbs as well.

It all seemed part of the whole Sun City concept – a mixture of fun, excess, kitsch and craziness. Fine, if you liked that sort of thing, and easily avoidable if you didn't. Sun City had also been memorable for one incident during the apartheid era, when John McEnroe had turned down a mammoth fee to play tennis there, and I for one relished the opportunity of recording at least one instance during McEnroe's life when he had actually behaved well.

CHAPTER 14

First Election Day

April 27 1994 was not like any previous day in South African history. This was to be the day of our first ever really democratic election – the first time that all our adult people were to have an equal vote to choose the first ever representative government of the people, by the people, for the people.

I woke up in Johannesburg to a fine sunny morning, and already long lines of voters were waiting at polling stations all over the country to cast their first real ballots. I thought of so much that had led to this day, and of those who had been determined to stop this election happening. In the weeks leading up to it I had travelled all over the country, meeting people in all walks of life and of all races and political groupings, asking what they hoped for from it and what it meant to them.

To blacks throughout South Africa the election meant everything. It was their final vindication as people of worth, and while not as many expected, as journalists said they did, that an ANC victory would mean immediate jobs, houses, cars and money for them all, everyone expected that there would be an immediate improvement in the quality of their lives, if only in terms of their reclaimed sense of dignity. And this had to be true, because the election was by now, in view of everything that had gone before, an achievement in itself.

There was excitement everywhere as all blacks, and a handful of whites, had to go through the bureaucratic procedures to get the right to vote, and because I had been so long in exile I had to do the same thing. I was glad I had to, because it helped me to appreciate all the more what a privilege I was exercising. It involved standing for hours in long queues, to get identity documents and photographs validated, and the voting papers issued, and although the lines were long and the process was tedious, there was a wonderful spirit among all the waiting voters-to-be. I was one of thousands being processed in a vast hall in downtown Johannesburg, with a queue snaking up and down to culminate on a large stage at the end of the hall, where the final procedure occurred, and as each person ascended the steps to the stage there was a raucous cheer of goodwill from the waiting masses. As I got nearer this stage I realized I was the only white person in the entire vast throng, and within moments of this realization I was recognized by some who had seen my picture in the paper and knew of the connection with the Biko story and the film *Cry Freedom*. The news spread that the white guy lining up to get his voting papers was 'uWoods', or '*lo wa se* Cry Freedom', ('the one involved in *Cry Freedom*') and with cheers and ceremony I was escorted to the head of the line and installed there while many surged up to shake hands or pat me on the back or shoulders.

Throughout all my visits to South Africa the relationship of South Africans to the film *Cry Freedom* had been an enlightening experience to me. Every black South African seemed to have seen the movie, some several times, partly because it had been the first major feature film to deal with apartheid and partly because, I discovered as I asked them questions about their opinion of it, they had been fascinated by the implications for the white family involved, namely mine.

When Richard Attenborough had first thought of making the film he had consulted African leaders as well as leaders and members of the African National Congress, the Pan-Africanist Congress, and the Black Consciousness Movement and had been told:

Tell the story through a white perspective. It is white Europeans and white Americans who have to be converted to see the enormity of apartheid, to help end it through sanctions and diplomatic pressures, so enable them to identify with the teller. Blacks don't need to be told how evil apartheid is, and blacks don't have the international economic power the white Americans and Europeans have to end it.

177

That the film had proved influential internationally in helping to mobilize indignation and support for anti-apartheid campaigners in countries all over the world, and in particular in places such as Japan, Switzerland, Indonesia and others which had not previously manifested knowledge of or interest in apartheid, was soon obvious. Hundreds of millions of viewers throughout the world saw the film, dubbed or subtitled in twenty-eight languages. But what had happened in South Africa had been dramatic. The apartheid government, concerned at reports in America and Europe that the movie would be censored in South Africa, had stated publicly that it would be allowed to be screened in public cinemas without cuts. Richard Attenborough, guessing that the apartheid authorities would mount a strong campaign abroad to try to discredit the film, had purposely understated a number of features of the story on the screen in anticipation of this. When the apartheid officials saw the film, which was screened for two showings in twenty-seven centres in South Africa to record audiences, and realized that it was scrupulously true and thoroughly researched, they knew they couldn't discredit it and sent in police units to confiscate the movie reels in the cinemas showing it. This, of course, had provoked international headlines and had done more harm to the apartheid cause, while getting more people abroad interested in seeing it, if only to see what the Pretoria government had been so scared of allowing on their screens. Years later during the hearings of the Truth Commission members of the cabinet of that time testified that one of their number had been in charge of preventing the screening of *Cry Freedom*, in two instances by having cinemas blown up so that others might be intimidated by bomb threats, and the screenings prevented 'for public safety'.

And Attenborough had had another reason for understating the film. He had learned after making a picture called *A Bridge Too Far* that public opinion pollsters had found that audiences had not believed an American general, as played by actor Ryan O'Neal, could be that young, although the real-life general being portrayed had actually been two years younger than Ryan O'Neal. Attenborough thereafter followed the dictum: 'A film must not only be accurately researched and true; it must also be credible. It's no good being accurate if audiences won't believe you.' Consequently in *Cry Freedom* several incidents were played down. One was a scene in which Steve Biko, being interrogated and slapped by a

Security Police officer supported by two others, jumped forward and slapped the officer back. In the real incident there had been seven Security men in that cell, but Attenborough said: 'Few people would believe that a man surrounded by seven officers would hit back like that. We know it happened, the Security Police even acknowledged that it happened. But we will understate it, to be sure our film is believed.'

For a year following the seizure of the reels from South African cinemas, there had been a surge in pirate videocassettes circulating throughout South Africa. After the release of Nelson Mandela and the commencement of negotiations for the establishment of democracy, the film was at last released and allowed to play fully to audiences in cinemas all over South Africa. The result was a record run in the country, beating *Gone with the Wind*, *The Sound of Music* and other long-running films. Yet, strangely, comparatively few whites said they had seen it, and some of those had been so shocked by what they had at first thought was fabrication, and later found out to have been carefully researched truth, that it must have been disturbing to many of them. At least two prominent anti-apartheid South African whites I knew well had at first disputed the facts about the Soweto shootings as shown in the picture, as they had been told at the time that the students had been shot by black policemen, but fortunately we had been in possession not only of eye-witness accounts but actual television and film footage showing that the shooting had been by white policemen, apart from the fact that black police constables had not been allowed at that time to carry firearms, but were routinely armed only with batons and spears.

But what had interested me most had been the feelings of black South Africans about the film, the first major movie to show honestly what had happened in Soweto in 1976 and what had happened to Steve Biko in 1977. Time after time after flying into Johannesburg I had been driven by black taxi drivers to the Rosebank Hotel in north Johannesburg, where I usually stayed when in the city, and time after time the same routine had ensued. After a mile or so the driver would ask if I was 'Woods' or 'Donald', the friend of 'the late Steve Biko' (always the phrase 'the late Steve Biko'), and invariably the driver would announce that this taxi fare was on him. This was moving generosity, because the fee was at least 150 rands, a lot of money to the average taxi driver, and I had always thanked him warmly but said not to worry, usually lying that the BBC or some newspaper was paying. It never worked, because the invariable reply was, with a broad grin: 'No, not paid by the BBC – by *me*!' Another variant was: 'This ride is on nobody but me,' or 'This is *my* ride.'

Another surprise I had when I asked what they had liked about the film was to be told, consistently, that it had been the fact that it had depicted whites 'giving up your home for us' or 'giving up your swimming pool for us' or 'giving up your Mercedes and big house for black people', and one of the cab drivers had said, laughing, that he didn't think he would have done that if he had been in my position. These were the general views voiced by blacks all over South Africa, so I wasn't surprised by the warm reception in the vast voter-registration hall in the week before the election.

Possibly out of self-consciousness at being the centre of attention on that stage, possibly out of exuberance at the experience of lining up with blacks so that we could claim our vote together, I couldn't resist a bit of clowning when it came to my turn to be fingerprinted. As a young law student and journalist I had seen so many blacks being fingerprinted, and afterwards rubbing their thumbs vigorously on the thick hair on the backs of their heads to try to get the ink off, that when I had had my thumb-print taken I had, in full view of the hall and with a big smile, exaggeratedly rubbed my thumb vigorously on the hair on the back of my head, whereupon prolonged shrieks of laughter hailed their recognition of my recognition of the gesture. After I received my voting papers I was loudly applauded out of the hall, waving at everyone as if I were royalty. We were all in such a boisterous mood that even the most feeble joke by any of us would have been received as hilarious, and never had I ever been as conscious of so much good nature among so many gathered together in one room, however large.

Unsurprisingly, not all South Africans shared this general delight at the advent of our first democratic election. A small minority, in fact, had been determined to prevent it, with bombs and firearms if necessary. Two weeks earlier in a small Western Transvaal town in the heartland of the right-wing AWB or Afrikaner Weerstands Beweging (Afrikaner Resistance Movement) I had been in a large bar where the locals, apparently AWB to a man, sat on stools at a horseshoe-shaped bar counter. To encourage them to speak freely, in Afrikaans among themselves if they felt like it, I did not deny that I was what they took me to be, a journalist from overseas.

They had debated briefly among themselves how frank to be, and had decided to be completely open, on the basis that what they knew would soon be known generally – apart from the fact that they had already been at the beer for a couple of hours. The gist of what they had to say was that there would be no election. They bragged that the AWB were ready and fully armed to 'prevent the takeover of the country by blacks' and that the whole world would soon see just what they, the AWB, could do.

This echoed what I had heard from the AWB in other centres, including Pretoria, where the claim had been that the country's leading experts in explosives were the white miners who were loyal AWB supporters and who had already stolen vast amounts of explosives over the past months for just such a day. They merely awaited the word from their leaders, it was repeatedly said. But just who these leaders were was another matter. Officially the acknowledged overall leader of the white conservatives outside the National Party was General Constand Viljoen, and I made an appointment to see him.

General Viljoen's office in Pretoria was impressive, both as to security and as to calibre of staff. In fact his chief of staff seemed to me more efficient and confident in his authority to speak for his leader than any other aide in any of the other parties taking part in the election. While waiting to see General Viljoen, who was always these days in collar, tie and formal suit rather than the military uniform I had last seen him in (when he had restrained P. W. Botha from going totally hysterical in his attack on me in Cape Town nearly twenty years previously), I suddenly thought I was hallucinating, because walking past me and into the general's office seemed to be the general himself, in a loud Hawaiian-type sports shirt, casual trousers and sandals. The general's aide saw my astonishment, winked at me and said: 'They do look alike, hey?' and I realized this was Viljoen's twin brother, Braam, whose politics were known to be far to the left of his twin, though the two were said to be close emotionally. In fact, Braam Viljoen had helped initiate talks between white farmers and the ANC, whereas Constand at that stage had been set against such contacts.

When his twin had left General Viljoen called me in, recalled with some amusement the P. W. Botha incident, and then talked quite openly about his pre-election fears. He doubted if the peace could be preserved, because although he was the nominal leader of the white disaffected right, there were many splinter groups among them, such as those following Eugene Terreblanche, who acknowledged no discipline outside their own structures. He felt that the country was spinning out of control, that the ANC were pushing too far, too fast, and that wholescale nationwide civil war might ensue. He himself was against military action of any sort, but he had accepted a leadership position and had realized he couldn't shirk that responsibility even if widespread conflict occurred. Increasingly all the signs he could see appeared to be leading to such conflict. The only hope, he felt, was if the ANC leadership showed willingness to consider allowing the white conservatives to set up their own territory, their so-called Boerestaat, or state for the Boers.

Only days before the election, General Viljoen had led his team in talks with the ANC leadership, who had surprised the white right with their readiness to address the issue of white fears, and most of the mainstream white conservatives seemed sufficiently satisfied with this attitude to back the general in the decision to take part in the election. But Terreblanche's group didn't see it that way, and prepared for direct action to stop the election.

Terreblanche himself had been much in the news. Bearded and invariably dressed in paramilitary garb with neo-Nazi trappings such as an emblem similar to the swastika, and with an élite corps known as the *ystergarde* (the 'iron guard'), he had tried often to evoke *volk* memories of the Boer War, for example by riding on horseback instead of in vehicles. A charismatic speaker and by some accounts a spellbinding personality (one English-speaking woman reporter sent to interview him was said to have fallen in love with him), he was also a poet of sorts and his speeches were a succession of resounding Afrikaans phrases. To his critics, however, he was a figure of fun, who had fallen off his horse in public and whose ringing prophecies were repeatedly seen not to be followed by fulfilment.

It was therefore partly out of frustration as well as partly out of wishful thinking that he and his followers saw an opportunity shortly before the election to demonstrate white power and resolve. There had been a strike in what had been one of the apartheid era 'homelands', and in the belief that they could put it down and establish a military power base before the authorities were able to act, the white right-wing militarists blundered into the area, near Mafikeng, in a display of force that soon went horribly wrong.

With the leaders of the operation uncoordinated and its objectives confused, rank-and-file paramilitaries began to go their own way, shooting blacks randomly in the streets and calling out racial insults. Then came the scene which publicly, on national television, put an end to one of the enduring myths which had long sustained right-wing white racists. Three of the whites in a convoy had fired on local black soldiers, who had fired back, immobilizing their car and killing one of them, and for more than a quarter of an hour the two survivors, sprawled outside the car, pleaded for their lives as they were guarded by a unit of black police. But as news of what the white convoys had done spread among the police, they became increasingly angry, shouting that the two were dogs, who should be shot like dogs. 'They have killed women, they are animals, not people!' one shouted, and another stepped forward and killed both men, each with a single rifle-shot to the head. And this incident, played and replayed on national television, exploded for ever the notion that whites would always have control of blacks through superior weaponry and resolve. In all its awful simplicity, the public execution of the two whites sent the chilling message to whites who might heed it that blacks could also use weapons now, and could also lose their tempers and act decisively to express their rage.

The shockwave that had swept through the country after this incident had been traumatic for many whites, and it had heralded the sudden downward spiral of white extremist resolve to impose authority by force of arms. Thereafter incidents of white resistance were few, and though frightening in the localities where they were experienced, they were no longer seen as possible election-stoppers. Shortly before the election a massive car-bomb had exploded outside the ANC offices in downtown Johannesburg, killing nine people and injuring ninety-two, and another car-bomb at a taxi-rank in Germiston had killed ten people. Bombs were thrown into several polling stations and then, finally, a large bomb exploded at Johannesburg airport.

And that, basically, was that. The nation absorbed these bombs, then ignored them and prepared to vote in huge numbers, in a mood of rejoicing South Africa had never known before.

183

From early dawn on the great day, in the sparkling sunshine and jubilant atmosphere, the whole country gave itself over to the most extraordinary event in its history. Even the criminals went on holiday and crime statistics, for three memorable days, dipped far below the norm while all the population, it seemed, black and white, so-called coloured, so-called Indian, rich and poor, law-abiding and crooks, took time off to register their vote.

For many, it was an all-day affair. The country had tried hard to prepare its polling stations, officials and facilities but was overwhelmed by the sheer numbers pouring in so soon and in such great numbers to all polling stations. Yet the festive air continued, and at all the polling stations I visited there was total goodwill throughout the day. Blacks and whites celebrated together, and possibly for the first time it could be seen that the election was a liberation of whites from their past guilts as well as a liberation of blacks from generations of oppression, and that the experience, itself, was therefore an occasion of joy for all.

Anecdotes abounded from this extraordinary day, one of the most popular being the one about the rich white madam driving her maid to the polling station, then saying on the way home: 'Doris, you know I'm not ANC, but today for your sake I voted ANC,' only to be told: 'But, madam, I voted DP for you!'

I went to vote at a Rosebank polling station, and finding the queue extending for half a mile down the street, I explained to the polling officials that I was a journalist covering the election, and was sent straight in to vote, with the support of all the nearby voters, who called out to me to vote and then go and describe what was happening. This was a huge contrast to the old South Africa, where officials wouldn't have risked taking the initiative in this way, and where those waiting wouldn't have had the good nature to approve such a move.

Contrary to dire predictions by the pessimistic or malevolent, the election, monitored by a large corps of international observers, was a huge success and pronounced to have been sufficiently free and fair to qualify as a true democratic test of the national will. As generally expected, the overwhelming winner was the African National Congress, and so the inauguration of Nelson Mandela as President was a day of high emotion throughout the country. For me and for many the final turning-point in our national history was emphasized in a dramatic moment with a flyover of air force jets in salute to our new President and our new democracy. The power had really been transferred.

Two days later I had the privilege of a private meeting with our new President in his new office, the very office where, many years before, one of his less illustrious predecessors, B. J. Vorster, had angrily dismissed my pleas for Mandela's release from prison with the bitter words: 'Mandela will be released over my dead body!'

Immaculate in a new tailored suit, Mandela was in typical good humour as he talked of the inauguration and the tasks now ahead, speaking with particular affection of those friends and supporters who had helped bring the great victory about, but also with generosity to opponents and adversaries.

He was conscious that he was now President of all, with an inclusive style totally new in that office and in our country – a consciousness of the South African nation as a people beyond any single faction or section or ethnic group. Struck by this fact in his presence, I became strongly conscious anew of how limited and small of political stature and spirit his predecessors had been because of their racial tunnel-vision. P. W. Botha, Vorster, Verwoerd, Strijdom, Malan, with their narrow, twisted perspectives, were now fortunately consigned to their rightful obscurity in our history, and South Africa could at last grow and develop as a real united nation.

CHAPTER 15

Resurgence in Sport

One of the earliest and most dramatic signs of a new feeling of national unity came through sport, especially the three major sports of cricket, rugby and football. And it was a nice irony that I, as one of many who had campaigned to keep apartheid South African sport out of international competition, should now be able to enjoy supporting our teams in the world arena now that selection was no longer racial.

When I first read that South Africa's cricket team, boycotted internationally for nearly a quarter-century because of apartheid selection, was now welcomed back by the sporting world, I dropped everything else I was doing, negotiated a publishing deal that would cover my costs to report the tournament, and flew off to join the South African cricket team for the World Cup of 1992, to be competed for in Australia and New Zealand. Thanks to Dr Ali Bacher and the United Cricket Board of South Africa, I was booked in with the team at all their hotels and on all their flights throughout the tournament. It proved to be one of the most enjoyable months of my life.

I was profoundly moved on the opening night of that World Cup when our cricketers ran on to the Sydney Cricket Ground in their dark green and gold strip in South Africa's first return to international cricket. I soon realized this was probably the most talented team in the tournament. Right from the start, their first match against Australia, one of the highest-ranked teams, at the magnificent Sydney Cricket Ground, the South Africans impressed the huge crowd of 72,000 with their spectacular feats in bowling, fielding and batting. Allan Donald, bowling at more than ninety miles an hour after a long run-up, took a wicket first ball, which was disallowed by an umpire who later confessed it had all happened too fast for him to take in. But Donald, and other fast bowlers such as Pringle, Snell, McMillan and Kuiper, shot the Australians out for a modest total anyway, then South Africa hit off the runs with ease. The historic victory was followed by a memorable party in the South African dressing room.

We flew from Sydney to Auckland, where South Africa were expected to annihilate New Zealand but suffered a surprising loss before 65,000 fanatical New Zealanders, and the same thing happened two days later in Wellington, where one of the lowliest teams, Sri Lanka, beat South Africa in the last few minutes against the run of play. We took off from Wellington to Christchurch, to my mind one of the most attractive cities in the world, to play the mighty West Indies, and surprisingly beat them handily. We had now lost to the two weakest but won against two of the strongest teams.

From Christchurch we flew to Brisbane to play another of the fancied teams, Pakistan, and during this match I was privileged to see the greatest single fielding feat in more than a century of international cricket history. As one watched one could scarcely believe it, as the whole thing seemed improbably defiant of the basic laws of gravity. It involved, of course, the man now regarded as possibly the greatest cricket fielder of all time, Jonty Rhodes, aged only twenty-two but already acknowledged as fielding's all-time great. The teams had been evenly matched and Pakistan were in fact threatening to overtake the South African batting total when the young batting genius Inzamam-ul-Haq ran for a quick single. Rhodes, fielding the ball, could have thrown it but he backed his own speed of movement and ran, diving five yards through the air and breaking the wicket a millisecond before the shocked Pakistani made his ground. We watchers stood with jaws agape, because the whole thing had happened so quickly, and when we saw the television slow-motion replay we realized we had witnessed one of the most extraordinary feats on any cricket ground in history. At the time Rhodes broke the wicket he was, according to the many pictures taken of the incident, parallel to the ground and about four feet above it as he passed over the bails. It was the decisive factor in the match, bringing South Africa victory, and the South Africans moved to third in the table in the World Cup.

The next match was against another of the strongest teams, India, in Adelaide, South Australia, at the beautiful Adelaide Oval stadium, and again South Africa shot India out for a modest total and knocked off the runs with time to spare, now looking like strong contenders for the world title at the first time of competing. Their next opponents, Zimbabwe, who beat England in the shock result of the tournament, were swept aside in Canberra at the beautiful Manuka Stadium. The South Africans had qualified for the final stages of the tournament.

At last we came to the marvellous Melbourne Cricket Ground, the biggest all-seat cricket stadium in the world, with a capacity of 115,000, second only to Calcutta with its overall total capacity of 122,000 including standing room. In Melbourne South Africa lost narrowly to one of the highest-ranked countries in the tournament, England, which then still had in their ranks their greatest all-round cricketer of all time, Ian Botham. But previous victories were enough to take South Africa through to the semi-finals, with Pakistan, England and New Zealand, the latter being the surprise survivors to this stage; out were such star countries as India, West Indies, Australia, all previous title-holders. We moved excitedly up to Sydney for South Africa's semi-final against England.

In this crucial game South Africa outplayed England generally in bowling, fielding and batting, and in my opinion were cruising along for a probable victory when, only moments before the end, rain intervened and some ludicrous rule imposed because of television scheduling in Australia changed South Africa's target from a gettable few runs to an impossible twenty-one in one ball! Even the capacity crowd booed the decision and applauded the South Africans as they did a lap of honour – but the absurd ruling prevailed, and England went through, eventually to lose a final against Pakistan that many critics thought South Africa would have won.

I was impressed by the sportsmanship of the young South African team. They had made a favourable impression all over Australia and New Zealand with their exciting hitting, aggressive bowling, spectacular fielding and good behaviour.

I had been smitten since childhood with the mystique of

Springbok sport – our international sportsmen were nicknamed after the highly athletic national buck, the springbok – and I had been reluctant at first to include my beloved Springboks in the apartheid equation. For years I had been one of those who had advocated the preservation of sporting ties with the international community, opposing boycotts on the basis that sporting contacts were more likely to convert racist South African whites away from apartheid than exclusionary sanctions.

I had, of course, been wrong. Though the boycotters were frustrated for years and all international sports links preserved, we had seen no significant move towards the inclusion of blacks in Springbok teams. After Steve Biko's death I had realized that longer-term methods were leading nowhere and that I should join the hardline boycotters.

Once this decision was made I sided with those opposing the Springbok cricketers and rugby players, and though this hurt me personally I could see it was the only hope of ending sports apartheid. I also travelled to New Zealand in 1981 at the invitation of New Zealand anti-apartheid groups to make sixty-two speeches throughout both North Island and South Island, and to take part in many radio and television discussions and interviews to support the movement to stop a forthcoming Springbok rugby tour to that country.

I was in New Zealand for two weeks, returning shortly before the tour was due to commence, to learn that a near civil war had broken out there between the demonstrators against apartheid rugby and the conservative backers of the tour.

In the event the tour was stopped, but not before violence had broken out with baton charges by police and vigilante action by right-wingers against the young protesters. One international fixture was cancelled after a New Zealand pilot bombed the Eden Park rugby field with flour bags shortly after the start of the match.

It was therefore with a special emotion that I was able at last, now that sports apartheid was dead, to support our Springbok cricketers and rugby players again, even though the new-era cricket side had only one black player, as did the first post-apartheid Springbok rugby team. In fact, our campaign against apartheid sport had never been against all-white teams as such – only against teams chosen from whites only – and now that South Africans of all races could legally be chosen for Springbok teams the racial composition of such sides was less important than the pool of choice. At last we had what we wanted, 'merit, not colour', and if at first the colour of the team was not fully representative of the ethnographic statistics of the nation, that was understandable. In time, we hoped, natural progression would ensure that future Springbok sides would accurately represent the demographics of the country.

In 1995 we had the heady experience of seeing our first non-racially based Springbok team competing for the first time in the Rugby World Cup. Though only one player of the fifteen was black, it was a genuinely representative team because these were our best fifteen players chosen on grounds of merit.

President Mandela entered into the spirit of the thing and in an inspired symbolic gesture he appeared at the World Cup final wearing a replica of the Springbok jersey with the number 6, the number of the captain, François Pienaar. From that moment, as Pienaar said afterwards, we had not 70,000 supporters at the stadium but 40 million supporters nationwide.

To get to the final South Africa had had to beat some top world teams. Australia, who had won the last World Cup, had been highly rated to retain the trophy, but at Newlands in Cape Town, before a crowd of around 77,000, the South Africans ran all over the Australians to win by a fair margin.

And as they progressed through the opening rounds they had to play some highly motivated teams, yet managed to win their way through convincingly to the semi-final against France in Durban. The match was played in torrential rain, before a crowd of more than 74,000, the South Africans winning a narrow victory through the power of one of the heaviest forward packs in rugby history. In the other semi-final New Zealand had annihilated England through the strength of the young giant Jonah Lomu, who with his size and speed seemed untackleable to the England players, so that when South Africa faced up to New Zealand in the final at Ellis Park, Johannesburg, before 80,000 spectators, Lomu was regarded as one of the major threats to Springbok supremacy. Unusually big, fast and strong, he seemed able to run through most tackles and against England had crossed the line with two or three Englishmen hanging on to his heels.

But the South Africans were ready for him, and I noticed from the first kick-off that whenever Lomu so much as looked at the ball, two or more dark-green jerseyed Springboks were waiting to crash into him, especially Japie Mulder and James Small, the centre and wing respectively. It was a tough final, as one would have expected from two such traditional opponents, who had been competing on the rugby field for ninety-three years, and when the final whistle was due to blow South African fly-half Joel Stransky put through a brilliant drop-kick to win the title.

Stransky was the *'span se Jood'*, it being an old superstition in South Africa that unless the Springbok rugby team had at least one Jew it would fail against the arch-enemy New Zealand, and when he put over the winning kick many an old rugby fan reaffirmed the old belief. The team Jew had pulled them through. A subtle nation we were not. But what the hell, to have beaten New Zealand was to have savoured one of life's richest rugby blessings. And what all this meant, too, was that in the late 1990s South Africa had the world's strongest national rugby team, the world's strongest one-day cricket team, the golf world championship and Africa's best national football team, which won the African Nations Cup. The rainbow nation was glowing in sport.

And sport was proving to be a healing agency in our national life. Old diehard racists who hadn't previously been able even to contemplate the dread possibility of a black man wearing a Springbok jersey were surging to their feet to applaud a black wing in a Springbok jersey crashing over the opposition line, and suddenly they weren't noticing his colour any more. It reminded one of Charles Morgan, the Alabama lawyer, who had said that black sports stars in America had brought white crowds 'to their feet and to their senses'.

But other healing agencies were necessary. For too long in South Africa political crimes had gone unpunished and dissidents had disappeared without explanation, while others had been imprisoned without trial and tortured with impunity. The response was one of South African genius – the Truth Commission.

CHAPTER 16

The Truth Commission

South Africa's Truth and Reconciliation Commission was to prove the bravest experiment yet in a country that had recently become noted for brave experiments. To mark the abolition of apartheid with the world's most tolerant constitution and to set goals in housing, education and health that would tax the wealthiest of countries, let alone one ravaged by injustice and poverty inflicted for so long by specific legislation against four-fifths of the population, was brave enough. But the Truth Commission was to prove the bravest of all these bold initiatives.

There had been attempts elsewhere to heal historic wounds through such hearings, but none had been as ambitious or far-reaching as South Africa's. It was from the start a unique approach for dealing with the results of a unique system of oppression, and the key to it was not punishment for apartheid's unique crime but exposure and examination of that crime through the testimony of its perpetrators as well as its victims.

As to whether the Truth Commission was an unqualified success, if a severe interpretation were placed on its terms it could never have succeeded because its task was impossible within the period of its remit. To arrive at the complete truth about the apartheid years would have required the testimony of millions, not thousands, and there was never a guarantee that the truth would bring reconciliation. Besides, the truth itself was given many facets by various witnesses, recalling the words of Pontius Pilate: 'What is Truth?' Nevertheless, the commission succeeded in its most important task – the shedding of light on the shocking extremes to which the apartheid policy had led over four decades.

Though black South Africans had been the main victims of apartheid, relatively few of them – and even fewer whites – had known of the monstrous excesses against some of the leading black activists. But, as South Africans, black and white, listened day after day to the admissions from former Security Police officers, corroborated by their underlings of the time, no South African could thereafter claim such accounts were fabrications.

These accounts, broadcast on live nationwide television, were of the most brutal and depraved tortures imaginable, culminating in the most callous murders, in some cases followed by dismemberment and burning of the bodies of the victims. And as lies were revealed, lies that the apartheid government had told over decades, even conservative whites were shocked at the extent to which they had been deceived.

Famous cases were dealt with, including the Biko case, and the whole nation could at last see the killers of their heroes squirming and wringing their hands as they testified about matters for which they had never been called to account, and about which they had for many years never thought they would be called to account. Some of the victims' families, including the Bikos, were critical of the process and said the killers should be put on trial, but prosecutions couldn't have succeeded without evidence, nor could convictions have been secured without proof, and to my mind the commission's hearings were the next best thing. To say the killers walked free from the hearings was simply not true. These men would never again know a day of freedom or peace in South Africa, and would be looking around them and behind them for the rest of their lives, because they were now publicly identified for their crime.

So the Truth Commission succeeded not only in educating many South Africans about their country's past but also in educating them about the real nature of their compatriots on both sides of the divide. Many of the families of victims said they were finally at peace after hearing what had really happened to their loved ones, and many said that being able to locate and bury their bodies meant more to them than revenge against their killers. As to whether the process achieved reconciliation, the answer had to be a mixed one, a yes and no. No, in the sense of replacing all resentment and bitterness with forgiveness and love, obviously. But yes, in the sense that there were striking examples of perpetrators and victims reconciling and even embracing. For as many who said the hearings were exacerbating rather than easing tensions in the country over the past, there were as many if not more who said that the ventilation of these evils and the remorse expressed by some of the worst offenders had indeed spread feelings of reconciliation and hope for the future.

With the publication in 1999 of the Truth Commission's report, the courage behind the entire proceedings was fully revealed, because not only the sins of the apartheid regime but also those of its opponents were now open to debate and examination. The two main liberation movements, the African National Congress and the Pan-Africanist Congress, were also accused of human rights abuses in torturing suspected informers, killing dissidents and risking the lives of non-combatants through the planting of bombs and land-mines and even in some instances of killings through mindless rage. And some previously revered leaders of the anti-apartheid struggle, such as Winnie Madikizela-Mandela, were shown to have given way in the last years of that struggle to excesses previously the preserve of their enemies.

Apart from the obvious inference that all human beings were capable in certain circumstances of plumbing the depths as well as scaling the heights of human behaviour, the main result of the report might well have become what its planners had probably hoped it would largely be – a final indictment of apartheid as the ultimate evil behind all these sufferings and a comprehensive lancing of the boil of South Africa's apartheid past to enable the new nation to put that past behind it and build its own hopeful future.

Unfortunately the launch of the report was marred because, in one of its most foolish decisions, the ANC tried through legal action to prevent or delay publication of the portion of the report critical of the ANC's own violations of human rights. A first-year journalism student could have told them of the inevitable consequence of this, as I was saddened to realize at the time, because I was in London on the day of the release of the report, and booked to be interviewed on its contents by seventeen television stations, including the main ones in America, Europe, Britain, Australia, New Zealand and parts of Asia, as well as twelve radio stations. But instead of being interviewed about the major conclusion of the report, the final indictment of the apartheid system for so much wrongdoing against so many, it turned instead into the question of why the ANC had tried to suppress the report, and emphasis was focused on that part of the report to which the ANC objected. It was a public relations disaster for them and it had resulted from the ignorance of those who simply couldn't or wouldn't understand how free media functioned. One occasionally saw actors falling into the same trap, and one could cite the case of an Oscars ceremony some years ago, with billions of people watching on television all over the world, as an actress claiming her Academy Award foolishly took the opportunity to condemn a Los Angeles newspaper for publishing some slur upon her. 'I just wanna deny here that I am an alcoholic or that I am addicted to cocaine . . .' And so to correct one medium, a newspaper with fewer than a million readers in one corner of California, she broadcast to billions all over the world the very defamation she had sought to correct.

This was what the ANC had done in turning what would have been a largely overlooked one per cent of the report that was critical of them into the main news item, so that instead of the emphasis of the world media being on how the report had indicted the apartheid regime it was now on the one per cent indictment of the ANC.

Fortunately the chairman of the commission, Archbishop Desmond Tutu, said exactly the right thing at exactly the right time, as he had done so often in South Africa's political past. In an appropriate put-down of the petty objectors he said South Africa had no intention of allowing new censors to replace the old, and his own stature ensured that the process kept its credibility. In fact throughout its operation the credibility of the Truth Commission had been guaranteed by the calibre of the commissioners and the leadership of Tutu and his deputy, Dr Alex Boraine. The country couldn't have put the process in better hands.

And so as the work of the commission drew to a close, the huge scope of its prodigious labours became apparent in the basic statistics. Beginning its hearings in April 1996, the commission took testimony from more than 21,000 victims of apartheid – a staggering achievement – and processed more than 7,000 applications for amnesty, most of which were rejected. To gain amnesty, perpetrators had to satisfy the commission that their actions had been political, as directed by a political organization, and that full disclosure had been made. It was the latter provision that scuppered most of the applications for amnesty, because former Security Police officers and other perpetrators obviously sought to get by with minimum disclosure of their actions and repeated the perpetuation of their original unconvincing versions of the facts. For example, Steve Biko's killers still stuck to the story that Biko's brain damage had resulted from an accident, when he had bumped his head against the wall during a scuffle with his 'interrogators'. But at least the South African public at last saw what these killers looked like, saw and heard them grilled and cross-examined for days by the skilled lawyer George Bizos, and knew finally exactly who had been responsible for Biko during his final days in Security Police control.

At the conclusion of the commission's work it was also learned that the chairman, Desmond Tutu, had been fighting cancer for much of the hearings, which made his leadership all the more remarkable. Knowing this great man for as long as I had, I had long regarded him as ranked alongside Mandela in stature of the spirit, and his modesty and humour had always been a delight. Once when he was invited as a guest of the MCC to Lord's cricket ground, the holy of holies of international cricket with more than 200 years of tradition, the committee man sent to meet him at the gate said he couldn't spot the Archbishop among the people waiting there – until someone pointed out Tutu in a tracksuit bottom and T-shirt. His MCC hosts were lucky it wasn't one of his favourite T-shirts – the one labelled CALL ME ARCH.

It has long been my belief that when Africa's great men of our time are acknowledged the five greatest will be Wole Soyinka of Nigeria, Ali Mazrui of Kenya, Julius Nyerere of Tanzania, and Nelson Mandela and Desmond Tutu of South Africa.

One of the ironies of the ANC's bungling of the launch of the commission's report was that it could have scored well out of the Truth Commission exercise, because in fact the ANC had generally a fine record of behaviour in its conduct of the armed struggle. Apart from a few lapses from the discipline of avoiding harm to non-combatants, and ill-treatment of some of their own people suspected of being informers, there had overall been careful ANC observation of the Geneva Convention compared with the National Party government, which had indulged in torture, poisoning, gassing, assassination and murder. The ANC had also come out of the armed struggle with a better reputation than the PAC, some of whose later commanders saw military valour in shooting church worshippers at prayer, or golfers in a clubhouse.

One of the saddest aspects of the long fall-out from the apartheid era was the plunge from adulation to disgrace, disrepute or at least dubious repute of some of the brightest and best of the heroes and heroines of the struggle, and their distancing for long periods, and in some cases for good, from their previous associates in many a gallant campaign against apartheid. The most notable of such fallen angels were Winnie Mandela and Allan Boesak.

For two decades while Nelson Mandela was held in prison on Robben Island, Winnie Mandela had won the admiration of all who opposed apartheid. Her undaunted courage, her leadership of the lost and despairing youth of the townships, her defiance of the Security Police and her refusal to be cowed regardless of the extreme actions the state took against her had won her the lasting affection and admiration of many millions.

The Security Police put her into solitary confinement twice, fire-bombed her house, did their best to torment her and taunted her with prospects of seeing her husband, then withdrawing permission for the visit at the last moment. Many wondered how she retained her sanity after all the years of agony and persecution, and some doubted today that she had. One body of opinion, which included some loyal friends of hers, rested on the firm belief that Winnie's mind had snapped finally, and some among her closest associates believed she had two personalities – that two distinct Winnies inhabited her body, one being the sweet-natured 'Mother of the Nation' and the other being a sociopath. One of her friends told me: 'I can tell instantly which Winnie is in her, even if her body is turned away from me. I can tell from the movements and gestures.'

Until the late 1980s Winnie Mandela hadn't put a foot wrong as a popular leader who was frequently called on for international comment and for instant response to some South African crisis. Her remarks and conclusions had been balanced, moderate and telling, yet none the less powerful in their controlled anger – all until the day she spoke angrily of liberating South Africa if necessary by the extremest of means, appearing to give support to the ghastly method of murder known as 'necklacing' – placing a tyre filled with gasolene round the victim's neck and igniting it. Though she later denied this was her intent, the impression had been created that it was, and it hadn't been denied soon enough to be convincing.

Then accusations against her began to increase, and ultimately she was convicted of kidnapping, accused of murder, and held generally responsible for some of the worst excesses of her corps of supporters and protectors known as the Mandela United Football Club, who were feared by many of the township dwellers and appeared to act as if they were a law unto themselves. Her marriage to the President broke down completely, through her own behaviour, and they were duly divorced in a sad end to a remarkable union that had begun as a strong love affair and had endured for two decades of enforced separation through his imprisonment.

Although she was said to have strong grassroots support and still held high office in the African National Congress, she was clearly alienated from the mainstream and the broad leadership of the ANC, still standing accused of misuse of funds and influence from the time she had held office in the cabinet. There was nothing in her manner that was contrite, however, as she held her head high and appeared to plead guilty to no offence, proven or otherwise. But one of the most adverse results of her actions was that the impression was created at home and abroad that past leaders of good repute remained acceptable to their followers no matter what they might or might not be thought to have done, and this was a Third World trait South Africa could happily do without as it sought to show a more sophisticated face to the world.

The Allan Boesak case had had some similar elements. At first when this remarkable man, one of the most charismatic of the younger leaders in the fight against apartheid, had been accused of misuse of funds donated for black anti-poverty projects, leading ANC figures had sought to play down the allegations. When Boesak had flown back to South Africa to stand trial accused of stealing from foreign donors, the Minister of Justice, Dullah Omar, head of law administration in South Africa, had shocked many by heading a welcome for Boesak and embracing him publicly. Remarks had been made about 'struggle accounting', in reference to unorthodox practices in the handling of foreign donor funds during the struggle against apartheid, in order to keep the apartheid authorities in confusion and to protect secret projects.

But it was soon pointed out that the theft Boesak was accused of had occurred after the downfall of apartheid, in regard to projects no longer secret and therefore no longer subject to the needs of 'struggle accounting', and the matter began to be increasingly embarrassing for the ANC.

An internal inquiry by the ANC had cleared Boesak even before the trial began, until it became obvious that the inquiry had not been sufficiently thorough and had not had access to all the evidence. Unfortunately both President Mandela and Deputy President Thabo Mbeki had early given the impression of being critical of the state prosecution, Mandela by questioning whether it should proceed and Mbeki by appearing to accept the internal report of the ANC too readily. But the professional prosecutors stood by their allegations and the trial duly commenced, and as it revealed how aid money had funded a lavish lifestyle while millions of blacks lived in squatter camps, support from the ANC leadership diminished and ultimately there were no prominent ANC leaders present in court to hear Boesak convicted of theft and fraud.

Yet elements of the case remained unresolved as he appealed the verdict, and long postponements protracted it beyond the year 1999. This litigation and the delaying tactics of his defence strategy meant that the nation had no detailed rebuttal from this popular leader of the misdeeds attributed to him, although he was clearly paying a heavy price in the court of popular opinion and had had his appointment revoked as South African Ambassador to the United Nations in Geneva. Eventually he was sentenced, in May 2000, to three years' imprisonment.

Another fallen angel in the South African firmament was 'the people's poet', Mzwakhe Mbuli, who had been found guilty in a Pretoria court of armed robbery. Mbuli, who until recently had been one of the most popular poets and senior figures in the ANC cultural department, had reacted to his arrest and conviction by claiming that he was innocent, and was being framed as part of a conspiracy to cover up drug trafficking by senior members of the ANC government.

Another leading light of the struggle who appeared for a long time to have been deserted or disavowed by his government was Robert McBride, who had been held on death row at one stage by the apartheid regime, awaiting execution for terrorism. Released and elevated to high office in the ANC government, he had been suddenly arrested in Mozambique and held on charges of arms dealings, and though his initial response had been that he had been investigating illegal arms trafficking on behalf of the government he was neither defended, spoken for nor represented legally by the government, and no government spokesperson mounted even a cautious defence on his behalf as the months passed with him in custody.

It seemed at the time that either those in authority knew something the rest of us didn't, and were distancing themselves from their previous heroes McBride, Mbuli and Boesak, or that if any or all were innocent this was callous abandonment by their former comrades.

At the same time it seemed to me, as I worked and lived in Johannesburg in 1997 and 1998, that the nation had not adequately recognized some of its major heroes, such as Steve Biko. There was no monument to his memory, and his grave in King William's Town was in appalling condition, overgrown with weeds in a neglected little cemetery.

It seemed to me also that inordinate recognition had been given to some who had featured in helping the struggle against apartheid, but that others who had done far more had not been publicly acknowledged. I had been to see President Mandela about this, suggesting that a number of prominent non-South Africans who had done the most to help should be appropriately recognized. I had mentioned particular activists such as Harry Belafonte, who had been the first prominent entertainer in the world to take up the anti-apartheid cause, long before it had become more widely supported, and had been a steadfast campaigner for many years. Others I mentioned to Mandela were John and Diana Collins, a British couple who had probably done more to keep our leaders and their families alive, maintained, legally represented and supported, than anyone else. Canon Collins had founded the International Defence and Aid Fund, which with donations from all over the world but mostly from Sweden, Norway, Denmark, Finland and Holland, had raised over £100 million, which had provided lawyers for South African political trialists and support for their families for more than three decades. I suggested that the President should invite these people, or in the case of Canon Collins his surviving spouse Diana, and in the case of Sweden's Olof Palme his widow, to confer honorary South African citizenship on them. Others I suggested for such recognition included Anthony

Sampson, David Astor, Anthony Lewis, Andrew Young, Corretta King, Madame Mitterrand, and several more who had been known to have 'gone the extra distance' over many years for the anti-apartheid cause.

President Mandela had been delighted with my list, feeling that such recognition would be appropriate from us as South Africans to these distinguished non-South Africans who had done so much to help. But within three weeks he said his advisers had been opposed to the plan, because 'others left out would be affronted'. Well, I had long believed that most good ideas should never be referred to committees, which were usually the kiss of death – here was proof!

Unfortunately the nation's thanks to others, who hadn't done nearly as much as the above, had in my opinion been inordinate. True, Colonel Gaddafi had helped the ANC and PAC in the struggle against apartheid, but he wasn't, as described, a 'comrade in the cause of freedom' because he still denied freedom to his own people.

As for Fidel Castro, while I agreed with acknowledging his aid in the Angola war and admired reputed Cuban achievements in literacy and child health programmes, I had met too many refugees from Cuba, including some, like the poet Armando Valladares, who still bore the scars from Castro's prisons. And I couldn't agree with too cosy a friendship with a dictator who feared the vote of his own people, wouldn't risk free media, and ran a country from which people almost daily risked their lives to escape. To call such a tyrant an ally in the cause of freedom was, to put it as gently as possible to our beloved President, unduly generous.

But, leaving aside the distinguished non-South Africans, it seemed to me quite wrong that the huge contribution of Steve Biko to the new nation had not yet been nationally and publicly acknowledged. Then good fortune took a hand.

CHAPTER 17

The Biko Statue

In 1997 and 1998 I ran the Institute for the Advancement of Journalism in Johannesburg, at the request of its founder, Allister Sparks, and board of trustees, and though I had at first been reluctant to do this, I was delighted finally that I had agreed, because it turned out to be one of the most fulfilling and enjoyable periods of my life, providing eighteen months of stimulation and inspiration drawn from this remarkable small organization doing such giant work.

At first I had been reluctant because it meant being away from my family for a year and a half, apart from regular visits, but Allister was eloquent that my help was necessary. President Mandela had asked him to take a leading role in cleaning up the South African Broadcasting Corporation and turning it into a real news medium, and at the same time his natural successor as head of the institute, Hugh Lewin, was away on Truth Commission duty. They wanted me to run things from Allister's departure until Hugh was finished with the Commission and could return to take over.

On arrival I was impressed with Allister's creation. South African journalism, and African journalism generally, badly needed upgrading, and the institute was able to provide intensive courses in radio, television and newsprint for up to 700 journalists a year from all parts of Africa. In only two decades Africa's number of democracies had gone from two to twenty-three – in varying stages of development – and it seemed to us at the institute that the best boost for African democracy, for its preservation and development, was the training of vigorously independent-minded journalists from all over the continent, to keep shining the flashlight of scrutiny, on the lookout for any signs of corruption, autocracy or authoritarianism by any government or leader in Africa. We had President Mandela's support, expressed in writing, as a mandate for us. After I took over, I became increasingly impressed at how the institute was going about its work. The lecturers were good, the courses well supported and the staff highly motivated.

From the moment I arrived until the day I handed over to Hugh Lewin, who in my opinion was the author of the best prison book to emerge from the struggle against apartheid owing to the modesty and skill of his writing about his years in political prison in Pretoria, I thoroughly enjoyed my time at the institute. It was located in a fine old randlord mansion set in several acres of lawn and garden on a ridge in Parktown. From my office window I could see my apartment block in Parkview, in the neighbouring suburb, where I had a flat overlooking the sports fields of Parkview School.

In early 1997 I was drinking wine and playing against my chess computer when there was a knock on my door. I opened it to find a woman who announced herself as follows: 'Good evening. I am Naomi Jacobsen.' Naomi Jacobsen was one of our nation's most distinguished sculptors, and when I had seated her, with a drink in hand, she told me she lived on the floor above and said: 'If you can raise the costs of it, I would like to do a large bronze statue of Steve Biko.' It was the start of a wonderful working relationship and resulted in a fine statue that was to help reset the new era of our nation's history.

Naomi had a studio on the top floor of our apartment block, and she began that week a huge nine-foot-high statue of Steve Biko, working from photographs I supplied. In the process I learned a lot about how to make a bronze statue. The first stage was to construct a sort of frame on which to pack plaster of Paris in the exact form of the final statue. The next stage was to cover this with wax to create a mould, which was transported to Pretoria, where the country's best bronze foundries were, run, inevitably it seemed, by Italians. There in the foundry the wax mould was filled with bronze, and in time the wax removed and the bronze left. The entire process took several months, and while Naomi was busy with it I was telephoning prospective donors to the statue. The first ones I telephoned were Richard Attenborough, who had produced and directed *Cry*

Freedom, Denzel Washington, who had played Biko in it, Kevin Kline, who had portrayed me, and Michael Williams Jones, who had been head of United International Pictures when the film was distributed internationally. Other donors included David Astor, Richard Branson, Frederick Mulder, Charles and Camille Morgan, my friends from Alabama, John Steele Chalsty, a South African who now headed one of America's largest corporations, Jerry Dunfey of Boston, the author Ken Follett, singer Peter Gabriel, and my former publishers, John and Janet Marqusee of New York.

Within twenty-four hours I had raised the total cost of the statue including the moulding, casting, transportation 500 miles to its erection site in the Eastern Cape, and ancillary costs. While Naomi worked on the statue I began work on finding a site for it. There were complicated political considerations to deal with.

For a start it was vital that Nelson Mandela should unveil the statue – but it was also a fact that some of his followers and advisers would oppose this, because Steve Biko had not been a member of the ANC and because Naomi Jacobsen was white and because I, organizing everything to do with the statue, was also white. It helped slightly that I was keeping totally in the background and that Naomi had done some of the first sculptures of black leaders in our history, but there were still mutters.

Two remarkable women helped to solve the first problem. Mamphela Ramphele and Thenjiwe Mtintso, former associates of Steve Biko who had major influence with Mandela, persuaded him to unveil the statue. The second problem was resolved by sheer speed. Naomi and I just went ahead with turning the statue into a *fait accompli*.

The most important question to be addressed was the exact siting of the statue, and my first idea was to try to get the East London City Council to agree on the site. My initial hope was to get the statue sited next to the Buffalo Bridge, the city's biggest and most imposing bridge, across which Biko had often been driven in custody by the Security Police transporting him between Fort Glamorgan Prison and the Security Police headquarters. I had hoped that if the councillors agreed to the bridge site, this might move them to rename the bridge itself the Biko Bridge. Its official name was still the Vorster Bridge, after Prime Minister B. J. Vorster of apartheid days, and this seemed to me highly inappropriate in the context of the new South Africa. I flew from Johannesburg to

East London and met with the mayor, deputy mayor and key heads of department of the city in what was now, change of all changes, an ANC-governed city. They were strongly supportive and I was thrilled when they said they would like to locate the statue right in front of the city hall – the most prominent site in the city. I was moved, and said this was the perfect place, and that the only reason I had asked for the bridge site was because I hoped this might cause them to rename the bridge. At this the mayor said: 'We can do that too! We'll call it the Biko Bridge and have the renaming done on the day the statue is unveiled.' From that moment the East London City Council were the epitome of energy, enthusiasm and efficiency on the question of the Biko statue. I was not aware of the complex infighting going on in ANC circles in the Eastern Cape, where some factions wanted the statue erected in King William's Town, while others didn't want it erected at all and yet others were prepared to use the issue to pursue their own agendas even if this meant post-poning or even cancelling the statue project. The key to all this was Mandela's consent to unveil the statue. I saw him at his official resi-dence in Pretoria, where he assured me he would do it, and two weeks later he gave me an unusual reassurance of his commitment to the project.

I was attending a ceremony at Witwatersrand University at which the biographer and close friend of Robert Sobukwe, Benjamin Pogrund, was presenting the Sobukwe papers to the university research library, when, in a typically generous gesture and salute to the memory of his former political rival, President Mandela suddenly appeared.

For the ANC leader to support the tribute to the deceased PAC leader was further testimony of Mandela's generosity of spirit, which also accounted for his readiness to pay tribute to Steve Biko's leadership of the Black Consciousness Movement which many in the ANC had viewed as a threat to it. As hundreds of admirers crowded around Mandela on his departure I had stood back, having seen him in private only weeks before to discuss the unveil-ing of the Biko statue on the twentieth anniversary of Biko's death, 12 September 1997, but as he went past, waving to everyone, he saw me at the back and called out: 'I won't forget, Don – see you on September the 12th.'

With him so publicly committed to the unveiling, some of the earlier opponents of the project now began seriously trying to stir up opposition to the statue. At one stage one of the leaders of the King William's Town faction had telephoned me to ask why the statue wasn't going to King William's Town, and my reply was: 'Because for twenty years you have grossly neglected the grave of Biko in that pathetic weed-grown little cemetery. If you couldn't even look after his grave why would you look after his statue?'

All that, however, was soon to change, because I had protracted negotiations with the historical monuments commission and with the magical name of Mandela behind everything, 12 September would be a memorable date indeed, on which not only would the statue be unveiled and the bridge renamed, but the Biko cemetery, weeded and walled, repaved and redesigned, would be declared a national monument and therefore subject for ever to state upkeep, as would be the Biko house in King William's Town, which we his friends had raised the money to buy for the family in perpetuity. In view of all this, Naomi Jacobsen donated a separate bust cast from the statue which was erected in King William's Town.

Richard Branson, one of the main donors to the statue fund, organized his airline, Virgin, to fly Biko friends from London, including Father Aelred Stubbs, the Biko family friend and priest of the Community of the Resurrection, who though elderly and frail gamely made the long journey. South African Airways also helped fly members of the Biko family and musicians who would be performing at the ceremonies, and my secretary, Marion Marais, worked miracles of communication in inviting prominent figures from all over the country to attend.

Some friends even came from as far afield as America, including Jerry Dunfey of Boston, whose family had steadfastly supported South African dissidents down the years. The East London City Council were magnificent, providing limo and escort services for the many VIPs and throwing a large evening reception on the night before and a grand banquet lunch immediately after the main ceremonies on the day itself.

Thanks to all the planning by the councillors, by Naomi, the bronze foundry people who had brought the statue from Pretoria to East London and the local ANC committee who stayed steadfastly behind the project in spite of snipings from other factions of the party in the Eastern Cape, all was ready when the great day arrived and everything went perfectly. My own private fear, that when Mandela pulled the cord the shroud around the statue would simply stay in place and have to be torn down, proved groundless, and more than 20,000 people and a large television audience shared the great moment when the shroud fluttered down and the magnificent statue stood revealed.

I heaved a private sigh of relief because so much could have gone wrong, and so many had tried to make it go wrong, that the day could well have been ruined instead of being, as planned, an important national event. The first assaults on the schedule had come from some negative elements in the Eastern Cape government. I had voiced the concern that timings should be adhered to punctually, because the weather was very hot, and excited crowds kept waiting too long before seeing their beloved President could get restless and occasionally downright dangerous, to themselves and others. The original arrangement was that the Mandela plane would land early on the day at East London airport, that the East London ceremonies including the unveiling of the statue, the renaming of the bridge and the municipal banquet would all occur first, as the waiting crowds would probably total close to 30,000 in a fairly concentrated area, and that the Mandela party would then move to King William's Town for the ceremonies at the Biko house, the cemetery and the graves of Griffiths and Victoria Mxenge, other famous local martyrs of the political struggle.

Somebody managed to turn the whole schedule around, placing the King William's Town events first, so that by the time the President reached East London and the statue site it was boiling hot, the huge crowd was highly volatile and already surging dangerously against the police barriers and seating area for the ceremony. Furthermore, a small group of anti-statue demonstrators, hugely outnumbered but highly organized, had started a regular chanting which was beginning to annoy the vast majority to what I thought was a dangerous extent.

Fortunately the situation was saved by some timely generosity. Richard Branson had flown Peter Gabriel 6,000 miles to the ceremony, and Peter sang his world-famous song 'Biko' to the crowd at the statue site while they waited for the President. It was a moving moment for me, as I had heard the song all over the world, in New Zealand, Australia, Germany, America, Brazil and several African countries, articulating the anger and mourning of the growing international army of anti-apartheid campaigners. To hear it now in Steve Biko's own area, on the day he was finally acknowledged before the nation and the world, was a highly emotional experience. Another helpful development was that the East London City Council had provided a number of choirs and dancers to perform for the occasion, and this helped the time to pass even as the day grew hotter and hotter. The final saving grace came from the remarkable President himself. The sight of him wiped away all the frustration from the huge crowd, and when the few demonstrators tried to set up a chant he was able to silence them with a few humorous words of reproof, ending by telling them as a grandfather might have told naughty children: 'Don't try to spoil this important occasion.' They responded warmly, and it must have galled their organizers that the demonstrators joined in the general applause for Mandela, the occasion, the statue and the entire day's acknowledgement of Steve Biko as the Eastern Cape man whose name had reverberated around the world in the struggle for the freedom of all South Africans.

There remained one final touch of Mandela magic to make the day even more special. After an eloquent speech in which he paid tribute to Biko's legacy to the nation, the President challenged all South Africans to unite in the spirit in which Steve Biko had tried to unite all factions, and directly addressing the three main party leaders on the stand behind him, he called each of them up to the microphone to state whether or not they would work together with the ANC for South Africa's future. Amid laughter at the humorous style of this challenge the leaders of the Pan-Africanist Congress, the Azanian People's Organization and the Inkatha Freedom Party took the microphone in turn to pledge to work with the President and the ANC in matters of common interest for the country's future. The Inkatha leader, Chief Mangosuthu Buthelezi, raised an extra laugh by reminding the President that he was already a member of the President's cabinet. After the unveiling of the statue, the national anthem was movingly sung by the large crowd, the bridge was renamed and the city completed its massive salute to one of the region's most extraordinary men, Steve Biko, in a tribute led by another of the region's most extraordinary men, Nelson Mandela. In the end, after months of planning and effort by many, Steve Biko had been granted his rightful place of public honour in the annals of the new nation he had given his life to help bring about.

CHAPTER 18

The Personal Side

The completion of the Biko statue, the renaming of the Biko Bridge, the cleaning up and paving of the Biko grave and cemetery and the declaration of all of these and the Biko house as national monuments signalled the end, as far as I was concerned, of what for twenty years had been an unfinished chapter in our national life.

Although Wendy and I and our five children were based in London, the children either married to or variously involved with British partners and our grandchildren little Londoners, and although we had dual nationality with British as well as South African passports, our ultimate intention from the time we went into exile had naturally been to return to South Africa when this was practical. However, family commitments were pushing this ever further into the future.

I had enjoyed my eighteen-month stint in Johannesburg at the Institute for the Advancement of Journalism up until the middle of 1998, and three of us in the family worked on South Africa-related projects in the field of education and development, revisiting as often as we could. Since my first trip back in 1990 I had, by April 2000, been back twenty-seven times, and on at least twenty of those occasions had managed to get to East London to see friends, relatives and old colleagues from the *Daily Dispatch* days. At least, now, I would be able to visit the Biko graveyard without finding it overgrown with weeds. At least, now, that grave was in a suitable setting.

But there was an even more important grave for our family than that of Steve Biko, and when I arrived in East London I often went to the Cambridge cemetery, where our youngest son, Lindsay, was buried. He had been only a year old when he had died in 1971 of a sudden attack of meningitis, and we often thought of him.

It is said that time heals all pain, but I think it more accurate to say that time eases rather than entirely heals the pain of bereavement, because although it wouldn't be natural to grieve every day for thirty years the pain nevertheless sharpens afresh every time one thinks at length of the loved one lost. When I visited Lindsay's grave it was never a morbid experience but always an intensely emotional one, because I still remembered the day of his death so vividly, following a lovely Sunday when we had all been in the pool. He had barely started walking and was a handsome child resembling our second son, Duncan.

On the following morning Wendy had found him sick and listless, and had called our family doctor who had had him admitted immediately to the Frere Hospital where he had died that afternoon.

Years later, in 1983, Wendy wrote a description of her loss as a mother so powerful that I can barely read it all these years later without intense emotional pain. She wrote as follows for the *Guardian*'s 'First Person' column:

I remember waking and knowing at once by the quality of light in the room that it was later than it should have been. Something else was wrong. I had drifted slowly and naturally into wakefulness. The silent absence of insistent infantile chatter from the next room boomed in my head.

I ran to the room. He wasn't standing up in his cot. He lay on his back, his eyes wide open and he looked at me absently from the depths of intense preoccupation with pain. His face was redder than it had ever been and his breathing was much too fast and too shallow. He had a little go at a smile and the fingers of one hand gave a rudimentary wave. I bent closer and could feel the heat coming from him.

I knew it was very bad and as I picked him up to undress him and sponge him down, I shouted to my husband to phone the doctor. I suspected that what we could do for him was probably not going to be enough and started to pray for him not to die.

The doctor came. He pushed the baby's knees towards his

stomach and tilted his head forward. The baby cried in pain. Spinal rigidity. I knew all about that. The doctor had done those tests dozens of times before on my other children. 'Why do you do that?' I'd asked. 'Testing for meningitis,' he'd said. The doctor, normally laconic and full of joking insults, went all nice. 'We must get him to hospital now,' he said.

They did a lumbar puncture and tests on his spinal fluid showed meningitis. 'But not one of the virulent ones,' said the doctor. 'We've got him on a penicillin drip.'

We went home and talked about what we'd do if he died and then sat in silence. I went out and did some grocery shopping, came back and we talked some more about what we'd do if he died.

In the afternoon the hospital phoned to ask us to come quickly. The fear, barely containable, doubled in intensity. At the hospital the sister said he wasn't responding to the penicillin and that he was having convulsions.

We waited, saying nothing to each other. Our doctor ran past the waiting room, dressed in squash kit. Very soon after that we heard the squeak of his shoes coming back down the polished passage. The footsteps were slow and then nearly stopped. It was then that I knew that the baby had died. The doctor didn't want to come in and tell us.

When he did his expression had a near-normal look. He had tried, but hadn't managed to hide his feelings. 'He's gone,' he said.

We asked to see him and were led into a room with a high narrow bed in it. He lay, small and still, in the middle of it, a white cloth covering his tummy and legs. I had expected him to look as if he was merely asleep.

But he didn't. He looked different. His eyes were not properly closed and his mouth hung open slightly. Several nurses stood around the bed. No one said anything. I bent and kissed him and nuzzled into his face. He wasn't hot any more. My husband followed suit and we walked out.

The fear had stopped and the pain that took its place seemed so distilled that it took me by surprise and I had to work to stretch my capacity to contain it.

Waking up the next morning was like waking into a nightmare. During the night I had 'forgotten' that he was dead and the rush of memory produced a shock so new that it seemed as if it had all just happened.

Household routine claimed our attention and energy, providing a framework for reasonably undemanding distraction. Every now and then I would come across my husband in some corner, crying. I found this distressing. I had never seen him cry so much or so often before.

Friends and acquaintances arrived, some diffident and awkward and others openly moved to tears. We found ourselves grasping their sympathy with an unexpected gratitude. Looking back, I realize we did this to relieve some of the loneliness of the pain.

For me the sudden physical absence of someone who had claimed so much of my time and attention left great gaps in the day which had me wandering around the house aimlessly, not able to use the time, only to pass it.

I missed him so much and several times a day I would go and sit in his room, to look at it and all his things. His mattress and pillow had the hollows where he had slept. I would press the pillow to my face, to get the smell of him.

For weeks living became a balance between needing distraction from the pain and needing to return to it. I could not go for long without allowing myself to know how much I wanted him and how I could never have him again.

Months later I was ready to clear out his room and to give his clothes and toys away. Now, years later, we make do with some photos of him and a soft toy ball crocheted for him by his grandmother.

CHAPTER 19

The Down Side

To appreciate South Africa's miracles of achievement within only one decade, a decade which brought the introduction of democracy, it seemed necessary to review the nation's down side in terms of trials and torments and problems both inherited and intensified.

It was clear as the new millennium began that South Africa had many major problems which would have been daunting challenges to any nation in the world, let alone one struggling to recover from centuries of discrimination and decades of extreme repression.

As in the former Soviet Union, the removal of a fiercely repressive police state bolstered by military backup had set loose a powerful culture of crime which for generations had been the only means of survival for the dispossessed. In South Africa, the death of apartheid, welcome for most, had also meant freedom for criminals to spread across the face of the land, beyond the townships into the wealthy white suburbs on a scale previously unknown.

By the end of the twentieth century, although certain areas of the major cities were more notorious for violent crime, no part of South Africa was free of the fear of criminals prepared to kill for gain. There were 20,000 murders a year on average, which for a population of 40 million was one of the highest figures per capita in the world, and in the major cities hardly a day went by without reports of horrendous murders, many of them apparently pointless and more than a few patently racial, as blacks took violent vengeance for apartheid.

Though whites were not the main victims of crime, blacks forming the overwhelming majority of the victims, the wealthier whites were increasingly being targeted for murder, robbery, rape and car hijackings. Even well-guarded properties with security gates were being breached by the criminals, who in some cases waited for dinner guests to drive through security gates to enter them themselves and kill or rob the guests and hosts for the evening. In my eighteen months in Johannesburg I became used to following carefully explained security instructions when accepting dinner dates, and although I never saw any crime of any sort throughout my stay, it was rare to encounter a group at any function who didn't have their own horror story of violence or murder. Everyone you spoke to had either had such an experience or knew of someone who had.

But in my eighteen months in Johannesburg I formed a deep affection and a strong respect for the Johannesburgers themselves, who simply wouldn't allow the criminals to change their lifestyles or social habits, and I always admired those revellers I saw, and they were many, in suburbs such as Melville, who openly dined out on pavement cafés or in beer-gardens as if the criminals didn't exist. It might have been careless, but it was also impressively defiant.

I spent an evening in Baragwanath Hospital in Soweto, one of the biggest hospitals in Africa, and watched horror scenes in the Friday night casualty department which was like a war zone. We could hear gunfire throughout the evening, and doctors there told me many of the wounds were akin to what they had read of Vietnam, with criminals using high-velocity bullets and the latest automatic rifles. The hospital was later named after Chris Hani, a member of the ANC's National Executive Committee, who was assassinated in 1993 by a right-wing Polish immigrant.

In addition to its horrendous crime rate, South Africa had by the end of the twentieth century one of the world's worst road casualty rates. As an example, although Britain had twice as many vehicles as South Africa, South Africa had many times more road accidents and deaths than Britain – an average of more than 10,000 per year. And this was no new phenomenon. When we had lived in East London, South Africa, near the corner of Devereux Avenue and Chamberlain Road, two wide and quiet streets seldom plagued with heavy traffic, scarcely a week went by without a ghastly crash at that intersection. First we would hear the squeal of tyres as brakes were applied, then the spectacular sound of collision. I myself was once stopped at that intersection, with its lights on red, when a vehicle had driven into the back of my car. In the court hearing which followed the driver said he hadn't been looking ahead at the time! Somehow that intersection seemed wired for weekly accidents.

Yet when we moved to London, that vast metropolis of ten million people, in twenty-one years we heard only two collisions, neither fatal, and saw no fatal accidents at all.

To a great extent the difference between both countries was a question of attitude. In Britain there was a noticeable courtesy and consideration shown by drivers towards other drivers. Cars yielded lanes to others, permitted them to enter traffic streams and were generally helpful, probably because this was the most efficient way to keep traffic moving. And within a year in Britain we found that the road courtesy was catching, that we were yielding to other cars as a matter of course and rather enjoying letting other drivers into our lane. Back in South Africa it had been so different. In our fairly small city of East London I had once had to wait eighteen minutes to be allowed out of a lane to leave a drive-in cinema. The few seconds it would have taken one of the other drivers to give way had been considered too much, for nearly twenty minutes.

Such road selfishness inevitably led to road rages and to lax road legislation. There were no re-testing regulations in South Africa such as in Britain, where all cars beyond a certain age had to be tested each year and re-licensed for roadworthiness. In South Africa the roads were flooded with unroadworthy vehicles, and this was at least part of the reason for the high toll of road fatalities.

Many road deaths in South Africa involved minibuses which were used as township taxis, crowding too many passengers into their confined seating spaces, and often operated with faulty brakes and steering and other defects. Drivers frequently stayed awake too long in order to make more money, only to fall asleep and crash the vehicle. One driver was arrested for having no steering wheel – he had been driving with a large wrench clasped around the steering column.

As well as the great number of unroadworthy vehicles on the road, there were many unlicensed drivers. It was known that a high proportion of driving licences in South Africa had been obtained through bribery rather than through driving tests, and it was an irony that this carnage was taking place on some of the best roads in the world, because generally South Africa's main highways were of the highest quality.

With such high rates of road deaths, murders, violent crimes such as rape and robbery and assault, South Africa towards the close of the millennium was suffering consequent losses economically. The tourism industry was being hit, with people from all over the world reluctant to risk being mugged or worse, and agriculture was also being affected, because of the murders of white farmers in many parts of the country.

In addition to all this, the high rate of unemployment was adding further to the social tensions. South Africa's official rate of unemployment was twenty-three per cent of the work force in 1997 and twenty-seven per cent in 1998, and if the underemployed were added the figure rose to thirty-eight per cent, while more than 300,000 school leavers joined the labour market every year.

Meanwhile standards were dropping in hospitals and clinics all over the country, a situation exacerbated by the increasing tendency of nurses to strike regularly for more pay, and teachers in many state schools were simply not turning up for work or were teaching for only a portion of the day. In one school I visited in Soweto the pupils took me to the teachers' common room to point out the errant teachers, six of whom were relaxing and smoking there instead of being in their classrooms teaching.

Official corruption was also on the increase during the 1990s, and accounts were common of graft and kickbacks in over-ordering supplies, in buying too expensive cars for government servants and in budget excesses unaccounted for and ignored. In the Eastern Cape in the first few years of local government since the democratic election, more than 200 government cars were either crashed or stolen.

Adding to the new government's problems was another phenomenon, also experienced by other countries newly emerged from authoritarian rule: international critics, including some foreign journalists, took aim at the easy targets they now saw in their sights. For example, in the former Soviet Union and certain satellite states such as Romania, it was now fashionable for visiting journalists to point to the unsolved problems and discontents of populations who reportedly yearned for the old days of organized repression. In these countries, as in South Africa, none of these commentators were kind enough to supply the answers and solutions they themselves demanded. Communist dictators had ravaged the economies of Russia and other Iron Curtain countries to a degree simply not fixable in a few short years, and in South Africa the Mandela and Mbeki governments had inherited another kind of wasteland – a post-apartheid nation of high expectation and inadequate resources.

To provide equal education meant massive expenditure. In the apartheid era the average white child had eleven times as much money spent on its education as the black child, so the new democratic government had to come up with much bigger education budgets. The same applied in medicine and health. Suddenly the new government had to find nine times as much money as the apartheid government had had to, because it had been concerned mainly with funding white education which was only one-ninth the amount needed to provide equality of basic educational services. And when the visiting critics pointed out these shortfalls in schools, housing, health and other spheres, claiming: 'See? Apartheid still lives', they unfortunately didn't go on to provide the answer of where to raise the money needed to achieve all these things. If whites still tended ten years after the collapse of apartheid to live in better houses than blacks, how did these critics expect Mandela and Mbeki to fast-forward the remedy – by confiscating white homes and moving blacks into them? And if so, how then were the new mortgages to be serviced? With government grants? Raised how? By taxing the newly impoverished?

Of course this was setting the stage for any demagogue to embarrass the new government by claiming it had forgotten its own people, or was neglecting its grassroots support, or was selling out to big business, and this, in turn, could draw silly responses from government spokesmen anxious not to appear outgunned in the anti-white rabble-rousing stakes.

The extraordinary truth, as the new millennium dawned, was that on balance the new government was generally handling its mandate rather well despite all these horrendous problems and despite those who sought to exploit them for passing advantage.

Unfortunately, however, the new government also shot itself in the foot over the issue, boiling up in March 2000, of racism in the media. That there were elements of racism in various media, as in most major sectors of South African life, could not sensibly be disputed, South Africa's recent history being what it had been. What could be disputed was the wisest way of dealing with it.

Central to the controversy was a man Wendy and I had known

for many years, Barney Pityana, the gifted deputy of Steve Biko in the old Black Consciousness Movement and for the last twenty-two years a leading member of the ANC. Barney and his wife Dimsa had been good friends of ours during the exile years, and Barney's brilliant younger brother, Sipho, had proved to be one of the younger stars of the new administration in the Department of Labour, being appointed director over many older candidates. When Sipho and his wife Nkulie were married in Birmingham I had had the honour of being chauffeur of the bridal car, and Barney, an ordained clergyman of the Anglican communion, had performed the nuptials.

After a distinguished career with the World Council of Churches in Geneva, Barney had returned home after the fall of apartheid to play a leading role in the new administration, and was appointed chairman of the Human Rights Commission to considerable acclaim. The commission, however, became embroiled in controversy and several of its leading members resigned, including the veteran anti-apartheid parliamentarian, Helen Suzman, and human rights activists, Rhoda Kadalie and Sheena Duncan. Controversy was compounded when the commission decided to investigate allegations of racism in the media.

Unfortunately the method it chose was general and undefined, issuing subpoenas and summonses upon editors unrelated to any specific allegations in the manner, if not the intent, of the old apartheid regime which had spent decades trying to bully journalists.

The incident sent shock waves around parts of the world previously well disposed to South Africa's new democracy, and there were reports and interviews on the issue in all the leading democracies, which had long accepted as central to democracy the notion that if any state body alleged a crime that allegation had to be both specific and particular, accusing an identified person of a defined offence. Here, on the contrary, appeared to be a state body making accusations over attitudes rather than actions, spilling over into the realm of thought rather than deed.

Fortunately common sense prevailed before editors could get riled enough to tell the commission to go jump in the lake and to court arrest and prosecution by defying the summonses and subpoenas, and the affair turned into a general discussion about racist attitudes and their effects in the media, which is what could have happened in the first place without blackening the eye of South Africa's fresh face of new democracy before the world.

The incident, like the attempt to stop publication of portions of the Truth Commission report, was a sorry example of complete ignorance of how the spirit, let alone the letter, of democracy is observed in a mature democracy where the spirit of tolerance is frequently as important as the letter of the law preserving it.

In both cases South Africa as a country and South Africans as a people were more damaged than they would have been by the original material complained of, bringing to mind that old saying of the cure being worse than the disease.

Then came an even more serious issue to test the statecraft of the new democracy. Robert Mugabe, Prime Minister of Zimbabwe, clearly losing popular support after twenty years in power, sought favour from the more militant members of his ruling party by encouraging them to invade and occupy farms owned by whites. The result was a rush to grab such land all over Zimbabwe, and in violent attacks on those farmers or their workers who tried to resist. By April 2000 the situation was out of control as the land grabbers, described as veterans of the liberation war of two decades previously, though many were still obviously teenagers, turned their violence not only on the white farmers and their loyal workers but on all obvious opponents of the ruling party. By May, several hundred had been seriously assaulted and eighteen killed, including several white farmers.

Mugabe rejected appeals by Britain, America and several European countries to apply the rule of law and call off the attacks, especially since Zimbabwe's own high court had ruled that the farm occupations by the invaders were illegal and that the police should act to clear them off such property. The police declined to act, saying they had inadequate staff, and Mugabe and other ministers backed the police attitude, publicly encouraging the squatters to ignore the high court ruling.

President Thabo Mbeki immediately led a strong diplomatic consortium of Southern African leaders in putting private pressure on Mugabe. Mbeki realized that the events in Zimbabwe might trigger off copycat land invasions in South Africa, in addition to driving hordes of refugees from the violence in Zimbabwe across the border into South Africa, thereby swelling South Africa's own jobless and homeless populations. By all accounts Mbeki showed masterful leadership behind the scenes, diplomatically saving the faces of several others in the consortium by using reasoned argument instead of blunt power.

Unfortunately, however, this diplomatic approach also saved Mugabe's face, and he made use of the respite to proclaim publicly that no other power would dictate to Zimbabwe how to act. Equally unfortunately, the diplomatic approach by the Southern African leaders, one of whom, Chissano of Mozambique, made the grotesque public statement that Mugabe was a respecter of the rule of law, also lent credence to the Zimbabwean claim that the land issue rather than the state-sponsored violence was the central issue.

In fact Britain had made available large sums of money over many years to enable the Mugabe government to address the question of land purchase from white farmers for redistribution to black farmers, but farms so acquired had been handed over instead to Mugabe cronies rather than to genuine black farmers, and the British had demurred at funding further such handouts to the favoured few in Mugabe's system of nepotism.

Unfortunately, also, the failure of Mbeki and other African leaders to condemn Mugabe publicly dealt a huge blow to the esteem, the economy and the future of the region in the eyes of developed democracies in the rest of the world.

In the view of these countries it looked like African leaders maintaining a typically blind Third World loyalty to one of their number regardless of his corruption, tyranny or even, as in this case, governmental incitement to murder. There was also a danger that lawless elements in neighbouring countries, such as South Africa, would be encouraged by this public loyalty to a lawless leader to take the law into their own hands in similar fashion.

Some sought to justify Mbeki's quiet diplomacy by saying this would achieve more than public denunciation would, but this was an unfortunate reminder of earlier attitudes by two Western leaders who had no great credibility as staunch upholders of democratic values. These were Ronald Reagan and Margaret Thatcher, who supported what they called 'constructive engagement', reasoning that they believed they would achieve more through quiet diplomatic friendship with the apartheid regime in South Africa behind the scenes than through public denunciation.

They were wrong, as was proved by the fact that during their

220

terms of office the apartheid government felt emboldened to invade more surrounding territories, kill more Africans, torture more dissidents, and generally behave more aggressively than they had dared to when the United States had a Democrat in the White House and Britain had a Labour administration. It was therefore doubly to be regretted that President Mbeki and his colleagues appeared to be following a policy of 'constructive engagement' with Mugabe, especially when the money markets abroad understandably reacted by plunging the South African rand to its lowest-ever levels against the dollar and pound.

Again, as with South Africa's other two public relations disasters – attempts to suppress the TRC report and the HRC's initial action in issuing subpoenas and summonses against editors – the most worrying aspect for friends of South Africa abroad was the apparent ignorance within South Africa of the seriousness with which international democrats viewed such matters. And for some South Africans to say, as they did, that governmental commissions in Britain and America also had powers to issue subpoenas and summonses was to make this ignorance of democratic sensitivities abroad even more serious, ignoring the fact that the essence of mature democracy is not to use all available powers except as a last resort. If any British or American government had issued summonses against editors as the HRC initially did there would have been a major national crisis in both countries, with heads rolling for such crass overuse of authority.

As to the inevitability of the rand's fall because of the nondenunciation of Mugabe, consider only the type of message sent out to potential investors abroad when one government in a region actually encourages its citizens to steal private property, to use violence in doing so and to ignore court rulings to the contrary, and other governments in the region give no immediate and public repudiation of this state-sponsored theft. Does that make investment money from abroad seem safe in this region?

More and more as time goes by it becomes clear that South African leadership should not only stop dealing too permissively with Mugabe, but should take a leading role in condemning his racist policies, his totalitarian bullying of opponents, his fascist clinging to power by undemocratic means and his contempt for the spirit or letter of democracy. And since the precedents so usefully set in international law in the case of former General Pinochet of

Chile, it should be spelt out clearly that nobody guilty of crimes against humanity, under whatever pretext, should travel abroad without risk of arrest and appropriate trial.

CHAPTER 20

The Up Side

Having detailed the problems and disadvantages facing the new South Africa, and without minimizing or underestimating them, one could nevertheless see by the beginning of the year 2000 that they appeared to be outweighed by the country's achievements, assets, advantages and opportunities. As South Africa's celebrated journalist, Allister Sparks, pointed out at the time, what the country had already achieved through negotiating itself from crisis to consensus was 'amazing, absolutely bloody amazing'. In only three years it had seen twenty-six political parties as widely divergent as any on earth managing to reach agreement on a range of issues that spanned the entire socio-political spectrum. It was difficult enough to imagine twenty-six parties reaching agreement on anything, said Sparks, yet these had done so without any foreign broker or facilitator. They hadn't had to be brought together on the White House lawn like Yasser Arafat and Yitzak Rabin, and there hadn't been any Untag force or Vance–Owen plan. The South Africans had done it on their own without intermediaries. And they had reached agreement not only on broad principles but on legalistic detail.

Sparks reminded his readers that South Africa was a country which only a short while before had had no tradition of inter-racial dialogue. 'It was an authoritarian society in which for generations whites had talked about blacks and decided what to do with them. In business as in government decisions were taken on high and handed down, and the idea of discussing issues with black people instead of deciding for them was not only unthinkable, it was downright subversive.'

For thirty years the major black political organizations had been outlawed, and it had been a crime to quote them, speak to them or say anything favourable about them. Yet in three short years South Africans had turned that 'no-speak' tradition around into a pervasive culture of negotiation. Sparks had observed during the multi-party negotiations something that had been notable by its absence during the Arab–Israeli negotiations or the Northern Irish peace talks – an inexorable process of movement to bypass or surmount all obstacles in the path of a solution. 'The negotiating moved from multilateral to bilateral forums and back again as it flowed like some glutinous substance around the obstacles in its path,' said Sparks, concluding: 'The rapid development of this new culture is what is going to save us. We were a divided and fractious nation, but learned the art of conflict resolution.'

It was indeed true that South Africa had confounded prophecies of doom and destruction on several occasions, and seemed of necessity to have learned the skills to survive challenges that might have smashed the resolve of others. Even the problem of the high crime rate had been addressed and the start of 2000 was beginning to yield some hopeful signs on this worrying front.

For example, except for some pockets of resistance in northern KwaZulu-Natal very little of the violence in the country was now political, and in the major cities there were already indications by late 1999 that certain categories of violent crime, such as murder and car hijackings, were on the decline. These crimes had been targeted in a special national police initiative, and police spokesmen said there were hopeful signs of further decrease in such crime. President Thabo Mbeki was known to be especially keen on the fight against crime, aware as he was of the link between tourist revenue and investment on the one hand, and South Africa's reputation for stability and safety on the other.

As for the economy, despite the doleful predictions of some, the South African economy actually grew consistently during the country's decade of democracy, averaging about 2 per cent growth per year, with a peak of 3.4 per cent in 1996. In some quarters, however, economists expected this high to be exceeded during 2000, possibly reaching 3.7 per cent. Inflation was also on the downward trend, finishing at around 6 per cent for 1999, and the producer inflation rate dropped from 7.1 per cent in 1997 to 3.5 per cent in 1998. As to the core inflation rate itself, economists generally agreed that inflation should dip below 6 per cent during the year 2000.

The South African Chamber of Business's index rose from 82 at the end of 1998 to 90.1 by September 1999, and with interest rates dropping steadily and Gross Domestic Product growth on the up, there was a clear basis for increasing business confidence.

Contrary to expectation the rand rate firmed up in the last few years of the 1990s and stayed fairly steadily at around ten to the pound sterling and at around six to the dollar, so that economists were remarking on the newfound stability of the currency. Though others warned that external factors could affect the rand either way, some commentators actually hoped the rand might firm further in 2000. This hope was, however, hit by the rand sinking to twelve to the pound following the Mugabe crisis.

The South African Reserve Bank had maintained high interest rates until early 1999 mostly because of speculative attacks on emerging markets in June 1988, but during 1999 interest rates fell from 21 per cent to 16.5 per cent. The Reserve Bank's repo rate was declining steadily and the prime overdraft rate at year-end was heading towards 15 per cent – the lowest in years. This trend was starting to have a positive effect on economic growth. As to productivity, despite low skills and low training levels South Africa's latest productivity statistics indicated large areas of positive improvement. South Africa's salary cost per unit produced in manufacturing increased by 231 per cent from 1970 to 1997.

This was worse than the United States (134 per cent), Sweden (194 per cent) and Italy (212 per cent), but better than France (269 per cent), Britain (396 per cent), Germany (439 per cent) and Japan (557 per cent). In labour productivity South Africa scored highly in the later 1990s, with a growth rate of 8.9 per cent, ahead of Sweden (6.6 per cent), France (6.4 per cent), Germany (6.1 per cent), Japan (5.5 per cent), the United States (5.2 per cent) and the United Kingdom (0.9 per cent) Although from a low base, these figures indicated a positive trend.

Regarding progress in black economic empowerment, in 1990 only 1 per cent of the companies listed on the Johannesburg Stock Exchange were black-controlled, but by 1999 this figure had risen to 5.5 per cent, with a total value of $9.2 bn, and another 10 per cent of Johannesburg Stock Exchange companies were partially black-owned. Unfairly, however, critics of black entrepreneurs accused black leaders such as Dr Nthato Motlana and Cyril Ramaphosa of amassing wealth with little regard for general black empowerment. They were thought to have made themselves billionaires at the expense of other blacks. But the facts were considerably different. Motlana and Ramaphosa had been asked to spearhead black entrepreneurship and had done so brilliantly, but at frightening risk, because when their New Africa Investments Limited, or Nail, had acquired a considerable chunk of white business, both found they were in deep debt. They had had to borrow hugely to buy the white interests, but after purchase their share value had plunged so far that they ended up owing more than they had made. They had shown the courage to take the requisite risks, but had been reviled for doing so by some who should have known better.

The income gap between black and white had narrowed considerably over the past two decades. Whereas in 1975 only 2 per cent of black households were among the 10 per cent of richest South Africans, by 1996 22 per cent of the richest South Africans were black, and by 2000 probably 25 per cent.

Spending on crime prevention had risen massively over the past decade. Between 1990 and 1999 there had been an increase of 456 per cent, resulting directly in a decrease in murder, public violence, theft, white-collar crime and drunken-driving.

As to health, since 1994 an additional 5 million people had been provided with access to health care, mainly primary health care, and 495 new clinics were built, 250 upgraded substantially and 2,300 upgraded to a lesser extent. Sadly, however, by July 2000 South Africa had more than 3 million people with AIDS, and a recent survey found that, although awareness of it was as high as 90 per cent in all parts of South Africa, the percentage of people taking preventive measures was as low as 10 per cent.

Housing was one of South Africa's success stories, with more than 1 million capital subsidies awarded to first-time home-owners in the five years up to 1999. Of these, about 900,000 had been converted into houses by the year 2000, and the capacity to maintain this rate of delivery had been built into the housing departments of the main provinces.

In the realm of transport, apart from the horrendous road fatality figures, South Africa was well provided with transport infrastructure. About 5 million cars used an extensive road network of half a million kilometres by the end of the 1990s, the three international airports handled more than 8 million passengers a year and the seven commercial seaports moved about 200 million tonnes of cargo. Durban was the busiest port in the southern hemisphere, busier than Sydney, Rio or any other port south of the equator.

Since 1994 more than 1.3 million new telephone connections had been made, with 35 per cent of the population now having access to telephones, and that figure was set to rise by existing licensing agreements to 75 per cent by 2002.

Water was another of the main success stories in South Africa, thanks to the energy and leadership of Professor Kader Asmal, who held the water portfolio until 1999. Since 1994 more than 3 million people had been given access to clean water and in 1998 and 1999 more than 1,000 projects had been started to provide access to an additional 5 million people. The latest estimates showed that almost 80 per cent of the population now had access to water and 50 per cent had access to modern sanitation. This was dramatic progress indeed in one of the most important basic commodities vitally needed by the populace.

In education there was also impressive progress. By 1998 more than 12 million pupils were enrolled in schools, over 90 per cent of the children of school age, and 860,000 students were enrolled at South Africa's twenty-one universities and fifteen technikons. While the pass rate was still woefully low, as a legacy of the past, it had improved since 1997 and the improvement curve appeared headed upwards. By 2000, Professor Asmal had been appointed to head the Education Authority.

Hard-headed businessmen in South Africa, usually disposed to be critical of all administrations, recently reported that among the most positive factors in South Africa over the five years to the year 2000 were:

Increased socio-economic delivery in housing, electrification, water, infrastructure and telecommunications

Fiscal and monetary discipline, low inflation, reduced budget deficits and low foreign debt as a percentage of Gross Domestic Product

Vigorous action to combat and reduce crime and corruption

Strong maintenance of the independence of constitutional institutions such as the judiciary

Evidence of a growing 'social middle ground'; an emerging black middle class and an increasing number of liberal whites, including Afrikaners

An established culture of negotiation to resolve industrial and other differences.

Apart from increased trading with Europe, Asia and America, South Africa by 2000 was experiencing an export boom to the rest of Africa, with R20 bn worth of exports representing a huge 335 per cent increase since 1992.

One of South Africa's leading political commentators, Dr Frederick Van Zyl Slabbert, came up with an interesting theory as to why South Africa was holding together so well, in contrast to such troubled regions as the Balkans.

Yugoslavia had for decades been created out of a forcing together of Croats, Serbs, Slovenes and Bosnians who had wished to remain apart, and as soon as the authoritarian regime compelling them to stay together had fallen, they had separated, whereas South Africa had had the opposite experience. Ethnic groups in South Africa had been forced apart by the apartheid system, and as soon as it had fallen, they had rushed to unite. It was, at the close of the twentieth century, an intriguing explanation of the South African success story.

As the world entered the year 2000, South Africans could say with justifiable pride that no matter what lay ahead in terms of triumph or disaster, failure or success, their first remarkable decade of entry into democracy had been a brilliant achievement.

To have moved, in only ten years, from pariah of the world to the world's favourite nation was little short of miraculous. And to have turned the national philosophy, in only a decade, from one based on hatred into one based on love was, no matter how flawed or imperfect, the wonder of the world.

The Rainbow Nation, whatever lay ahead, had truly been redeemed.

CHAPTER 21

Facing the Future

South Africa, once the most wretched of countries with a government hated all over the world, had within only one decade become the most loved and most warmly embraced new democracy, with a first President, Nelson Mandela, more admired than any other contemporary political leader in the world. Now, with the dawning of the year 2000 under its new President, Thabo Mbeki, it seemed fitting to consider more thoroughly South Africa's place in the world, its possible role in international affairs, and options and initiatives that it might take to make its own positive impact on the world.

Looking inward had been vital. This had been a country in turmoil for so long that it had initially to address its own internal priorities before even beginning to consider its role in the world. But having done so, it now had to see that the next step, contemplation of its continental and international destiny, was no less important.

To begin with, South Africa, the new democratic South Africa, obviously had a key role in Southern Africa. It was the most powerful and advanced industrially of any of the southern countries, which included Zimbabwe, Namibia, Zambia, Lesotho, Botswana, Swaziland, Malawi, Mozambique and Angola, and it seemed inevitable that one day it would have a leading role in a large federation of democratic states of Southern Africa. Economically, that development would make such a federation a world power because while South Africa had enormous wealth in gold, diamonds, platinum, uranium, manganese, ferrochrome and other valuable minerals, it had no oil, but there were rich oil reserves in Cabinda, Angola and other fabulously wealthy emerald and other mineral resources in the rest of Southern Africa. Furthermore, Southern Africa had huge agricultural potential, and if intensively cultivated could feed not only all of Africa but Asia and South America as well.

The image of Africa as a poor, unhealthy continent had long been inappropriate. Africa was now acknowledged generally as the richest continent of all in natural resources and mineral wealth, with the most benevolent climate known on earth, with few of the extremes of heat and cold that afflicted North and South America and Asia. Africa had little experience of ice and snow, but was generally warm or temperate, with all varieties of climatic condition varying from desert to tropical rain forest but mostly temperate savannah or grassland. Perhaps it was because it had for so long been so favourable for human habitation that Africa was now acknowledged also as the site of the earliest traces of human life.

President Mbeki had called for an exciting role for Africa, for an African Renaissance – for a flowering of African talent and skills to usher in a new era of progress for the continent. And a necessary prerequisite for such a major leap forward for Africa was something Steve Biko had always called for, to make Africanism something positive rather than negative. His constant message had been: 'We must stop looking to the white man to give us something.' He had meant not only that blacks should stop depending on whites but that blacks should stop blaming their own shortcomings on whites. 'We have to create our own future!' he had proclaimed, and he had railed against myths not only about white superiority but also about black inferiority.

It seemed to me as the year 2000 dawned that South Africa had many glorious opportunities to enter into its heritage and fulfil its destiny not only in Southern Africa but throughout Africa and the world, and that its leadership could be progressive and imaginative. Perhaps South Africa could play a leading role in long-needed United Nations reform.

In March 2000 there were wonderful images of South Africa on television screens all over the world – images of young South African soldiers, black and white, rescuing Mozambicans trapped by floodwaters, during a tragedy which highlighted one of the greatest shortcomings of the world organization since its inception. It has been incomprehensible to me for many years why when floodwaters render multitudes homeless, or people lose their lives in disasters such as mud slides in Colombia or Venezuela, or earthquakes in Japan or Turkey, the international community reacts first with shock, then horror, then compassion before belatedly sending help. To me the ideal United Nations Organization should have twenty-four-hour-a-day readiness for such disasters. Around the clock there should be air crews in readiness, with aircraft pre-filled with medicines, bandages, food or whatever equipment is needed in such crises, ready to take off minutes after official notification of such disasters, instead of days or weeks later. And the same thinking should be brought to bear on military crisis situations. There should be a standing United Nations force, armed and equipped in readiness for authorization to take action in trouble spots all over the globe, such as Bosnia, Serbia and other Balkan states in the last days of the last millennium, needing only the swift clearance of Security Council approval before acting. Such United Nations forces, given the moral authority of the necessary votes by most of the world's acknowledged democracies, would be able to deal more adequately with assaults on the human family whether by natural disaster, famine, or military attack.

A natural partner in leadership for South Africa on the African continent is Africa's other major country – Nigeria, a nation of 120 million people. South Africa could learn a lot from Nigeria because the Nigerians, given the chance, are the world's ultimate traders, dealmakers and operators. The other great thing about Nigerians is their self-confidence. Today's Nigerians have never known subjection on the basis of race, nor had a feeling of inferiority inculcated in them by others. On the contrary, they often show signs of feeling superior to non-Nigerians. When visiting Nigeria I more than once wished Steve Biko had been with me, knowing how he would have relished this particular trait of its people because along with the arrogance for which we chide many Nigerians goes a great dynamic energy and a readiness to tackle huge projects and concepts. Nigerians, I have found, have a strong interest in South Africa and in South Africans, and I believe they could team up well with South Africa in many a major enterprise.

In conclusion, let me say that the new South African Constitution was such a masterpiece of draftsmanship, and such an inspiring achievement with its wise provisions so far in advance of those of any other constitution in securing for its current and future generations the optimal liberty consonant with the general good of citizens, that I was moved to draft a preamble to it as my own private salute to the Rainbow people as they face up to the future:

A PREAMBLE FOR THE CONSTITUTION

After centuries of conflict, culminating in the severest system of racial repression ever inflicted by a minority upon a majority, this nation now resolves to redeem itself and to reconstitute its purpose and its people in dedication to democracy with full freedom for all.

Conscious of the suffering of so many for so long, we bind ourselves to heal these hurts and to make this land, once reviled for its racism, now revered for its reconciliation.

Knowing from our past the wrongs that result from rule of the unrepresented by the unrepresentative, we hereby complete the fullest consultation ever engaged in by our people, and in setting our national course for good governance as mandated by the majority we pledge to consider the concerns of minorities in all our standards and statutes, opposing all tolerance of intolerance and all patience with prejudice, within the strict rule and proper processes of law.

We declare the primary principle of this and future laws to derive from continued consultation between the governed and the governors of this land as lawfully elected, requiring public response from those publicly responsible and public account from those publicly accountable, and securing for all time the right of due dissent and the full freedom of all media.

Mindful of the problems new nations confront in turning principles into practice, we ask all the world to witness these our high resolves, to aid us in their attainment, and to call us to account if we fail in their fulfilment.

Now therefore we constitute this constitution, commending its clauses and passing its principles to future generations to guard as our national charter for the enactment of all legislation henceforward.

Postscript

On 30 June 2000, Wendy and I celebrated our wedding anniversary, following a marvellous five-week trip to South Africa to catch up with all the latest buzz there. We indulged ourselves totally, travelling on the Blue Train from Pretoria to Cape Town, staying at fine hotels all over, but the highlight of our stay was at beautiful Knysna, at Belvidere on the lovely lagoon and then at Phantom Forest, an eco-sanctuary on a wooded cliff overlooking the lagoon all the way to the bluffs of the Knysna Heads. Here all the chalets were like five-star treehouses, with the best views imaginable from the luxurious bathrooms. Drinks were served in the most scenic bar we'd ever seen, also perched high up among the trees overlooking the lagoon and river, and the cuisine was first-class.

We drove from George via Port Elizabeth and through much of the Eastern Cape which looked as green as we'd ever seen it. In Grahamstown we attended the ceremony at which our friend Colin Legum received an honorary doctorate of laws from Rhodes University, and during his acceptance speech he made one of the most important points any South African could make to the watching world. Pointing out that European countries and other developed democracies had taken centuries to progress to mature democracy and material well-being for their people, but that nevertheless some critics and commentators, inside and outside South Africa, expected South Africa to achieve these miracles of advancement in a few short years, Legum pleaded eloquently for patience and understanding in assessing progress in the new democracy.

We paid a visit to Shamwari, a progressive type of game reserve in the Eastern Cape where extensive research is financed by the

Born Free Trust to relocate rescued big cats. One such was Ricky the Leopard, bought from a circus where he was closely caged, kept in a sanctuary in Kent where he got used to more space, then transferred to Shamwari where he had a whole bush area practically to himself. Wendy was very excited because she had given money for his rescue back then, never dreaming that she would once see his final home in such perfect circumstances right in our own Eastern Cape. Shamwari was also bringing other species of wildlife back to the region, such as elephants, which had been hunted out a hundred years before.

In other parts of South Africa we stayed with friends and family, and by the time we got back in early May we were reflecting on what an eventful year it had been. For me, from a health point of view, it had been a hard year. A routine check-up after I turned sixty-five revealed unexpectedly that I had two malignant cancers in my right lung and one in my left kidney, so the entire right lung was removed in July 1999, and the entire left kidney in December. Fortunately I recovered well from these, thanks to expert surgeons, and by the time we got to South Africa I was able to play two rounds of golf, one in Durban with my brother Harland.

And in many other ways it had been a lucky year, in which we were able to delight in our two little twin granddaughters, and I had been able to keep on with my work for the Institute for the Advancement of Journalism and with some other initiatives I had become involved with. One was, increasingly, Northern Ireland. In recent years I had been invited to speak in various parts of Northern Ireland, where the people believed South Africans could help their own peace process with practical advice gleaned from our own peace negotiations. After a number of such visits I felt increasingly attracted to the people of Northern Ireland, from both contending sides, recognizing immediately that many were victims of the same sort of bigoted upbringing that white South Africans had received from their parents for so long, and that their inherited hostilities had flourished because of the virtual segregation of one community from the other in various areas. It was to be hoped, therefore, that a similar coming together of negotiators and their supporters there, as in South Africa, might have similar educational results, leading finally to a similar peace. But there was clearly a long way to go in Northern Ireland, and a lot of history to overcome.

As part of the process I was invited to a conference in Washington, DC where President Clinton was promoting new initiatives to restore the peace process in Northern Ireland. The event was highly successful, and at a dinner at the White House for delegates I was able to meet the President and his wife, both of them being more intellectually gifted than most political leaders.

On 16 May I had the honour to be received at Buckingham Palace where the Queen appointed me a CBE. The full title resounds with the history of the past, being Commander of the Order of the British Empire, and I received many congratulations and considerable kidding in consequence. On the same day two famous ladies, Elizabeth Taylor and Julie Andrews, became Dame Commanders of the same Order, but I never plucked up the courage to chat to these two Sisters in Chivalry although we shared the same reception area of the palace prior to our decorations.

By now having both British and South African nationality, Wendy and I were based in London because of all our children and now grandchildren, but were able to keep travelling often to South Africa and to keep working on concerns important to us. Wendy was still sending thousands of books to rural schools in South Africa, and I was able to help in areas additional to my South African journalism training project and the Northern Ireland peace projects. One was an impressive Australian project to reduce blindness among black South Africans. Sponsored by the Fred Hollows Foundation of Sydney, the project funds large-scale campaigns to operate to remove cataracts in South Africa at far less cost than the usual cost of such operations, and I set off for a tour of Australia and New Zealand in July to help raise financial support for the Hollows Foundation's South African drive.

Another project I became involved with was a plan to try to get a statue of Nelson Mandela erected in Trafalgar Square, sculpted by Ian Walters, who had created the fine bust of Mandela near the Royal Festival Hall years before Mandela was released from prison. Trafalgar Square seemed appropriate because South Africa House is there, and the South African High Commissioner, Cheryl Carolus, gave her blessing to the project which we envisaged from the start as a gift from the British people, or possibly people from all over the Commonwealth, to the people of South Africa in salute to our greatest South African of all time, in London's most famous square.

So as the millennium year of 2000 entered its final months it seemed to me ever more true that each waking day was to be relished, in order to keep working to improve things for people everywhere, and that I had been blessed not only in my friends but in my own family and relatives, my wife and children and brother and sister and, in Xhosa tradition, my ancestors and other relatives.

I had been enriched not only by being born in South Africa with its extraordinary people and places, but also to have been hospitably received in the country of my ancestors, Britain, and felt a great love for both places and their inhabitants. I would also, because of my experiences in each, have a great affection for Ireland, for America and Canada, for Australia and New Zealand, and especially for Denmark, Finland, Norway, Sweden and Holland for their extra support for freedom and development in South Africa, far above normal expectations and hopes, and for that giant of Africa, Nigeria, which would one day, I felt certain, share with South Africa the great task of African regeneration.

Wendy and I visited our former home in East London, Eastern Cape, in April 2000, finding it was now a nine-room bed-and-breakfast place tastefully adapted and renamed Villa Devereux. The owners had remodelled the great house well, and had thoughtfully left the bullet holes the Security Police had fired into it during our last days there. We walked again in the large garden where we had planned our escape, far from the microphones in the house, and I thought of the amazingly eventful two decades that had elapsed since our escape.

If anyone had told me then, on the eve of that frightening and amateurish departure, that we would escape unscathed, be given a worldwide audience on arrival overseas, be received by presidents and prime ministers, have a major film made of our story which would be viewed all over the world in many languages, be able to help influence foreign policies against apartheid with books, speeches and lecture tours, and be able, eventually, to see the triumph of the South African people over that unspeakable insult to the human race, it would have been astonishing, encouraging and exhilarating.

Yet if anyone had told us authoritatively that the contrary would be true, that we would be ignored, ineffectual and futile, I doubt if it would have led us to any different course of action, because the truth was at that time and in that place that after witnessing the death of our friends and the excesses of our enemies, we knew only

237

one rational purpose in life from that moment – to raise as much alarm in the world as we could; to convey as much outrage as possible, and to help to hound the guilty ones out of power as soon as possible.

That, and to relish with our compatriots the great process of South Africa's liberation in the dawn of the new millennium.

Index